Secrets from the Sand

Contents

Introduction

It is dusk now. The Giza plateau is empty but for the scattered guards who stand watch over the ancient monuments. The tombs and temples are quiet, abandoned by the long-vanished families of the dead who lie just below the spot upon which I stand. The setting sun blazes a brilliant orange as it slips beneath the western horizon, illuminating for a moment the timeless symbols from which mankind takes comfort, beacons to those who seek the poetry of eternal life. The pyramids stand fast, unchanging and unmoving, although the bodies they were built to protect disappeared shortly after being put to rest.

I bear the responsibility for these ancient monuments now, and it is both a great honor and a great burden. As director general of the Giza Pyramids, Saqqara, Heliopolis, and the Bahariya Oasis, a position I have held since 1987, it is my job to guard and protect these treasures, to preserve them for eternity. This is not an easy task, and I must wear many hats. First, in order to protect the monuments in my charge, I must be an administrator, managing millions of visitors and those in the business of tourism and also overseeing the day-to-day running of my office and a staff of five hundred people. I must be a politician, fighting for the preservation of the monuments and to keep the dangers of modern life from overwhelming and destroying the site. But I am, above all, an archaeologist, supervising my own excavations at Giza, Saqqara, the Bahariya Oasis, and Heliopolis, as well as the work of foreign expeditions to all of the sites under my jurisdiction. I must find time to write scholarly articles and academic books, which record and convey the details of my work to other Egyptologists, and books like this one, designed to reach the general public everywhere. I serve as an ambassador to the world, meeting with leaders, celebrities, journalists, and television crews from all over so that I can share my adventures among Egypt's ancient monuments with millions of people. And I must do battle daily with the forces of Seth, ancient god of evil and chaos and the enemy of success, who appears in the form of careless tourists, greedy politicians, jealous colleagues, and the destructive forces of nature that threaten to destroy our heritage. But I have the strength for all these tasks because I love my work. It is my passion, my love, my reason for living.

Since 1987 I have carried out a number of important archaeological projects. At Giza, I developed a unique site-management plan, and primarily as a result of this plan, I have made

My right arm, Nashwa Gaber, helps me keep track of the many details of my working life. Here we are in my office at Giza, headquarters for many of my recent excavations.

many wonderful discoveries. I have found several important new features in the complex associated with the Great Pyramid of Khufu, including a satellite pyramid, a causeway, a valley temple, a harbor, and the possible remains of a palace and a pyramid city. In addition, I have carried out new work around the valley temple of Khafre and found evidence for a second harbor, completed important conservation work on the Sphinx and the pyramids, and discovered a pair statue of Ramesses II near the Pyramid of Menkaure. My good friend Mark Lehner and I have unearthed important evidence of the men and women who were responsible for the actual construction of the Giza pyramids; Mark is currently excavating the ancient Royal Installation, as we call it, where rations and tools for the workers were produced and distributed, and I am uncovering the tombs of the pyramid builders. At Saqqara my team is working in the complex of the 6th Dynasty king Teti (c. 2345–2323 B.C.), where we have been clearing the complexes of two of his queens. We have made exciting discoveries, including the tomb of his crown prince, Tetiankhkem, and the pyramid of his chief queen, Khuit. At Heliopolis my teams have been excavating and conserving two tombs of the 26th Dynasty (664–525 B.C.); I am also instituting a site-management plan for this endangered area. And last, but far from least, we have made spectacular discoveries in the Bahariya

Oasis, far out in the Western Desert, where we have uncovered an enormous Greco-Roman cemetery—the Valley of the Golden Mummies—and a number of important 26th Dynasty tombs.

I am lucky to be aided in my work by an excellent staff, many of whom I am training in archaeological and conservation methods. My personal assistant, Nashwa Gaber, is my right hand. She sits near me and keeps track of all the people I need to talk to and all the things that I need to do. One of my favorite archaeological assistants is a young man named Mansour Boriak, whom we sent, with the help of the Getty Conservation Institute, to Cyprus for training in conservation and to the Field School in Chicago to learn archaeological techniques. He is an excellent archaeologist and is now at a new field school in Upper Egypt where he is helping to train other young archaeologists. Mansour likes to gossip and I always ask him for news, just for its entertainment value. He has assisted me in the excavations of the tombs of the pyramid builders at Giza and has also worked for three seasons at Bahariya. Sometimes I have been hard on him, but it is only because I want him to be excellent. I always tell him that it is not enough to be a good archaeologist; you must also be a good administrator. To do good work, you must be modest and strong. And as a leader, you must leave a distance between yourself and the people who answer to you. That is the secret of success.

Mansour Boriak, one of my most experienced and trusted excavators, holding a statue from the cemetery of the pyramid builders at Giza.

Left: Tarek el-Awady, one of my favorite and most promising protégés, is climbing here to the top of the Great Pyramid. He is now in Prague, working on his doctorate.

Right: Ramadan Badry, now at Brown University, also assists me with many of my excavations; here he is in the Bahariya Oasis.

Below: My assistant Mahmoud Afifi, who is now working with me on his doctorate at Cairo University, and I are at the entrance to one of the tombs at Sheikh Soby, Bahariya Oasis.

Tarek el-Awady assisted me in all my work during the first, second, and third seasons at Bahariya and helps me in the preparation of my lectures and books. He understands exactly what I want to achieve with only one look. He is very intelligent and completely dedicated to his work. When I was writing my recent book *Valley of the Golden Mummies,* I sent him to my New York publishers to deal with the photographs. Although it was the first time he had left Cairo, he worked so hard on the book that he didn't even go to see the Statue of Liberty or the Metropolitan Museum of Art. I was able to arrange, through my close friend Miroslav Verner, for Tarek to go to Prague to study for his doctorate, and he left for the Czech Republic in January of 2002.

Another important protégé of mine is Mahmoud Afifi. He is a very sensitive man, but he is also strong and a good leader. He finished his master's degree at Cairo

University and is now working with me on his doctorate. He is writing about the history of the first part of the 6th Dynasty, and I hope that he can finish within the next three years, because I think he could eventually hold a position high in our Supreme Council of Antiquities. I consider him a son, although I am only eight years older than he is.

I have two well-trained archaeologists working with me in my office. The first is el-Hussein Abdel Bassir, an excellent if somewhat impatient young man who helps me prepare many of the articles I write for the *el-Ahram* newspaper. I am hoping that Abdel Bassir will go to Johns Hopkins University to continue his education. Ramadan Badry, who also acts as my teaching assistant, has worked with me in the excavation of the complex of Teti at Saqqara and at the Valley of the Golden Mummies. He is now at Brown University on a fellowship, studying with Leonard Lesko.

I am also privileged to work with several gifted artists and epigraphers. The best is Noha Abdel Hafiz, who has brilliant hands, although, like many artists, she can be very moody. She has done excellent drawings in difficult places, such as on top of the Great Pyramid and inside the five relieving chambers above the burial chamber of Khufu—spaces that are difficult even for an athlete to enter. Noha also works with me in the excavations of the tombs of the pyramid builders at Giza and in the Valley of the Golden Mummies.

Two specialists in architectural restoration, Abdel Hamid Kotb and his assistant Nevien el-Maghraby, are an integral part of my team. Abdel Hamid is an extremely promising young architect, and Nevien is very intelligent and dedicated. Their work is unique and has no real precedent, and I have enormous faith in them. My chief restorer is Moustafa Abdel Kader, who has done a great deal of important work for me.

These young people are our future, and it is exciting for me to watch them learn and grow. I hope that they will all do better than I have done, but I also hope they will also be strong enough to face Seth and the jealous people who resent the success of others.

* * *

During the last two years, I have received a great deal of national and global recognition for my work. The foreign press in Cairo gave me the Pride of Egypt Award, and Mansoura University, which has a branch in my home province of Damietta, honored me for my contributions to Egyptian society and to the archaeological community

A vital task at every excavation is recording the reliefs and inscriptions. I depend on the excellent work of Noha Abdel Hafiz, who is hard at work in the tomb of Djed-Khonsu-efankh, Bahariya.

worldwide. I received the Distinguished Scholar of the Year for 2000 from the Association of Egyptian-American Scholars, and I was presented by the Russian Academy of Natural Sciences with their Silver Medal. In addition, I have been chosen to serve as a member of the jury for the Agha Khan Award for Architecture, and the National Geographic Society has chosen me to be their eighth Explorer-in-Residence.

The most important honor I have received is the First Class Award for Art and Science, presented to me by President Hosni Mubarak in recognition of my achievements in the conservation of the Great Sphinx. Another very special award was given to me by the people of my home village in a ceremony held in the courtyard of the school where I received my primary education. The governor of the Damietta region attended, and there were many speeches in my honor. When I saw my uncles, aunts, friends, and all their children smiling at me, I felt tears running down my face.

The American Academy of Achievement awarded me a Golden Plate, placing me in the illustrious company of several Nobel Prize winners, as well as Mikhail Gorbachev, Jeremy Irons, Paul McCartney, Edna O'Brien, Benezir Bhutto, and the presidents of Latvia and Bulgaria. During the four-day celebration, we met with four hundred of the world's most outstanding honor students and talked to them about our paths to success. I told the young audience the story of how I came to be in charge of some of the most important and fascinating monuments in Egypt, and how I found my life's passion along the way.

It has always been important to me to let both the scholarly community of Egyptologists and the general public know about the wonderful things I am finding. I have written many scholarly works, and I am also involved in editing several important volumes, including *Egyptology at the Dawn of the Twenty-First Century: The Proceedings of the Eighth International Congress of Egyptologists*. In recent years, largely through the encouragement and support of Mark Linz, my close friend and publisher of the American University in Cairo Press, I

One of my proudest moments was receiving the Golden Plate that the American Academy of Achievement awarded me in 2001.

have also written or contributed to many books designed to reach a wide audience. Foremost among these publications are my international bestseller, *Valley of the Golden Mummies,* and *Silent Images: Women in Pharaonic Egypt,* which I wrote at the request of Mrs. Suzanne Mubarak for the International Conference on Women in Beijing.

In *Secrets from the Sand,* I will tell you the story of my adventures as an archaeologist—of how I came to be who I am today and of the wonderful discoveries I have made during my thirty-three years of searching for Egypt's past. The last decade has been particularly fruitful, and my work continues as I write this book. The life of an Egyptian archaeologist is busy, exciting, and sometimes dangerous, and in the following chapters I will tell many stories about my excavations, of the spectacular discoveries we have made, and of my struggles to save the ancient monuments of Egypt. As I was finishing this manuscript, I was promoted by Egypt's minister of culture, Farouk Hosni, to the post of secretary general of the Supreme Council of Antiquities, the top antiquities job in Egypt. This new position will allow me to put into practice many more of my ideas about how to effectively explore and at the same time preserve our past. The sand of Egypt has been generous to me, and it is my great pleasure to share my discoveries with the world.

This is the plundered granite sarcophagus of Khufu, seen here in situ inside his granite-lined burial chamber.

Chapter I. My Path to the Pyramids

Finding My Life's Passion

Late in January of 1974, while I was serving as inspector of antiquities at the Nubian site of Abu Simbel, I was called by the late Gamal Mokhtar, chairman of the Antiquities Department (whose official name was then the Egyptian Antiquities Organization and is now the Supreme Council of Antiquities), to accept an appointment as first inspector of antiquities for the Giza Plateau. At that time, the pyramids had not yet captured my heart. General Auda Ahmed Auda, Dr. Mokhtar's chief adviser, explained to me that the plateau needed the sort of courage and discipline I had shown in my previous positions. There had just been a major theft—thieves had broken through the wall of a storeroom and stolen boxes full of antiquities—and they wanted me to come and restore order to the site.

When I arrived at Giza, I immediately arranged a new system for the guards, and I went every evening to inspect the monuments, often coming back to the plateau at 1 P.M. to be sure that everyone was in his place. I discovered that many of the guards were taking little bribes for themselves instead of charging admission, so I began to watch them, and I even sent in some foreign friends as spies. I moved half of the guards away and fired others.

I joined my good friend Ahmed el-Sawi, then director of excavations for the Antiquities Department (and now professor of Egyptology at Sohag University), to help the police search for the stolen artifacts. We became friends with the police officer in charge, a very intelligent man named Major Abdel Wahab el-Hellali. One day, the major called me to tell me that they had found the missing artifacts in the Mansouria Canal: the thieves had become frightened and dumped their loot into the water rather than get caught and be prosecuted.

Once the artifacts had been recovered, I decided to concentrate on the excavation and restoration of the Giza monuments. I was amazed to find that the inspectors sat around doing nothing, and I was determined to change things. I lived in a beautiful rest house built by Ahmed Fakhry, a great Egyptian archaeologist who had worked at Giza in the 1960s. I had a wonderful cook named Rabee and the best balcony in the world, where I would sit for hours in my favorite chair, working, meditating on the pyramids, and spending time with the friends who came to visit. When the sun set, I could see the three great pyramids outlined in gold.

Everyone knew that I was there to watch the pyramids day and night and that the monuments were well protected.

By 1977 I had things pretty well in hand with a core staff of people I trusted. My assistant Atef Hassan was an excellent archaeologist who had excavated with me at sites such as Abu Rawash and Merimda Beni Salama; he later left the Antiquities Department to become a tour guide, which was a great loss to Egyptology. My driver, Omran, whom I called "Uncle" as a gesture of respect, said to me once, "I have worked with many archaeologists before. I would take them to the office at 9 A.M. and bring them home in the afternoon. I am an old man, and with you, I will die soon!" He died in the 1980s, while I was studying at the University of Pennsylvania, and I cried like a child when I was given the news.

During my early years at Giza, I lived in a beautiful rest house, with a balcony that overlooked the pyramids.

I first came to Giza in January of 1974, and I have worked hard to restore order at the site. Here I am as a young man in front of the Great Pyramid of Khufu.

I had heard stories and read in books about people who claimed to have slept for a night inside the Great Pyramid, although it was absolutely forbidden; one man even bragged that Khufu had come and talked with him! One day in November 1977, one of my sources told me that Hefnawi, a tour guide known worldwide as the Champion, whose claim to fame is that he can climb the Great Pyramid in seven minutes (it takes me forty-five!), and one of the guards were going to let a group of

Americans into the pyramid at 2 A.M. so they could meditate. I was surprised, since I liked the Champion very much. I later found out that in his opinion, which was shared by some of the guards, this activity was not wrong, but I was determined that nothing of this sort would go on under my jurisdiction.

I told everyone at my office that I was going to the Bahariya Oasis for an inspection. Omran drove and I took Atef with me. We left Giza in the afternoon (with as many witnesses as possible) and drove toward the Faiyum Road. After ten miles, I told Omran to stop and let me out, and I explained my plan. Atef wanted to come back to Giza with me, but I told him that I needed him to go all the way to Bahariya (about a seven-hour drive in those days, before the road was paved). He agreed, and he and Omran drove away. I took the bus back downtown and spent the day with friends.

At midnight I left my companions and took a bus to Giza. I walked from the bus station to the plateau, careful that no one should see me. I ran through the tombs west of the Great Pyramid in the dark, and when I reached the tomb of Hemiunu, the architect responsible for the Great

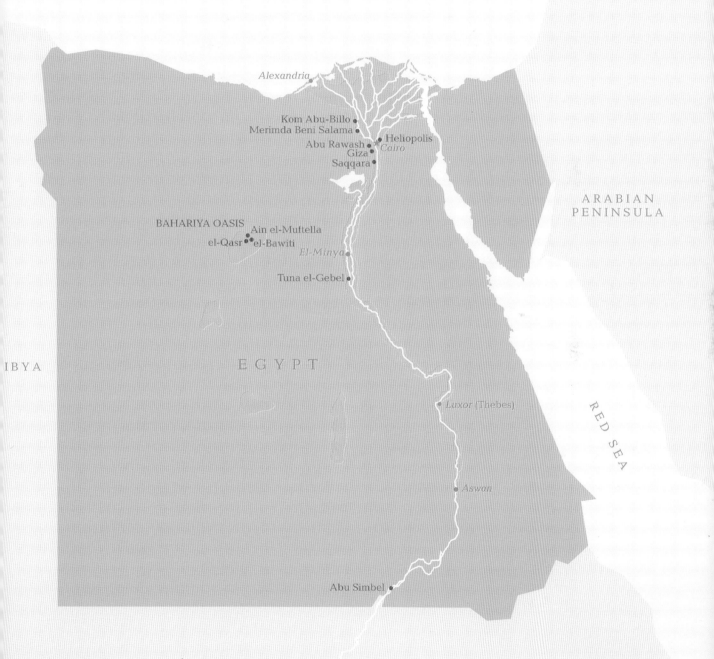

MEDITERRANEAN SEA

Alexandria

Kom Abu-Billo

Merimda Beni Salama

Abu Rawash

Giza

Saqqara

Heliopolis

Cairo

ARABIAN
PENINSULA

BAHARIYA OASIS

Ain el-Muftella

el-Qasr   el-Bawiti

El-Minya

Tuna el-Gebel

EGYPT

LIBYA

RED
SEA

Luxor (Thebes)

Aswan

Abu Simbel

SUDAN

Pyramid, one of the guards, a man named Saied, saw me. He couldn't see who I was, so he called for me to stop and pointed his gun at me. I was very frightened and yelled, "Don't shoot, I am Inspector Zahi Hawass!" Much to my relief, Saied lowered his gun and apologized, adding that he hadn't thought it could be me, since everyone knew that I was at Bahariya.

I took him with me back to my rest house and ordered him not to tell anyone of my presence; I even threatened that he could lose his job if anyone found out. I asked him to wake me up at 3 A.M. When he knocked at my door, at 3 o'clock sharp, I arose, got dressed, took the key to the Great Pyramid and a flashlight, and set off on my adventure.

I walked alone to the Ma'amun Entrance of the Great Pyramid, which was reportedly dug by Arab soldiers in the ninth century A.D. I unlocked the door carefully and entered a pitch-dark realm full of an enveloping silence. I felt as if I was wrapped in a blanket of night, and my heart began to beat faster with fright. This was the first time I had entered the pyramid alone at night, and I was overwhelmed by my childhood fear of the dark. I turned off the flashlight and sat down for ten minutes to catch my breath and listen for intruders. I could hear nothing except the noise of rats running inside the holes in the walls. I laughed to myself, wondering if the person who claimed that Khufu had spoken to him had been listening to the rats.

These thoughts relaxed me and I began to think more clearly, although I wondered exactly why I was doing this dangerous thing. But I believed then, and I believe now, that in order to excavate properly and protect our ancient heritage, there must be stability at every site. As Egyptian archaeologists, we are responsible for everything under our jurisdiction—for the safety of the monuments and the

artifacts, for restoration, conservation, and administration, and also for excavation and publication. It is not possible to do all of this in an atmosphere of chaos and instability.

Thinking about this, I began to move toward the ascending passage, which is only about 3 feet wide and 4 feet high. I went on my hands and knees in the dark for almost 120 feet, until I was able to stand up. I turned on my flashlight and was immediately overwhelmed by the grandeur of the Grand Gallery in which I stood. It was one of those moments in my life I will never forget, the instant when I confronted one of the greatest marvels of ancient architecture, standing alone in the dark with only the rats for company.

I thought I should search first in the "Queen's" Chamber (which has nothing to do with queens, who had their own small pyramids). No one was in this room, so I returned to the Grand Gallery and walked slowly up toward the King's Chamber, where Khufu was once buried. As I walked, bathed in the quiet and peace of the place, I made an important decision that changed my life. I decided to go on to graduate school and study Egyptology, focusing on the Pyramid Age. It took several more years before I would be able to act on this decision, but it was at that moment that I dedicated my heart and my life fully to the passion that has guided me ever since.

I reached the King's Chamber and found no one there. I even moved some wooden beams covering the north side of the sarcophagus, which was a mistake because when I moved the beams back, they made a horrible noise. This startled me so much that I ran back down the Grand Gallery and scrambled through the ascending corridor. After a minute, I calmed down enough to think about searching in the subterranean chamber of the pyramid, but I decided that no one would be there and that it was time for me to go. So I left without finding unauthorized visitors; instead, I found my life's passion.

Word of my exploits got around, and the rumors stopped. No one entered the site free of charge anymore, and there were no more overnight visits by seekers for eternal truth. I changed the padlocks on the pyramids and

Opposite: The Grand Gallery is a great corbeled passage leading to the burial chamber of Khufu. This incredible feat of engineering is one of the marvels of ancient architecture.

kept the keys in a safe in my office. For the next few months, I sat on my veranda and thought a lot about my own life and the future of the monuments under my care. I spent many nights watching the moon look down on the pyramids, bathing them in white light. I strengthened my determination to dedicate my life to these monuments, and as a reward they have given me more than I ever could have asked. In them I have found the beauty and peace that are the gifts of the gods—they have become my lover, and I have received their passion in return.

The Egyptian Delta, where I grew up, is a lush, fertile land of fields, palm trees, and villages built of mud brick.

Early Years

During my nights on the veranda at Giza, I thought about how fate had led me to my new passion for archaeology. I was born in a small village called Abeedya in the Damietta Governate. It is a very small village of only a few hundred people, located on the east bank a few miles from where the Nile meets the Mediterranean at the sea-side resort of Ras el-Bar. My father, Abass, was a farmer who owned land in the village; he also owned cows, water buffalo, and a beautiful horse.

My father married my mother, Aisha, when she was only fourteen, and together they had six children, of whom I was the first son. Growing up in my small village taught me a lot about life and the importance of community. On the day of my circumcision, a great occasion in the village, my father bought me a nice yellow suit with short pants. He put me up on a horse and walked me around the streets near our house with a band playing. When I got home, I sat in a chair, and all the villagers came to give me money and gifts.

This tradition goes back to ancient times and is part of what binds our communities together. For important rituals, such as weddings and circumcisions, everyone comes and gives money that we call "nuqta." You write the amount each person gives in a notebook, and when they have a celebration, you give them the same amount back, or increase it if you can. This is the spirit that built the pyramids: every household in Egypt would help the king by sending workers or grain or food; in return, the families did not have to pay taxes. On the evening of my circumcision, my father brought in a singer, and everyone sang and danced until dawn.

That was the day I became a man (at the age of five!), and from that day forward, my father began to teach me. Just as the ancient sage Ptahhotep had instructed his son, so my father taught me: be honest and never take anything that is not yours; love people and never hurt another person; but at the same time, be strong and never show your weakness to anyone except those who are closest to you. He also told me that he didn't want me to work as a farmer. "You can come and watch me work, but never put your hand into the dirt. You will be educated, and will be a great man."

This formal portrait was taken on the occasion of my graduation from the University of Cairo in Alexandria.

My father sent me to a man named Sheikh Yones to learn Qur'an. The sheikh was blind, but somehow he could always see if I tried to do anything wrong! I was also sent to a storyteller named Sheikh el-Dosouki to hear tales from history and fables from the Arabian nights. There was no electricity in my village. On nights when there was no moon, you could not see your finger in front of your face. The dark was always my enemy. Perhaps I got this fear from the tales my grandmother and Sheikh el-Dosouki loved to tell me. The heroes in their stories had swords and were strong and brave, but I was too young and weak to fight the devils that awoke in the night. If my father asked me to go and buy something from the store after sunset, I was so afraid that I would refuse unless my younger brother Mahmoud came to guard me.

My father died suddenly when I was thirteen. I cried for days, and felt as though I had lost everything I valued in life. I was the oldest boy, responsible for my three sisters and two younger brothers. But my mother was still young, and my father had left us well provided for. So I continued my education, going to school and reading a lot on my own. I devoured the works of many famous writers, both Egyptian and foreign. Every week I saved enough money to buy a book or go to a movie; even now, it is a great treat for me to read a good novel or see an excellent film.

When I was fifteen and a half, I finished high school and left home to attend the university in Alexandria. I had dreamed all my life of becoming a lawyer, but after one week of reading boring, convoluted law books, I decided that the law was not for me. Discouraged and disoriented, I went to the Faculty of Arts to see what other futures were possible. A new archaeology department had just opened and, although I didn't even know the meaning of the word, it seemed like a field with lots of opportunities. I spent four years at the university, majoring in the Greco-Roman Period. I was only partly engaged by my studies, however; I spent much of my time involved in campus politics (I was president of the Student Union) and had a very active social life.

In 1967, at the age of twenty, I finished my studies, and a year later I went to Cairo to join the Antiquities Department as an inspector. Before reporting for active duty, I spent three more months completing my training to join the Ministry of Culture, under whose jurisdiction the Antiquities Department falls. There were sixty of us taking classes together, and I was the only archaeologist. The others were involved with the theater, movies, books, or other cultural fields. Many of those who trained with me have gone on to become movie stars: every day, I sat next to Abdel Aziz Makhion, who is now a famous actor, and had classes with Nour el-Shereif, the Harrison Ford of Egyptian films. What they were doing seemed like much more fun than archaeology.

Those three months made me question whether or not I should be an archaeologist. Four years of studying Greco-Roman archaeology in Alexandria had not touched my heart, and I could not imagine myself working in a field that I did not love and was not even appreciated by the Egyptian public. To add insult to injury, one of my dates even laughed at me when I told her what I did.

After I finished my additional training, I reported to the Antiquities Department and was disappointed to find that the other archaeologists wanted only to sit in their offices and do paperwork. Most of them had no interest in fieldwork, except for one man named Ahmed el-Sawi, who is now a close friend of mine. I had heard that he was excavating at a site in the Delta called Tell Basta, where he had discovered an Old Kingdom temple and a large cemetery dedicated to the cat goddess Bastet.

The head of the Antiquities Department was Dr. Gamal Mokhtar, who issued a decree assigning me to the

Here I am with my mentor, Dr. Gamal Mokhtar, who guided me in the formative years of my career as an archaeologist.

position of assistant inspector at Tuna el-Gebel in Middle Egypt, about 150 miles south of Cairo. This seemed like a terrible idea to me, since it is in the middle of nowhere. Staying in Cairo didn't seem much better, since it meant mountains of paperwork, but I just couldn't imagine moving to the desert, away from my friends and all the things I liked to do. So I decided to become a diplomat instead.

I spent six months reading books about politics, geography, history, and economics, and then I tried to join the Ministry of Foreign Affairs. I passed the written exam, but during the oral exam, one of the examiners asked me, "What can an archaeologist do in the diplomatic service?" I answered him, "Our history is one of the most important in the world. People come from all over the globe to see our monuments, especially the pyramids, mummies, and King Tut. I can use the magic of the past to make more friends for my country." My examiner somehow found this offensive, and I failed my oral exam.

Just after this disappointment, I ran into Dr. Mokhtar on the stairs of the Antiquities building behind the Cairo Museum. He was surprised and very angry to find me in Cairo rather than at Tuna el-Gebel. Despite my insistence that I could not possibly live alone in the desert, he threatened that if I did not go to Middle Egypt immediately he would ban me from the Antiquities Department forever. I was terribly upset and wailed that I couldn't possibly go to a place where the telephones didn't even work, but he stood firm.

Alone in the Desert at Tuna el-Gebel

I spent five hours riding the train south from Cairo to a little town called Mallawi on a hot and humid day in 1969, and I arrived in the Middle Egyptian desert feeling rather sorry for myself—angry at the world in general and at Dr. Mokhtar in particular. During the trip, I thought about my life, wondering how I had managed to get myself trapped in a career I did not like or want.

From Mallawi, I took a taxi to Tuna el-Gebel, and when I reached the village, I discovered that the site of the same name, where I would be living during my tenure as inspector, was three miles from the town. There were no cars or taxis available, so the mayor of the village arranged for me to be given a donkey. Rather dismayed, I loaded up my bags in front of me and set off for the site. I arrived sweating and exhausted and was received by one of the guards, who took me to Ahmed Saied Hendi, senior inspector of the site. He was waiting for me inside a rest house built of mud brick, fronted by a garden and lying only a few hundred feet away from the site. I could not believe, as a young man of twenty, that I was coming

The ancient city of Hermopolis lies in the floodplain near the desert site of Tuna el-Gebel, where I spent two years as an inspector, my first archaeological job. The patron god of the area was Thoth; this statue represents a baboon, one of the animals sacred to this deity.

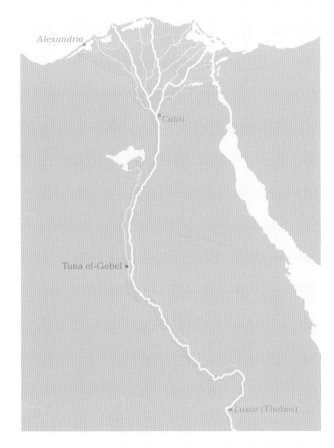

people that they continue until they reach the town of el-Ashmunein, about four and a half miles away. At el-Ashmunein, which was also under our jurisdiction, the principal monument is a temple to Thoth, the ancient god of wisdom, which was built first in the Old Kingdom and then rebuilt or modified a number of times throughout Egyptian history.

Top: The tomb of Isadora is one of the most beautiful tombs at Tuna el-Gebel. It was built during the Greco-Roman Period (332 B.C.–A.D. 642) by Isadora's bereft lover after she drowned in the Nile.

Above: Here you can glimpse the underground catacombs at Tuna el-Gebel, where ibises and baboons sacred to the god Thoth were buried. In the walls are niches where the mummified animals were kept in pots.

to stay in such an isolated place. I remember thinking that if anyone had a heart attack here he would die.

The next day, Hendi showed me around the scattered ruins, which include an extensive necropolis of the Greco-Roman Period (332 B.C.–A.D. 642). One of the most beautiful tombs in this cemetery is the tomb of Isadora, which dates to the reign of Antoninus Pius (second century A.D.). Isadora had lived in a town on the east bank of the Nile. She was in love with a man from the village, and their passion was the talk of the town. One day she went swimming in the Nile and drowned. Her devastated lover wept and built her this tomb, inscribing on its walls a poem in Greek telling of her life and death. Every day he would walk three miles to visit her tomb and light a candle as witness to their eternal love.

A large part of the Greco-Roman cemetery is occupied by a maze of corridors and galleries that were used for the burials of mummified ibises and baboons, animals sacred to the god Thoth. These catacombs cover at least thirty acres underground; there is a legend among the local

I stayed at Tuna el-Gebel for almost two years, and it was an important time for me. A few years earlier, before I graduated from college, I had come to this site and spent one night. I enjoyed myself then, but to live and work in this place was not fun at all, at least in the beginning. Later, however, I found it a place to think, and I learned to be alone. The senior inspector was away with his family in Cairo most of the time, leaving me alone for all but a few days each month. I liked this, since it made me feel independent.

I had plenty of time to visit the archaeological sites that surrounded me and to study them in detail. Every morning I would take my notebook and walk alone to the tomb of Petosiris, an early Ptolemaic tomb (c. 323 B.C.) that represents a wonderful blending of Greek and Egyptian traditions. This monument is dated to the reign of Philip Arrhidaeus, short-lived successor to Alexander the Great, under whom Petosiris was high priest of the temple of Thoth. His tomb is unique because it is shaped like a temple. The decoration was done by Egyptian artists, but with many Greek elements mixed in. I used to visit this tomb daily to enjoy the colors of the scenes.

The site became very quiet in the afternoon: the few tourists would have come and gone, and the cook would have made my lunch and dinner and then gone back to the village on his bicycle. I would take this time to visit the other monuments and explore the secrets of the site. One of my favorite monuments was a boundary stele (inscribed stone slab) of the New Kingdom "heretic" king, Akhenaten (c. 1352–1336 B.C.), whose capital city lay across the river. The stele stands in a rock-cut shrine cut into a cliff just outside the main entrance to Tuna el-Gebel, and it is the earliest monument on the site. Akhenaten

In this relief from the tomb of Petosiris (c. 323 B.C.) you can see the blend of Greek and Egyptian traditions that characterizes the monuments of the Ptolemaic Period. This image shows part of a traditional Egyptian tomb scene, but the participants are wearing Greek clothing.

had fourteen stelae carved to mark the boundary of his new capital, Akhetaten; this one marked the northwest limit of the agricultural area associated with the city. I used to sit and gaze at this shrine while the sun set.

In the early evening, I would often go to sit with the administrative secretary of the Inspectorate, Mr. Abadeer—a nice man and a religious Copt—who would tell me stories of people who had worked at the site. Around 9 P.M. I would leave to get my dinner and go to bed. I lived in a large rest house with plenty of empty bedrooms, a very nice reception hall, and lovely gardens. The house was lighted in the evening with a generator that frequently broke, leaving me without electricity for long stretches of time. There was no refrigerator or television; my only companion was a radio on which I could listen to the news. On the rare occasions when the telephone was working, I could call my friends and chat for a few minutes, which was always a great treat. I was in love at that time with a young lady from Alexandria and wanted to talk to her as often as I could.

With my long nights, I had lots of time for dreams and would often wake up suddenly from my sleep. There was no light to read by, so I would lie with my eyes open, staring at the ceiling and listening for the voice of the guard outside to take away some of my fear of being alone in the darkness. I fell into the rhythm of using all of the daylight for reading and exploring the site and the night for talking to Mr. Abadeer and sleeping.

Once Mr. Abadeer took me to an empty rest house nearby. The house had belonged to the former minister of education, Taha Hussein, who had been born blind but who overcame his handicap and traveled to Paris to earn his doctorate. Before the revolution in 1952, which overturned the Egyptian monarchy, he fought for free education for all Egyptians and wrote many useful books about literature. He had built this house to live in for a few weeks each year, during the winter season. He loved the story of Isadora, and he would go to her tomb every day and light a candle he had left inside. I decided to continue this tradition, and every evening before the sun set I would go to the tomb and light a candle, thinking of the grieving lover and of the great Taha Hussein.

One day at noon, I was sitting in my office when Mr. Abadeer came in with a man and wife who had come to visit the site. The man was a physician, and his wife had a degree in business. While we were drinking tea, the doctor told me that although they had been married for eight years they had not yet been able to have children. They had gone to every known doctor of gynecology in Cairo and Alexandria, to no avail, but they had not lost hope. Some people in their village had told the husband about a magic place inside the temple of Thoth that contained a monument to Min, the god of fertility. If his wife stood above a specific stone, she would get pregnant. I laughed and said, "How can a man with your education believe in something like this?" He answered that everyone in his village believed this, and so did he.

I asked the chief of the guards, Sheikh Moselhy, to take them to the temple of Thoth and Min, and I didn't give them another thought. But a year later, they came to see me and brought their three-month-old son! They gave me a box of candy and told me that they had dedicated him to Min, the god of fertility. I could not believe my eyes!

My ongoing fight against the theft of antiquities started during my first tour of duty at Tuna el-Gebel. The market in stolen antiquities is now and always has been a serious problem for archaeologists. Taking an artifact out of its archaeological setting strips it of the information that makes it more than just a beautiful object. The piece becomes truly dead, robbed of the context that brings its history to life.

One day the chief of police for Mallawi called me and said he had received some information about a family from el-Ashmunein who had been finding antiquities in the courtyard of their house and smuggling them to a known thief in the village. This thief was a guard at the temple of Thoth who had become rich and influential from the antiquities trade. I arranged with the police to be picked up at dawn on a certain date so we could pay a surprise visit to this house. When we arrived, the police knocked, but the man refused to open the door. So they broke it down, and inside we found the illegal excavation this man and his family were carrying out. He yelled at me, "Why are you here? This monument belongs to me, it belonged to my ancestors, and you have no right to take it!" We found some broken statues and pottery, and the police took the man to jail.

A few months later, we heard that there had been a car accident in the town of Maghagha, just north of el-Minya. Three men, one of whom was the antiquities thief from Ashmunein, died in the wreck. In the back of the car, the police found a bag full of antiquities that the men had been planning to sell in Cairo.

I also learned that our antiquities are threatened by more than just human thieves. One night, I was sleeping deeply when I was awakened by a knock on the door. Sheikh Moselhy cried out in a loud voice, "Sir, get up! There is a fire in the galleries of ibises and baboons!" I got up quickly, put on my clothes, and ran to the catacombs. There was smoke coming from the south galleries, which were filled with hundreds of highly flammable mummified animals buried in clay pots. I ran to call the fire department and the police, but of course the phone wasn't working. I had to get to town, and the only way was to take the pick-up truck. I made it to town in fifteen minutes, woke up the mayor, and called the fire and police departments. The fire department arrived at the village first. I hopped onto their truck and drove with them to the site, where they pumped water into the galleries for hours. Later, all the police from the nearby towns of Mallawi and Minya came. Samir Ragab, then reporter and now chief editor for the newspaper *el-Gomhoria,* wrote a story with the headline "Thoth is Burning." This was one of the most intelligent and accurate stories I have ever seen in a newspaper. Mr. Ragab stayed with me for a few days and reported news of the fire daily.

At noon on the first day, the fire department stopped pumping water, but the smoke came back. We fought the mysterious fire for ten days, but it kept burning. Finally, Dr. Mokhtar sent in an architect named Mamdouh Yacoub

to find a solution. At his suggestion, we built a wall at the entrance to the burning galleries so that the air supply would be cut off and the fire would burn itself out. Another young architect, Salah el-Nagar, came and stayed with me in the rest house, and two or three times a day we would go and put our hands on the wall to see if it was still hot. It took two weeks, but finally the wall felt cool; when we broke it down, we found that the fire had gone out, leaving behind the burnt-out remains of the burial pots.

We will never know for certain what started the fire, but the final report suggested that a careless visitor might have dropped a cigarette. Whatever the cause, I will never forget the weeks when Thoth burned.

The site of Kom Abu Billo, about forty miles northwest of Cairo, is where I did my first excavations, began to learn my craft, and fell in love with archaeology.

Salvage Excavations at Kom Abu Billo

In 1970 I moved, at my own request, from Tuna el-Gebel to a post as inspector of antiquities at Alexandria, stopping along the way to serve as interim inspector for the important site of Edfu. After only one month at Alexandria, I was chosen to join an excavation at Kom Abu Billo, about forty miles northwest of Cairo. I traveled directly to the site, which is in the western Delta, and met the rest of the expedition: the head of the team, the other archaeologists, the draftsmen, the photographer, the architect, and the overseer of the workmen.

The Antiquities Department was planning an extensive salvage operation to explore three miles along the projected route of a canal that would run through an archaeological site. When the importance of the salvage area became evident, the excavations were greatly extended. I spent six seasons here; this is where I learned my basic excavation techniques, and where I fell in love with archaeology.

A cache of flint tools, which was discovered by workers dredging the canal, provides evidence that the site may have been occupied as early as Predynastic times. The pharaonic town, known as Mafket, grew into an important trading center called Terenouthis during Greco-Roman times. Occupation in the region continued into the Coptic Period. During my time at Kom Abu Billo, we excavated many graves, dating from the Old Kingdom through the Greco-Roman and Coptic Periods, found traces of an Apollo temple and two Roman baths, and excavated a small section of the ancient settlement, most of which unfortunately lies under the modern town of Tarana and the surrounding farmland.

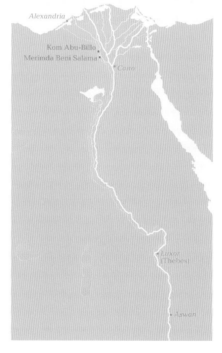

Our work focused on the extensive Greco-Roman and Coptic remains at the site. We uncovered and recorded more than six thousand tombs that dated from approximately 300 B.C. to the fourth century A.D. Most of the tombs had rectangular or square superstructures with barrel-vaulted roofs resting on platforms; there was usually an offering table of mud brick and a niche in the eastern face of the superstructure. Inside the niches were stelae or painted scenes depicting the deceased, sometimes with their families; the art showed a mixture of Greek and Egyptian elements. The Greco-Roman burials contained no coffins, just bodies placed directly into the ground, with, in many cases, a coin clutched in the left hand. This coin may have been to pay Charon, the ferryman to the Land of the Dead. Some of the burials contained personal objects, of which the most outstanding were statuettes of faience (a coarse silicate) representing Aphrodite-Isis, the goddess of love and beauty. We also found a single large pit containing fifty corpses, all of which showed traces of violent death, with arrowheads frequently embedded in the bone.

The archaeologist in charge of the excavations when I arrived stayed for only a few months, and in spite of my youth, I was made senior assistant to the man who succeeded him, Abdel Hafiz Abdelal. When he retired, Ahmed el-Sawi became head of the excavations. We became very close, and I learned a lot from him. When he left to finish his doctorate at the University of Prague, I was put in charge of the site. Dr. Hassan Sobhi el-Bakry, head of Pharaonic Monuments for the Antiquities Department, would often come and stay with us because he was interested in publishing the funerary stelae that we discovered inside the niches of the tombs; he too taught me a great deal. Another archaeologist, Loutfi Sherief, whom I had met earlier at Edfu, joined us during the second season. He and I became good friends and shared many adventures.

Working with us were over thirty well-trained men called Quftis, who came from a village in Upper Egypt named Quft. Men from this village are highly prized as archaeological workers. They were first trained in excavation techniques in the late nineteenth century by Sir William Flinders Petrie, who is often hailed as the father of Egyptology, and ever since, they have been teaching their sons and the sons of their sons to work in the excavations of both Egyptian and foreign scholars.

I had two mentors at Kom Abu Billo: the overseer of the workmen, whom we called Reis Doctoor, and Hag Mohammed Yasseen, our restorer, both of whom were from Quft. To my sorrow, both have now passed on. They taught me fundamental techniques, such as how to use a brush to clean a skeleton and bring a statue safely out of a tomb; they also taught me patience and wisdom. Over the course of six years, I learned from them the basics of field archaeology.

Reis Doctoor's father had also been an archaeological overseer, and his grandfather had worked with Petrie. One day during his excavations at Abydos, Petrie found a 2 1/2-inch high ivory statuette of King Khufu, builder of the Great Pyramid at Giza, seated on a throne. Petrie was thrilled, since this was then, and still is, the only image of

Khufu ever found; unfortunately, the figure was missing its head. Petrie asked the workmen to go to the nearby towns of Balyana and Sohag to buy sieves so that they could scour all the sand at the site in search of the tiny head. The workmen sieved the sand for days, until, according to family legend, Reis Doctoor's grandfather finally found the head.

Reis Doctoor was a tall man who walked with a limp and spoke with an Upper Egyptian accent. I believe that his family named him Doctoor because they knew how talented he would be. He used to take me by the hand in order to show me how to deal with an artifact, and he also used to tell me stories about other archaeologists, both good and bad. He would tell me that a strong personality is essential for a good archaeologist.

Hag Mohammed had dark skin and thick lips and always wore a white galabia robe and headdress. He was a strong man, and very sensitive, with the most golden hands I have ever seen; thanks to his delicate touch, he could handle fragile artifacts without damaging them. He was an excellent restorer and worked with me for many years. During my first days of excavation at Kom Abu Billo, Hag Mohammed asked me to come and see a tomb that he thought was intact. I took my tools and started carefully clearing away the sand. It was July, and the weather was hot and humid, but I forgot about the heat in the excitement of my work. I was excavating a niche inside when I saw a streak of blue. As I carefully brushed away the sand, a statuette of faience, my first major artifact, began to emerge. Before I tried to remove it, I asked

Above: The most highly trained archaeological workers in Egypt come from the village of Quft in Upper Egypt. The ancestors of today's Quftis were trained in excavation technique by Sir William Flinders Petrie, *the father of Egyptology. Here two Qufti overseers clean a faience statuette.*

Above right: A Roman funerary stele from Kom Abu Billo that shows the deceased lying on his funeral bed, drinking wine.

Hag Mohammed to treat, or consolidate, it with chemicals, because I was afraid that the faience would turn to powder when it was exposed to the air. After he had done his work, I began to use my brush. Suddenly, two beautiful eyes appeared, the eyes of Aphrodite-Isis. As I picked the piece up and held it in my hand, I could feel the passion for archaeology enter into every part of my body. During my time at Kom Abu Billo, I gave up many of the other things in my life and began to dedicate myself to the study of ancient Egypt. I started to feel that every artifact I found was a part of me. The light I saw coming from the eyes of that statuette touched my heart, as if I were falling in love at first sight with a beautiful woman. At that moment, I knew I had found my true love, archaeology.

There are millions of people who love their jobs, but often their work becomes routine. They will get up, go to the office, and come back home and focus on other things. But passion is something else. I live for my work; when I am not excavating, I am thinking about my discoveries, about how I will record them for scholars and how I will bring them alive for the public. I try to find ways to make each artifact breathe, whether it is of gold or of clay. There is no important or unimportant job: with passion, any job can be the most important job in the world, a job to inspire the young and help them reach their full potential. I believe that my enthusiasm encourages young people all over the world who want to become archaeologists to write to me. I always find the time to answer their letters.

My journey to passion did not end with my first find. I still had demons to overcome and work to do. At Kom Abu Billo, we found a Roman well which was about seventy feet deep. The workmen would tie one man to a rope, and three or four others would lower him to the bottom. If I looked down into the blackness below, my childhood fear of the dark would come rushing back. Hag Mohammed asked me if I would like to go down, but I said no. I thought about it for ten days and finally decided that it was time to get rid of this fear once and for all. I went to Hag Mohammed and told him I was ready. He tied me to the rope, and three men lowered me slowly

into the darkness of the well. My heart pounded faster and faster, and I was overcome by a feeling of panic. I closed my eyes and held tightly to the rope, and then suddenly, it was over. I was at the bottom of the well, safe, and rid of my fear of the dark.

Life at the excavation was an adventure. The expedition built two large camps on the site, one for the excavation team and one for the workmen, and rented the house of a rich farmer in the nearby village of Ezbet Moustafa. We would get up early and work until 2 P.M., braving snakes, scorpions, and the hot desert sun. After we ate a lunch of bread, garlic, and onions, we would write in our diaries, finish taking photographs, record our discoveries in the big excavation diary, or draw the artifacts we had found that day. We stopped work in the evening because there was no electricity and we had to use lamps. After dinner I would go and inspect the guards at the camp or meet with the Qufti workmen. It was their habit to greet us and offer us cigarettes. I didn't smoke at the time and used to give the cigarettes to Loutfi, but eventually I started to smoke like everyone else and didn't stop until 1993.

We used to store the artifacts that we discovered in a large tent on the excavation site. At the end of each season, I would take all the artifacts, many of gold (I myself found more than five hundred golden artifacts over the course of the excavations), to the Cairo Museum in a truck guarded by soldiers. The first year, as soon as I had unloaded the artifacts and had the curator sign for them, I received a call that an aunt of mine had died. The second year, after I had delivered the artifacts, someone called to tell me that an uncle had died! The third year, I told Ahmed el-Sawi that I was afraid that the same thing would happen again, and I asked him to send someone else instead of me. He laughed and said, "You know you don't believe in things like this." Two minutes later, a telegram came to the village saying that my beloved cousin Fayed, who was working in Libya at the time, had died in a bad accident. I don't believe in the Curse of the Pharaohs, but that was the last year that I agreed to take the artifacts to the museum.

Unearthing Prehistory at Merimda Beni Salama

After the excavations at Kom Abu Billo had ended, I was put in charge of the Inspectorate of Imbaba, which encompassed the antiquities sites from Giza in the southwest to Kom Abu Billo in the north. My territory included the important prehistoric site of Merimda Beni Salama, located thirty-seven miles northwest of Cairo. This site, one of the most important Neolithic (c. 7000-3200 B.C.) settlements in Egypt, was excavated from 1928 to 1939 by Hermann Junker, one of the great German Egyptologists. The high ground on which the site lies covers an area of more than forty-four acres; at the height of its occupation, there were probably as many as five thousand people living here. It is the earliest known farming settlement in the Nile Valley, ideally situated on a desert spur high enough to protect the inhabitants from the annual flood and cradled by the Rosetta branch of the Nile (now dried up) to the north and desert pasturelands to the south. The Neolithic villagers grew crops in the fertile plain, grazed their animals in the desert savannah, and supplemented their diet by fishing and hunting.

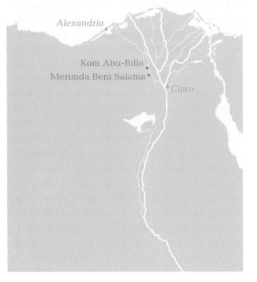

When I arrived at the site in 1976, I discovered that the modern inhabitants of the nearby village of Beni Salama were planting crops on antiquities land and digging up parts of the mound to use as fertilizer. I wanted to start excavating in this area again so that the local authorities would see for themselves how important the site was, and I asked the Antiquities Department for twenty thousand Egyptian pounds (about $4,500) to carry out a season of work.

That same year, I gave a talk in Cairo about Kom Abu Billo at the First International Congress of Egyptology and announced my plans to excavate at Merimda Beni Salama. The scholars at the conference were very skeptical, believing that I was too young and inexperienced to work at such an important prehistoric site. I began to talk to the other archaeologists, both to win them over and to ask their advice. I took with me to the site Manfried Bietak, current excavator of the site of Avaris in the Delta; Rainer Stadelmann, one of the foremost experts on Old Kingdom pyramids; and Jean Leclant and Alan Zivie, both French archeologists who are now excavating at Saqqara. I explained to them my plans for the excavation, and they were supportive of my ideas.

My work at Kom Abu Billo had been salvage archaeology, a matter of rescuing as much as we could before the new canal was built. At Beni Salama I was involved in a real excavation for the first time, and it was vital that we use the best techniques available so that we could gather as much information as possible. At that time, there were no field schools, so I bought a book by Mortimer Wheeler, excavator of the Indus Valley civilization, and began to study the techniques that he outlined. I was confident of my abilities and the skills I had learned at Kom Abu Billo and decided to start the excavation in October of 1976.

As my crew chief, I took with me Abdel Wahab, who had worked with me at Kom Abu Billo and who told me before the dig that he had dreamed we were doing a different kind work at Beni Salama, with grids and a very slow and careful pace of excavation. I also brought Hag Mohammed Yasseen, the restorer from Kom Abu Billo who had witnessed the moment when I first fell in love with archaeology. The other principal members of the expedition were Abu-el ela Sharawy, our photographer

This photograph from my excavations at Merimda Beni Salama shows me with one of my workmen using mud to restore the walls of a prehistoric shelter.

My excavations at Merimda Beni Salama were a great success. We began by excavating one square as far down as possible to familiarize ourselves with the basic stratigraphy of the site—which meant looking at a cross section that showed the different layers of occupation and analyzing them in order to determine how they related to one another temporally. We sieved every single grain of sand and collected grain, flint tools, pottery, and other artifacts. I used a mirror to reflect the sun's rays onto the excavation section so that I could read the levels as accurately as possible.

We stayed for three months and excavated three five-meter squares, as well as several test pits and trenches. In that small area, through careful work, we were able to gather some radiocarbon dates and make a number of important discoveries; a German expedition continued our work, digging at the site from 1977 to 1982.

Merimda Beni Salama was occupied as early as the beginning of the fifth millennium B.C., and our work demonstrated that it was settled for a very long period of time, about nine hundred years. We found the remains of some houses, which were oval and made of mud brick and wickerwork; they were very small, barely big enough for one adult and several children. Most of the daily activities took place outside; around the houses there were hearths, grinding stones, stone-carving workshops, sunken water jars, and storage containers (baskets, mud-lined pits, and huge clay jars buried up to their necks). There were also large threshing floors, where the ancient Merimdans may have worked collectively to prepare their grain for grinding.

We found evidence from plant materials and bones that the inhabitants of Merimda Beni Salama cultivated emmer wheat, barley (which we found for the first time), lentils, and vetch and raised sheep, goats, cattle, and pigs. They supplemented their diet with desert game, such as antelopes and gazelles, and ate a lot of fish; more than twenty different species have been identified at the site. We also found some hippopotamus and crocodile remains; hippo would have been an excellent source of food, and a

at Kom Abu Billo, and Hag Ismail Sadek, a draftsman working with me for the first time. Atef Hassan was my archaeological assistant.

Since it was too far to travel back and forth to the village every day, we all lived in tents in the desert (in contrast to Junker, who had housed his team in quite an elaborate expedition house). We spent one week surveying the site and establishing a grid of five-meter squares, and then we started our excavation. Life in our camp was very pleasant. We began work at 7 A.M. and ate bread, garlic, and onion for lunch, sometimes with egg, tomato, or potato. I had my own tent, with a bed and a table for studying, and we went to sleep early. One night I was in a deep sleep when a high wind came and blew away my tent! I was so soundly asleep that I did not even notice until the guards began yelling. When I opened my eyes, I found that I was looking straight at the stars.

number of hippo leg bones were found used as doorsteps, probably for ritual reasons such as the warding off of evil spirits. There were countless pottery sherds from simple dishes, bowls, and jars, the most interesting of which had stood on appendages modeled to look like human feet. The site was very rich in artifacts, many made from the various raw materials that were available nearby, and others from materials imported from both the northeast and the south. There was a vast repertoire of stone tools, many of imported stone; there were mace heads, spindle whorls for weaving, sling stones, hammer stones, small alabaster palettes for grinding eye paint, beads, and a few small, poorly made hard-stone vessels. Other tools, such as scrapers, needles, awls, harpoons, and fishhooks, were made of ivory, bone, or horn.

Burials were made within the settlement, and all of the skeletons we found were of women and children; it is possible that the men were buried in a separate cemetery that has not yet been found. The bodies were placed in shallow oval pits and laid on their sides in a contracted position, usually without any grave goods at all, although grain had been placed in front of the mouths of some of the dead as an offering. Many of the children were not even given proper burials but were simply thrown into rubbish pits.

One of the most interesting artifacts that we found was part of a female figurine. Neolithic female idols are much more common than males, which confirms the importance of women during this period. The inhabitants of this ancient site understood that the woman was the core of the society and that without her there would be no Egypt. Without Isis to nurse and raise him, there would have been no Horus to take revenge on his uncle Seth and reclaim the throne of Egypt. In the historical period, according to Ma'at (the Egyptian conception of the proper way of the world), women could not rule the country (although, in fact, we know of at least four female monarchs), but kings could not rule without their queens. Women in Egyptian society were highly respected as wives and especially as mothers, and they had many

rights, more than any other women in the ancient world: they could inherit or purchase land, houses, or goods and dispose of them as they wished, and they could initiate or act as witnesses in court cases.

When we had finished the season, I wrote a report to the Antiquities Department, telling them that we had excavated about fifteen square meters of the site and detailing our finds. I received an angry letter back, asking how I could have spent twenty thousand Egyptian pounds to excavate such a small area. I decided not to answer, since I knew that the head of the department was not an archaeologist and did not understand how careful one must be at a prehistoric site. But I was proud of myself and of the fact that I was the first to explore this site after the great Hermann Junker.

Early Dynastic Graves at Abu Rawash

The site of Abu Rawash is most famous as the site of the pyramid complex of Djedefre, son and successor of Khufu. There are also cemeteries of the Old Kingdom, and an Early Dynastic cemetery of large, extremely rich tombs. During my tenure at Imbaba, the Giza Governate decided to change the route of some sewage pipes, one of which ran through Djedefre's complex. The new route was not through antiquities land, but ran very close to it. In my first years at Imbaba and Giza, I had made a map of all the antiquities lands under these jurisdictions and marked areas nearby that need to be watched. Anyone who wants to develop land in the marked areas is required to hire workmen from the Antiquities Department to make sure that no archaeological materials are destroyed.

One day I was informed by the chief of the guards at Abu Rawash, Sheikh Ashour, that ancient remains had been encountered along the line of the new pipes. I saw quickly that this was an important site, so I stopped the construction completely and initiated a systematic excavation of the area. We set up camp at the site, and established a grid of five-meter squares. During our two-month season we uncovered three tombs from the reign of Hor-

We found three graves from Dynasty 1 at Abu Rawash, site of the later pyramid of Khufu's son Djedefre. Some of the artifacts we found were a pottery vessel, two alabaster vases, and some ivory bracelets.

Alexandria

Abu Rawash Cairo
Giza

Aha, first king of Dynasty 1 (c. 3000 B.C.), which had been cut into the desert marl. The tombs were rectangular in shape, about six feet long and three feet wide. Two of the tombs contained skeletons (a man in one and a woman in the other); the third had been robbed and contained only fragments of bone and pottery sherds. The two intact tombs contained great artifacts: slate palettes, alabaster vessels, beautiful pottery, beads made of carnelian and lapis lazuli, and fragments of ivory, bone, and copper bracelets.

It was difficult for us to sleep at night because of the enormous mosquitoes that left huge welts on our hands and bodies. After the first night, I had to send Abdel Wahab and my photographer, Abu el-ella Sharawy, to buy netting to hang from the ceiling and cover our beds. Even so, the mosquitoes would come like rockets during the night and break through the netting to suck our blood. It was so bad that Hag Mohammed, our master restorer, preferred to travel all the way home every night—not an easy journey—and return before we began work at 7 in the morning.

We spent every Thursday and Friday, our days off, in Cairo. We would put all the artifacts that we had discovered in a tent and leave them under the care of six antiquities guards under the direction of Sheik Ashour. One Friday morning, I decided to go back to Abu Rawash to inspect the excavations. My driver took me, and we arrived at about 12 noon. To my surprise, not a single guard was in sight. I entered the tent where the objects were stored, and no one was there; the guards had left the antiquities completely unprotected.

I asked my driver to come and help me load everything into the car, and we went back to Giza. We brought the boxes into the office, and then I waited. An hour later, Sheikh Ashour came crying to me that all of the excavation artifacts had been stolen, and he had no idea how it had happened. I asked him if he had left the site, and he admitted that they had all left to go to Friday prayer. I made him sweat for a while, and then I showed him the objects. He could not believe his eyes, and the smile came back to his face. All of those guards certainly learned an important lesson that day!

To Abu Simbel, and Finally to Giza

In November 1973, I was asked to serve a three-month term as inspector of antiquities at Abu Simbel. I stayed in Nubia from December 1973 through February 1974, and during my tenure there my love affair with Egyptology grew more intense. In the 1970s the site was still remote, and there were far fewer visitors than is now the case, when three to four thousand people visit the temples every day. I spent my time studying the beautiful rock-cut temples of Ramesses II and his wife, Nefertari, puzzling over the scenes that cover their walls. I enjoyed meeting the tourists and scholars who came to see the sights and to eat the fresh fish that was caught in the lake in front of the temple.

My uncle Mahmoud Riad, who had been a general in the army before the revolution in 1952, came to live with me. I learned a great deal from this man, and during our time in Nubia he became like a second father to me. He told me that there was no one alive that I needed to fear, which is advice I have taken to heart. During my months blanketed in the solitude of this remote site, absorbing the wisdom of my uncle, I thought about my life and about

*Above: The rock-cut temple
of Ramesses II at Abu Simbel
dominates the surrounding
landscape. From 1959 to 1963,
before the Aswan Dam was
completed, an international
team of experts worked together
to dismantle the temple and
move it to higher ground, out of
the reach of Lake Nasser.*

*Opposite: These are some of the
first excavations I supervised at
Giza. The style of my clothing
should give some clue about the
date!*

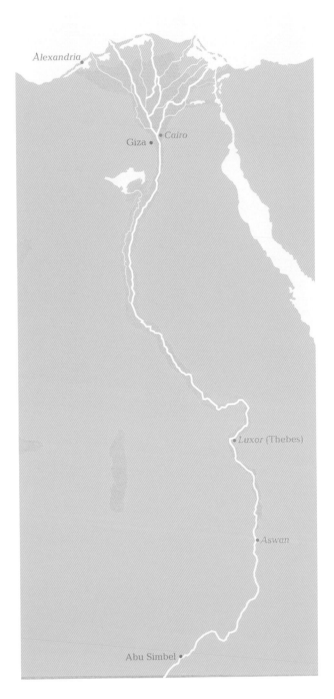

Alexandria

Giza • Cairo

Luxor (Thebes)

• Aswan

Abu Simbel •

how archaeology had become part of my soul. When I received the call from Dr. Mokhtar that would bring me to Giza, I was ready to go, eager to move to the next stage in my career.

The years from 1974 to 1980 in Giza were busy and productive, and I took a great deal of pleasure and pride in my work. In addition to restoring order and financial stability to the site, I began to excavate in the area of the Sphinx and made some important discoveries there. I enjoyed the physical labor, which ranges from the back-breaking to the painstaking; I liked the intricacies of managing people and the building of long-term working relationships with colleagues; and I reveled in the excitement of uncovering glimpses of the past. I realized that I had found my place in the world, that I had found the work to which I would gladly dedicate my life. And in 1977, inside the Great Pyramid, I had the epiphany that changed my life.

It was during these years that I became close to Gamal Mokhtar, who had done such an enormous amount for Egyptology. He was the first president of the Egyptian Antiquities Organization, the successor to the Egyptian Antiquities Service set up by August Mariette in the mid-nineteenth century. He was honored by everyone in the field for his knowledge, dedication, and many important achievements, which included arranging for the salvage of the temples of Ramesses II at Abu Simbel and the temple of Isis at Philae. During his tenure, the King Tut exhibition traveled to six cities in the United States, as well as to Japan, Europe, and Canada, setting off a surge of worldwide fascination with ancient Egypt. Dr. Mokhtar traveled all over the world, taught at many universities in Egypt, and supervised many master's theses and doctoral dissertations. He was very diplomatic and never said a negative word to anyone, not even in his own defense.

I always asked his advice on everything in my life. We met at least once a week for lunch or dinner and talked on the telephone almost every day. One day he came with me to discuss a master's thesis at Sohag University, and while we were there, he fainted. The doctor told Dr.

Mokhtar that he had a heart problem and sent him to Cleveland, Ohio, for surgery. When he came home, he couldn't walk and had to be in a wheelchair for almost a year, but he continued to work hard, and he attended meetings until 1998, when he became so sick that he had to go into the hospital. He was there for about a week, and I visited him every day. On the last night, he could not talk, but when I was leaving, he opened his mouth, and I realized that he was saying goodbye. He died the next morning.

Gamal Mokhtar was one of the few people I have loved in my life. He was like a father to me. He smiled at my successes, for they were his successes, too. I owe much to his wise advice and his love for me. I will never forget him and the wonderful stories he would tell about the salvaging of the Nubian temples and the traveling exhibition of King Tut. I will always keep him in my heart.

After my initial success at Giza, which included a flurry of attention from the press, an older man with a senior position in the Antiquities Department began to attack my name everywhere. He thought that he should have all the credit for our discoveries there, even though he had not done any of the work, and he was jealous of all the attention I was given by the press. I would complain about this

Here my archaeology professor at Penn, Dr. David O'Connor, watches a colleague cutting a cake shaped like the Step Pyramid of Djoser at Saqqara.

man to Gamal Mokhtar, who gave me the best advice I've ever had. He said, "You are a strong man. Try to protect yourself, but never give back hatred. Work hard and produce good things, and let him destroy himself."

I took Dr. Mokhtar's advice. One of the things that this man, minion of Seth, would say was, "How can Zahi Hawass be in charge of the pyramids with only a B.A. in Greek and Roman archaeology?" He had a point. I had already decided that I wanted to continue my studies, so in 1978 I went to Cairo University to earn a diploma in Egyptology. In my first year, I would go to school every day from 4 to 8 P.M. It was at the university that I took my first big step toward understanding the ancient monuments and where I made some lifelong friends in the field of archaeology.

I graduated with honors in 1979 and began to be known throughout Egypt for my work, but this made Seth's representative, who had managed to earn a doctorate without learning much about Egyptology, even more jealous, and he began to say that without a doctoral degree I was nothing. Several foreign archaeologists had offered me the opportunity to study abroad for my doctorate: Jean Leclant in Paris, Rainer Stadelmann in Germany, and Manfried Bietak in Vienna. Many Egyptian

My professor of philology at Penn, Dr. David Silverman, at the Middle Egyptian site of Bersheh, where he has worked for a number of seasons.

This is a formal portrait taken at the time I received my doctorate from the University of Pennsylvania.

Egyptologists go abroad to study through the foreign expeditions that work in Egypt, but this puts them in the position of owing favors to the people with whom they study. Even though these three Egyptologists are wonderful people and close friends of mine, I did not want to be put in this position.

At this point, I met Frank Blanning, who was the head of the Fulbright Commission in Cairo. He was a good man who appreciated my work, and he told me that Fulbright was planning to offer a program of study for an Egyptian in any branch of science to go to the United States to earn a Ph.D. Students in the fields of medicine, engineering, and science had been sponsored through this program, but never an archaeologist. I decided that this would be my best route, and I applied for the grant. As part of my application, I had to write a proposal stating why I wanted to study in the United States and I had to be interviewed by members of the Fulbright Committee in Cairo and the Egyptian Committee from the Academy of Scientific Research. In my proposal and the interviews, I stressed the importance of sending an Egyptian archaeologist to study in America. I emphasized that the Egyptian monu-

ments were treasures that shouldn't be used just for the benefit of the Egyptian economy, and I insisted that we needed long-term strategies for both conservation and restoration.

I was chosen from a field of more than five hundred applicants, and I chose to attend the University of Pennsylvania because it was on the East Coast and because it was the school with the best programs in both archaeology, taught by David O'Connor, and philology, taught by David Silverman. I was also interested in the collections at the University Museum: all of the artifacts there have been excavated, rather than bought on the antiquities market, which means they can be studied within their historical contexts.

I arrived at Penn on October 2, 1980, a day I will always remember. I met the two Davids and asked them to forget that I was an Egyptian official, just to treat me as a student eager to learn. It took me three and a half years to finish my courses and exams, and another three years to write my thesis and dissertation. Many important things happened to me during my years in Philadelphia. I began to learn how to lecture effectively, in a way that would engage both the public and scholars. Through the Education Department at the museum, I gave lectures at public libraries all over the state of Pennsylvania. In my second year, my lectures were so popular that I often had to speak more than three times a week. I also worked with Gene Kiefer, president of a company called Global Concepts, which was marketing lectures by foreign scholars in the States. Through his organization, I traveled and lectured all over the country, and I had the opportunity to share my passion for archaeology with many people. I had a lot of interesting experiences giving these talks; once I arrived to find the front row filled with people wearing pyramids on their heads!

During this time, I met Ambassador Abdel Raouf el-Reedy, Egypt's ambassador to the United States. We discovered that we were both from the Damietta Governate, and we became close friends. He would call me in for anything concerning archaeology in Egypt. When a group of artifacts from the time of Ramesses II toured Canada and the United States, Ambassador el-Reedy asked me to travel with him to a number of cities to publicize the exhibition. He used the magic of archaeology to make friends for Egypt, meeting with congressmen, senators, and the mayors of all the towns we visited.

I received excellent training at Penn, and my love affair with Egyptology grew during my years there. I chose a fascinating subject as my doctoral topic: "The Funerary Cult of Khufu, Khafre and Menkaure at Giza during the Old Kingdom." In this dissertation, I studied the archaeology of the Giza Plateau in detail, reviewing all of the previous excavations and scholarship and using all the available evidence to examine the royal cults that flourished there. My experience at Penn, in conjunction with my previous fieldwork, gave me a very solid foundation as an Egyptologist.

I came back to Egypt in June 1987 and took the position of director general of the Giza Pyramids, Saqqara, and the Bahariya Oasis. (Since 1998, I have also held the title of undersecretary of state for the Giza Monuments, but I always preferred my title of director general.) Upon my return, I plunged right into the thick of things, dealing with problems that had arisen with the nearby village of Nazlet es-Samman; setting up controls to collect fees from everyone entering the site and to limit the number of people entering the pyramids; fighting off a ring road that would have run near Giza and threatened the monuments; and setting up a site-management plan that includes both excavation and preservation.

As a result of this program, I made a number of important new discoveries. The great Egyptian archaeologist Selim Hassan was the last to excavate at Giza before I came. After his last season, he stated that the plateau was finished, that everything worthwhile had been found. But the last fifteen years have proven him completely wrong! So come with me to Giza, and learn about the wonderful new discoveries we have made.

Here I am in front of the Great Pyramid at Giza.

Chapter II. New Discoveries at Giza

The Giza Plateau, on the outskirts of modern Cairo, is one of the most extraordinary places in the world, and I feel its magic every day. I love to walk over its windswept stones and sense that the ancient monuments are welcoming me and thanking me for my stewardship. It is a rugged place, full of rocks and sand, but it is also an inviting place, offering incredible vistas, fresh air, and the chance to enjoy some of the most amazing achievements of the ancient world.

Over a hundred pyramids have been found in Egypt, but the three kings' pyramids at Giza, and especially the Great Pyramid of Khufu—the largest of all the pyramids—are by far the best known of these. These massive stone mountains and their companion, the Great Sphinx, dominate the horizon for miles around. They have fascinated mankind for millennia and generated all sorts of outlandish theories about how, when, and why they were built. We have overwhelming evidence that they were built by the ancient Egyptians over a period of three generations, c. 2589–2503 B.C., as monumental tombs for three specific kings. But all of the hard data that Egyptologists have gathered over the years has not stopped the "pyramidologists" and "pyramidiots" from "proving" that the pyramids were built by ancient astronauts, or men from Atlantis, or whoever else, and that they were designed as maps of the stars, mathematical maps of the universe, or launching pads for rockets. I tell people at my lectures that anyone can make a lot of money from the pyramids: Just make up an idea, the crazier the better, and write a book about it!

But some very important Egyptologists got their start on the fringes of the field. W. M. F. Petrie, one of the founders of scientific Egyptology, first came to Egypt as a believer in the theories of Piazzi Smyth, who believed that the Great Pyramid was "God's Message in Stone." And my good friend Mark Lehner, with whom I have worked closely for many years, originally came to Egypt under the auspices of the Cayce Foundation, a group that believes in many things that fly in the face of archaeological reality.

I met Mark for the first time in 1974 at a party. He was very quiet and told me only that he was interested in the field of Egyptology. I liked him and asked him to come and visit me at my office at Giza. I was young then, only twenty-seven, and my hair was still completely black.

Mark did come to see me, and he told me that he was studying Egyptology at the American University in Cairo. He explained that he had come to Egypt as a disciple of the American psychic Edgar Cayce, who has been called "The Sleeping Prophet." Cayce was a poor carpenter who apparently discovered that he had psychic abilities. He would close his eyes, loosen his tie, go into a trance, and give out prescriptions to people who were sick and suffering. His advice often cured his patients, and even though he was not a doctor, his prescriptions were accepted by physicians all over the United States (although many would also note that at least 60 percent of people recover from whatever ails them without any help). One day, his son Hylan Cayce supposedly became blind. Many doctors saw him and tried to treat him, but no one could cure him except his father, who by some miracle was able to open his son's eyes and make him see.

When Cayce was asked about his past, he closed his eyes and said that he had lived in Atlantis and that his name had been Ra-Ra. When the continent where he lived was destroyed, he was able to collect all the technology of the ancient Atlanteans and fly with it to Egypt. He used this technology to build the Great Pyramid and buried a box containing the records of his people under the right paw of the Sphinx.

Mark had met Edgar's son Hylan when he was a young man of seventeen and had been given a scholarship by the Cayce Foundation to study in Egypt with the ultimate goal of finding the lost technology of Atlantis. I told Mark that he was crazy—that all this was an American hallucination, but I liked and respected him, and we became good friends. By 1977, after facing the realities of archaeological fact and the physical evidence from the Giza Plateau itself, Mark had begun to have doubts about the Cayce mythology.

Later that year, Mark and I traveled to about ten cities in the United States to give joint lectures in the form of debates. These were very interesting, because Mark was beginning to think that we Egyptologists were right. While we were on this tour, we went to a party in Virginia

My good friend and colleague Mark Lehner and I have spent many years searching for evidence of the pyramid builders of Giza. We found it south of the Wall of the Crow, where this photograph was taken recently. I am working in the cemetery where the laborers, their overseers, artisans, and minor officials were buried, and Mark is excavating the royal installation where the workers received their tools and rations.

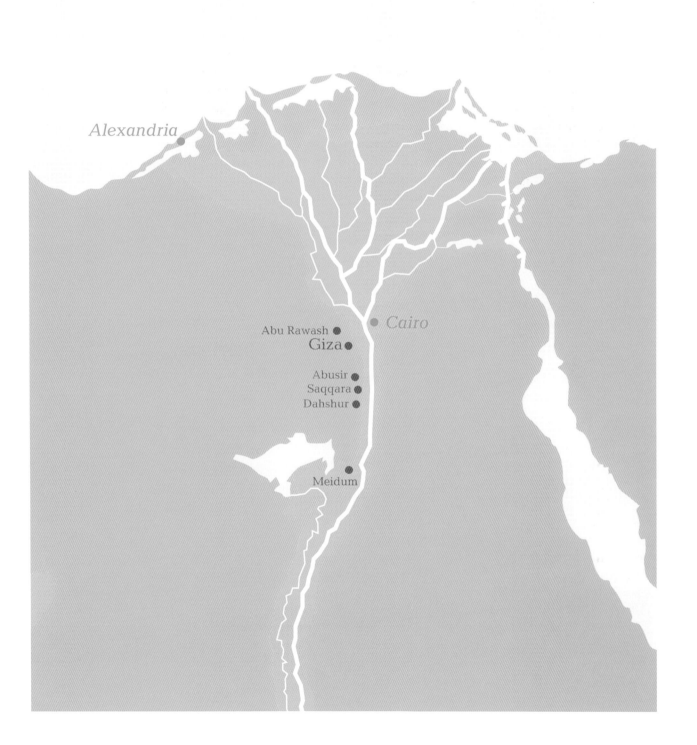

Alexandria

Cairo

Abu Rawash
Giza

Abusir
Saqqara
Dahshur

Meidum

Beach, where the Cayce Foundation is headquartered. On the way to the party, Mark said to me, "I do not believe in Edgar Cayce anymore. My studies in Egyptology have shown me overwhelming evidence that the Sphinx belongs to Dynasty 4 and not to ten thousand years ago, as Cayce claimed."

At the party, we met a famous psychic who professed to be able to predict the future. I myself have never believed in this sort of thing, but it was fun to watch him as he covered his face and began to speak in a language that no one could understand. He said that the records of Atlantis would be found in the year 2000, when there would be peace all over the world, by two men, one an American and one an Egyptian, meaning, of course, Mark and me. The party continued until late in the evening, and I reflected on what a strange world we lived in.

The tour was great fun, and Mark and I developed a bond that has grown stronger over the years. Mark, who went on to get his Ph.D. and to teach at a number of prestigious institutions, has been excavating at Giza for the past twenty years and has contributed a great deal to the field of Egyptology. We have grown up together, excavating, working, and lecturing all over the world. Sometimes, you can have a brother that is not born of your father or your mother. Mark is such a brother to me.

A Brief History of Giza

It is the monuments of Giza, perhaps more than any others, that have come to symbolize ancient Egypt. This great cemetery, watched over for eternity by the Sphinx, was founded by the second king of the 4th Dynasty, Khufu ("Cheops" in Greek), who came to the throne in about 2589 B.C. According to the standard chronology, he ruled for twenty-three years, but I believe that he actually reigned for at least thirty or thirty-two years. At the outset of his reign, Khufu moved his court and administration from Dahshur, where two pyramid complexes and the capital of his father, Sneferu, were located, to the foot of the Giza Plateau ten or so miles to the south.

The Great Pyramid of Khufu is the largest and finest of all of Egypt's pyramids, the fourth of the "true" (straight-sided) pyramids that developed from the stepped pyramids of the 3rd Dynasty, which in turn grew out of mounds built over the burial shaft inside earlier tombs. The pyramid forms part of a large complex called "the Horizon of Khufu," in which the standard elements of the Old Kingdom pyramid complex (mortuary temple, valley temple, causeway, satellite pyramid, queen's pyramids, nobles' tombs, and boat pits) appear in their entirety for the first time. Pyramid complexes, in addition to serving as sepulchers, were elaborate temple precincts, where both the king and important national gods, especially Re (the sun god), Hathor (his wife and daughter), and Horus (their son and totem of the king), were worshiped. Horus is also known as the son of Osiris and Isis, but the cult of Re rather than the cult of Osiris was dominant in Old Kingdom pyramid complexes.

After the death of Khufu, the throne was inherited by his son Djedefre. Instead of staying at Giza, Djedefre chose to build his pyramid complex at the remote site of Abu Rawash, five miles to the north, the site where I had excavated an Early Dynastic cemetery earlier in my career. Djedefre planned a relatively small monument, but he died after reigning for only eight years, and his pyramid complex was left unfinished. His half brother Khafre (Chephren) then seized the throne and came back to Giza.

Khafre built the second Giza pyramid complex, called by the ancient Egyptians "Khafre is Great," south of his father's monument. His pyramid lies on slightly higher ground, so that it appears to be the same size although it is in fact a bit smaller. In addition to the standard elements, Khafre added the Great Sphinx and its temple to his complex. I believe that the Sphinx represents Khafre as Horus facing east to worship his father, Khufu, as the sun god Re. This conclusion is borne out through the name

Overview of Giza, showing the Old Kingdom remains and highlighting the areas where new work has been carried out in recent years.

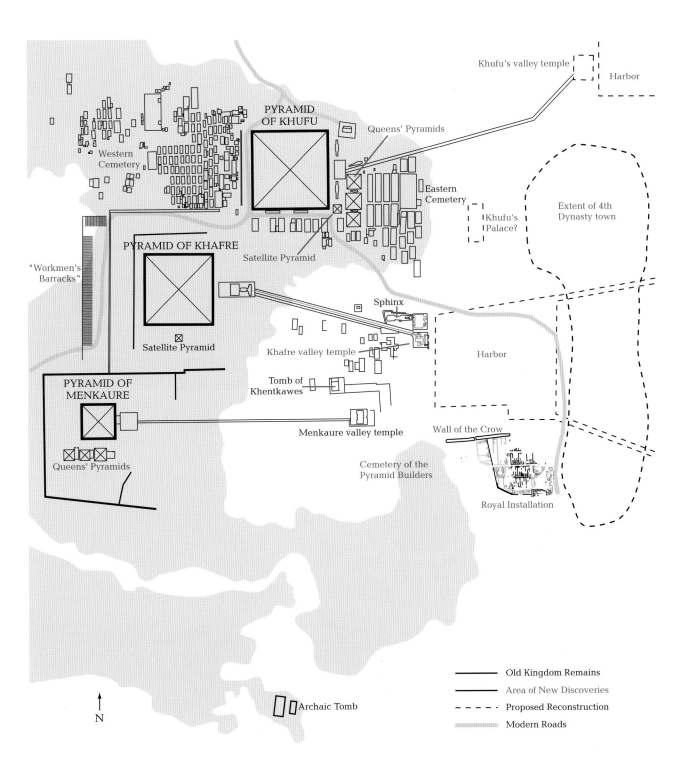

Khufu's valley temple

Harbor

PYRAMID
OF KHUFU

Queens' Pyramids

Western
Cemetery

Eastern
Cemetery

Khufu's
Palace?

Extent of 4th
Dynasty town

Satellite Pyramid

PYRAMID OF KHAFRE

"Workmen's
Barracks"

Sphinx

Khafre valley temple

Harbor

Satellite Pyramid

PYRAMID OF
MENKAURE

Tomb of
Khentkawes

Menkaure valley temple

Wall of the Crow

Queens' Pyramids

Cemetery of the
Pyramid Builders

Royal Installation

N

Archaic Tomb

Old Kingdom Remains

Area of New Discoveries

Proposed Reconstruction

Modern Roads

45

Right: The Great Pyramid of Khufu is the largest of all the Egyptian pyramids. It was built over the course of about twenty-five years and represents a monumental achievement of engineering.

Opposite, top: Khufu's son and successor, Djedefre, began his pyramid at Abu Rawash, five miles to the north of his father's, but the complex was left unfinished. Here we can see the entrance to his burial chamber, open to the sky.

Opposite, bottom: The pyramid of Khafre, seen here from the fields that lie to the east, is only slightly smaller than his father's, but it was set on higher ground and thus appears to be the same size.

Great Pyramid, date from the fifth year of Khufu's reign. These tombs are mastabas (named for low rectangular benches, which can still be found in the courtyards of modern Egyptian houses) belonging to officials and priests. Beginning in the twelfth year of Khufu's reign, members of the royal family were buried in neat rows of mastabas to the east of his monument. Nobles and priests continued to be buried at Giza until the end of the 6th Dynasty (c. 2181 B.C.), for as long as the cults of the Giza kings were still active.

Since my return to Giza in 1987, I have developed and instituted a site-management plan designed to focus primarily on conservation and restoration. In the process of

of the Sphinx, "Horus in the Horizon," which is found in monuments of the New Kingdom and later.

Khafre was succeeded by his son Menkaure (Mycerinus), who built his complex, "Menkaure is Divine," at the southern edge of the Giza Plateau. Menkaure's pyramid is much smaller, in part because he used the relatively expensive material of granite to case the lowest third of the monument. He died before his complex was finished, and his son and successor, Shepseskaf, finished his temples in mud brick. The last ruler to be buried at Giza was a queen named Khentkawes, who provides the link between the 4th and 5th Dynasties: she was a daughter of Menkaure, wife of the first king of the 5th Dynasty and the mother of two 5th Dynasty kings.

Many nobles, officials, and priests built their tombs on the Giza Plateau around the monuments of the kings whom they served. The earliest of these, to the west of the

The pyramid of Khafre's son Menkaure (seen here with its small queens' pyramids) is considerably smaller than its predecessors at Giza, but it was cased to a third of its height with the relatively expensive material of granite imported from Aswan far to the south.

executing this plan, which involves a great deal of clearance and cleaning, we have made a number of important discoveries that have shed much new light on the history of the 4th Dynasty. In the complex surrounding Khufu's pyramid, we have found new tombs, part of the pyramid construction ramp, Khufu's satellite pyramid (a much smaller pyramid that served a ritual purpose), and in the flood plain to the east (now covered by the modern suburbs of Cairo), remains of his causeway, valley temple, harbor, possible palace, and glimpses of his pyramid city. We carried out work, including the dismantling of the old Sound and Light Theater, in the area of Khafre's valley temple and we discovered a number of new features and traces of his harbor. In our clearance around Menkaure's pyramid, we found a double statue from the reign of Ramesses II, who ruled more than a thousand years later, carved from a granite block that had fallen from the pyramid face. Mark Lehner and I have also begun to find traces of the workers who built the pyramids: the settlement where the artisans and workmen lived, the royal installation where their supplies were produced and distributed, and the tombs in which they were buried.

The Master Plan

The creation and execution of our official site-management plan—which deals with issues of conservation and restoration, the management of tourism, the threat of urbanization, the dangers of vehicular traffic, and a sensible plan for excavation—is one of my chief tasks and the achievement of which I am the most proud. This is vital work; without it the pyramids themselves would be in great danger.

It has not been easy, and I have encountered many obstacles along the way. One of the most difficult problems is the resistance I have encountered from powerful local families. Before the Antiquities Department was established, families in the village near the plateau used to own the pyramids. They named the pyramids after themselves and kept all the income from the site for their own use. When the government took the site away from them, they were furious, and they still are. Now they are afraid that we will take their land away from them and leave them homeless, and they attack me for that. However, the plan puts the ancient monuments, from which they all derive enormous benefit, first.

Giza is one of the most difficult and complicated sites in the world, and one of the most frequently visited. The site-management plan balances the importance of tourism for the economy of Egypt with the long-term preservation of the monuments. My strategy has become a standard for UNESCO, which has invited me to conferences on tourist management all over the world and published my plan in many languages. Without such a program, the pyramids, which have survived for so many thousands of years, would crumble and be lost forever.

One of my primary responsibilities has been to manage the flow of tourists. When I first arrived at Giza, many people were entering the site for free or giving *baksheesh* (tips) to the guards instead of paying admission. Many tourists came on big tour buses and paid an admission fee to the company as part of the price of their ticket, but the Antiquities Department never saw any of this money.

This artist's rendering of the Giza Plateau shows the three major pyramids and their associated complexes.

In order to insure that we had complete control, we built simple gates at the only two entrances—at Pyramid Road and Sphinx Square. Before this, only visitors who actually entered the pyramids were asked to pay admission; now, anyone who enters the site must pay. This simple change increased revenues tenfold. We also created fees for cars, which helped to limit the number entering the plateau as it raised revenues. Finally, we added a special ticket for entrance into the Great Pyramid. Since then, we have introduced and implemented many new plans for tourist control (see Chapter V).

The Giza Plateau is a large site with many wonderful monuments that are well worth visiting. Unfortunately,

tourists are usually guided to only three places. They enter the Great Pyramid, go on to the valley temple of Khafre, and finish with a visit to the Sphinx—all in about two hours. This puts a great deal of pressure on these three areas and causes tourists to miss many of the most fascinating places on the plateau. And the interior chambers of all three of the big pyramids at Giza have suffered greatly from the effects of tourism. Each visitor produces nearly an ounce of moisture with a high saline content through their breath and perspiration. This results in the accumulation of salt, which leeches into the limestone and plaster and gradually causes them to crumble into powder. In addition, many visitors over the years have found it

Several of my conservators are working here to remove graffiti from the interior of Khufu's burial chamber. This is difficult and painstaking work, and the archaeologists must wear gas masks to protect them from the chemicals they use in their cleaning.

amusing to leave their mark by writing on the walls, with no regard for the sanctity of the ancient monuments. Earlier conservation efforts have been only partially successful, and in some cases older work has needed to be updated.

An example of this is the work was recently performed in the interior of Menkaure's pyramid by a team of Egyptian architects and conservators, headed by Abdel Hamid Kotb. The complex system of chambers leads to a vaulted burial chamber lined with granite, inside which a beautifully worked sarcophagus of dark stone containing fragments of the bones and wrappings of a man was found in the mid-1800s. Unfortunately, the sarcophagus and its contents were lost at sea off the coast of Spain on their way to England soon after their discovery, so they were never analyzed. I have been trying to convince Bill Ballard, discoverer of the *Titanic* and one of my fellow National Geographic Explorers-in-Residence, to join me one day in an underwater expedition to recover this sarcophagus.

We closed the pyramid for a year while we cleaned salts from the walls and restored weak sections and cracks with mortar. We also removed modern graffiti from the king's burial chamber and installed a ventilation system to insure that the air is renewed every two hours, thereby reducing humidity. The electrical system was also improved. We reopened this pyramid to visitors in March 1998.

Our restoration efforts continued with the closure of the Great Pyramid of Khufu on April 1, 1998. This pyramid is one of the most famous and most frequently visited monuments in the world, and theories about its construction and purpose abound. However, the true story of the pyramid is more interesting than any of the outlandish explanations that have been proposed. The pyramid shape echoes the *ben-ben,* the symbol of the sun god, Re. In the original plan of the Great Pyramid, a descending passage leads below ground level to a chamber carved roughly into the bedrock. Long before this passage was completed, I believe that a change in royal ideology led the builders to modify the design by constructing a second chamber in the body of the pyramid, the so-called Queen's Chamber, which is approached by an ascending passage and then a horizontal passage. Yet another change in plan extended the ascending passage into the Grand Gallery, an awe-inspiring corridor which leads to the granite-lined King's Chamber. Most kings before and after the reign of Khufu—with the exception of his father, Sneferu—placed their burial chamber beneath their pyramid. Traditional royal doctrine held that the king during his lifetime was an embodiment of Horus (the prototypical king) and became Re (sun god and king of the gods) after he died. The changes in the interior plan of his pyramid suggest that Khufu began his reign as Horus but later (probably in the fifth year of his reign) claimed the role of Re while still living. By raising his burial chamber high above the level of the ground, Khufu identified himself with the Re, ascending from the horizon within his ben-ben. It is interesting to note that his son and successor, Djedefre, used the title "Son of Re" (which then became a standard part of the royal titulary) for the first time in Egyptian history.

Inside the King's Chamber is Khufu's red granite sarcophagus, which was open and empty by the time the first European explorers arrived. Both the Queen's and King's Chambers have small square tunnels, nicknamed airshafts, cut into their north and south walls and leading all or partway to the pyramid exterior; this is a feature unique to the Great Pyramid.

In 1998 we discovered that the many visitors who had passed through Khufu's pyramid had increased humidity inside it to a frightening 80 percent and that the walls of the Grand Gallery were covered in some places with as much as three-quarters of an inch of salt. Over a period of twelve months, we cleaned the salt from the walls of the Grand Gallery and the three chambers, repaired cracks that had appeared in the walls, removed modern graffiti, installed new lighting and ventilation systems, and introduced a television monitoring system. When we reopened the pyramid, we added an extra entrance fee and limited the number of visitors allowed inside per day to three hundred. The first and second pyramid chambers were opened to the public for the first time, too.

As we worked on the new ventilation system in the Great Pyramid, we asked the German Archaeological Institute in Cairo to help us explore the so-called air shafts, which are, in my opinion, model corridors through

which the soul of the king could travel north to join the circumpolar stars or south to reach his solar boats (see p. 54). The engineer Rudolph Gatenbrink designed a series of robots, nicknamed Wepwawet after an ancient god of the dead, small enough to travel through these shafts, which measure only about eight inches square. The northern shaft leading from the Queen's Chamber runs for 57 feet before it ends; after traveling for 135 feet through the southern shaft, Wepwawet II encountered a slab of limestone with copper pins. There has been great excitement all over the world about this slab, and on September 16, 2002, we went behind it on live television in a National Geographic special broadcast from Giza. And the mystery deepened! Behind the first slab is a wall, which we will now study and penetrate when we are fully prepared to do so safely.

I do not like to call this slab a door, since it is very small and is inside an inaccessible shaft. I believe it is a stone that was used to smooth and polish the shaft, and when the architect abandoned the Queen's Chamber, he also abandoned the shafts and left the slab inside. But I will also say that one never knows what secrets the sand of Egypt hides, and I look forward to solving this mystery.

We closed the Pyramid of Khafre in January 1999. His burial chamber, which was cut into the rock at the base of the pyramid, is approached by a horizontal passage formed by the junction of two passages leading from the north, one descending from midway up the face of the pyramid and the other descending from just outside the pyramid at ground level. A black granite sarcophagus was found inside the burial chamber; when Belzoni explored the sarcophagus in 1818, he found the bones of a bull inside.

In order to clean and restore the interior of the pyramid, we removed all the modern graffiti that visitors had left on the walls of its passageways and chambers, removed the salt buildup from the walls, treated the floor by removing some blocks around the granite sarcophagus that had been placed there during a previous conservation effort and replacing them with others that better suit

This limestone slab with copper handles blocks the southern "air-shaft" leading from the Queen's Chamber in the Great Pyramid. I believe the slab was used to smooth the sides of the shaft.

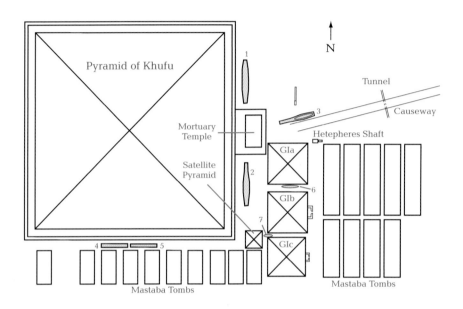

Pyramid of Khufu

Mortuary
Temple

Satellite
Pyramid

N

1

3

Tunnel

Causeway

Hetepheres Shaft

GIa

2

6

GIb

7

GIc

4 5

Mastaba Tombs

Mastaba Tombs

1–7 Boat Pits

the original stone floor. We also installed a new lighting system, replaced the stairs, removed some of the old mortar that had detached from the walls, and refinished the walls with a stronger mortar composed of sand and lime.

In order to protect the interiors of the pyramids for the future, I have established a rotation system so that each year one pyramid is closed for cleaning and renovation, while the other two remain open to the public. We have also opened more of the smaller pyramids and the tombs of the nobles, so that some of the pressure will be taken off the three large pyramids.

Discoveries in the Complex of Khufu

The central element of Khufu's complex was the pyramid itself, which represented both the primeval mound on which the creator god stood to form the Egyptian world, and the ben-ben, within which Khufu was buried. Khufu's architect, his nephew Hemiunu, planned the pyramid around a nucleus of bedrock, adding approximately 2.3 million quarried blocks of limestone, each weighing an average of two and a half tons. The exterior was cased with trapezoidal blocks of fine limestone that would have shone blazing white in the hot desert sun. The completed monument was originally a bit over 480 feet high (the top 31 feet are now missing), and the base covers a total area of about thirteen acres. The sides are inclined at an angle of 51 degrees, 52 minutes, and they are aligned very accurately to the cardinal directions.

Surrounding this pyramid are the remains of an elaborate complex that served the king for eternity. Nestled against the eastern face of the pyramid was a mortuary temple, of which only foundations and the remains of the basalt pavement can be seen today. The plan of this temple was enlarged when the change in ideology took place; I believe this was done in order to accommodate an expanded repertoire of relief decoration, fragments of which have been found both here and reused as fill in Middle Kingdom pyramids at Lisht. A causeway leads east from the entrance of the temple across the plateau and toward the floodplain below. We have recently been able to follow the route of this causeway—which turns and heads southeast partway down—to the remains of Khufu's valley temple, the temple that lay in the floodplain at the eastern end of the causeway and served as a ceremonial entrance to the entire complex. South of this temple, we discovered the foundations of a monumental building from the Old Kingdom that may be Khufu's palace. We recently caught glimpses of a vast settlement at the foot of the plateau, the northern part of which may be Khufu's pyramid city, also called the "Horizon of Khufu." We also found traces of a harbor to the east of the valley temple, where boats delivered fine limestone for casing the pyramids and decorating the temples, basalt and granite for temples and statues, and supplies from the far-flung estates that served the needs of the living king and his cult of eternity.

East of the pyramid and south of the mortuary temple are three small pyramids that were built for queens, each with its own small chapel; a group of large mastaba tombs built for members of the royal family; and, newly discovered at the southeast corner of the pyramid, the satellite pyramid of Khufu. There are five boat-shaped pits to the east of the Great Pyramid. One of these pits lies parallel to the causeway just east of the mortuary temple; I believe it was connected with the cult of Hathor, daughter of the sun god Re. Two others are at the base of the pyramid flanking the mortuary temple. These are oriented north-south, and I think they were used symbolically by the deceased king to control both Upper (southern) and Lower (northern) Egypt. The last two boat pits are associated with the northern and central queens' pyramids. Two more, in this case rectangular and actually containing disassembled wooden boats that I believe were solar boats in which the king would have traveled with (or as) Re across the sky, are located directly to the south of the pyramid, as are the remains of the construction ramp, which led from the quarry to the pyramid; to the west are mastabas belonging to officials and priests. East of the pyramid, south of the subsidiary pyramids, are two north-south embankments that may represent the remains of Khufu's workshops, where construction tools, food for the cult, and cult objects would have been produced.

The building of the Great Pyramid provides us with important insights into the reign of Khufu. From a political perspective, we see how he controlled the wealth and the population of the country, organizing households all over Egypt to participate in the pyramid project by providing labor and food. From an architectural perspective, the pyramid shows the skill and brilliance of Hemiunu, Overseer of All the King's Work, and his architects. Furthermore, it highlights the Egyptian achievements in science, astronomy, art, and mathematics that were necessary for the building of this great tomb.

THE SATELLITE PYRAMID OF KHUFU

An important area addressed by the site-management plan is the east side of the Great Pyramid of Khufu, which includes three queens' pyramids and many noble's tombs dating from the twelfth year of Khufu's reign through the end of the Old Kingdom. This area was chosen because of its archaeological value and because many of the monuments here were in danger. We have made some wonderful discoveries in the process of carrying out our plans for clearance and restoration.

In the 1950s, a paved road for tour buses had been built along the east face of Khufu's pyramid. I had always been appalled by this road, which ran far too close to the Great Pyramid and even allowed cars and buses to drive

This is an overview of the area directly east of the Great Pyramid. In the center of the photograph is a basalt pavement, all that is left of Khufu's mortuary temple. Flanking the pavement are boat pits used symbolically by the deceased king to control Upper (southern) and Lower (northern) Egypt. Khufu's causeway leads eastward in this photograph, diagonally and up to the left. At the upper right we see a queen's pyramid and boat pit and a number of mastabas belonging to members of the royal family.

Here archaeologists are breaking up the paved road that was built in front of the east face of the Great Pyramid that enabled cars to drive over the pavement of Khufu's mortuary temple and covered up important remains. Removing this road was an important part of our site-management plan.

One of the boat pits east of the Great Pyramid.

over some of its most important architectural features, including the basalt pavement of Khufu's mortuary temple. So we began to dismantle this road and in the process made several very important finds.

Work began in 1984 and finished in 1995. Three types of conservation work were done in the queens' pyramids, which have belonged, from south to north, to Henutsen (queen of Khufu and mother of Khafre), Meritites (principal queen of Khufu), and Hetepheres I (Khufu's mother, whose burial was moved at some point, perhaps soon after the end of the Old Kingdom, into a nearby shaft; her burial equipment and a sealed but empty sarcophagus were found in a shaft nearby). First, we did interior conservation, which included removing the salt from the pyramid entrances, cleaning the modern graffiti from the pyramid interiors, and installing ladders and electrical systems for lighting. Second, we worked on the architectural restoration of the interiors. The plan for the area

included the restoration of the Late Period Isis temple (a usurpation of the original mortuary temple of Henutsen), which is located east of the southernmost small pyramid.

To the north of what remains of the funerary temple of Khufu was a boat pit that was filled with sand in 1950 so that the paved road could run over it. This boat pit had never been photographed, and tourist buses had been driving over it for decades. After we removed the road, we began to clear the pit (about 120 feet long, 27 feet deep), which took almost a year. Inside we found ancient graffiti naming some of the gangs, or groups of workers, who built Khufu's complex. A restoration program was established for the pit.

I was eager to know if the pyramid of Queen Henutsen also had a boat pit, since both of the other small pyramids had boat pits on their southern sides. We did not find one, but I did discover that the pyramid had been left unfinished when I found two crossed lines carved into

In this view of the platform of the unfinished pyramid of Queen Henutsen (GIc on plan, p. 62), you can see the architect's markings and a limestone casing block in situ.

the bedrock where the corner would have been, and the area to the south was prepared for a pit that was never cut. Perhaps Henutsen died and was buried before they had time to finish her pyramid.

At the southeast corner of the Great Pyramid was a large mound of sand. In 1991 I told my assistant Ala el-din Shahat to begin clearing this so that we could see what was underneath. One morning, my driver came to pick me up at 8:30, as usual. I read the paper in the car, as I like to do, and just as we got to the Pyramid Road, I fainted. I thank God my driver didn't waste a moment. He turned the car around and drove right to the Pyramid Hospital, only a few minutes away, where I was taken to intensive care and given the injection of heart medicine that saved my life. I was in the hospital for twenty-two days.

As soon as the doctors moved me out of intensive care, my good friend Nabil Swelim, who wrote a very good dissertation on the history of the 3rd Dynasty but is now working as a tour guide, came to see me. After saying hello, he told me, "Congratulations, you found a pyramid!" I was thrilled at the news. Petrie had excavated in this area in 1881; the American archaeologist George Reisner had been here in the early 1900s; and Selim Hassan had done further clearance in 1940, just before the new road was put in. So we had no real expectations of finding anything new, especially something as important as a pyramid. When I left the hospital later and examined the newly discovered monument, I saw that it had a square base, the typical shape for a pyramid; its position, at the southeast corner of the upper pyramid complex, identified it immediately as Khufu's missing satellite pyramid.

The satellite pyramid is an important element of the Old Kingdom pyramid complex, but its function is still subject to debate. Some scholars think it was a symbolic burial place for the *ka,* or spirit double, of the king; others think it was for the burial of the king's placenta, canopic

The newly discovered satellite pyramid of Khufu sits at the southeastern corner of the Great Pyramid. It was dismantled in antiquity and covered by a large mound of sand.

jars (for viscera removed during mummification), or crowns; and still others believe it was a solar symbol. I believe that it might have been connected with the Sed Festival, a celebration whose exact meaning is still uncertain. This was clearly a very important occasion and included a number of different ceremonies. It is often called the royal jubilee, as it was generally celebrated for the first time after thirty years of rule, but history shows us that it also could occur earlier. Some historians think it reconfirmed the king as ruler, guaranteed his royal power, or renewed his life and his strength. I believe the festival was held by the king to commemorate his victories and to announce that he had finished all that the gods had asked him to do, that is, he had finished his mortuary complex. The satellite pyramid could have served as a sort of changing room, from which the king might have emerged wearing his ceremonial kilt and bull's tail, holding the flail, ready to perform a ritual dance in the pyramid court.

The pyramid complexes of Khufu's immediate predecessors and successors all have satellite pyramids south of their main pyramids. In pyramid complexes during the rest of the Old Kingdom, the satellite pyramid is typically placed at the southeast corner of the pyramid enclosure. The fact that Khufu didn't seem to have a satellite pyra-

These blocks, from the causeway of the 5th Dynasty king Sahure at Abusir, were discovered by my front-loader operator, who was clearing the area to prepare it for tourists. The four newly found blocks are decorated with scenes from the celebrations that would have taken place when the pyramidion was installed on top of its pyramid, marking the completion of the building project.

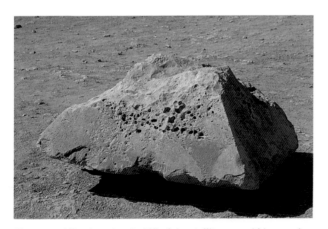

The pyramidion (capstone) of Khufu's satellite pyramid is one of the oldest known. Only the recently discovered pyramidion from one of the pyramids of Khufu's father, Sneferu, is older.

mid was always a mystery, and this new find fills a major gap in our knowledge of the development of the pyramid complex.

The newly discovered pyramid is aligned to the cardinal directions; it was originally thirty-five feet square, with a slope of about 51 degrees and 51 minutes, almost exactly the same inclination as the Great Pyramid. It was built of crude masonry and debris and cased with fine white limestone from Tura. When we found it, some of the foundation slabs and casing blocks were still in their original places, but many others were scattered around the area, and the entire center section of the pyramid had been removed, leaving the interior chambers open to the sky. This substructure is T-shaped, with a north-south entrance passage leading to an east-west "burial" chamber. The walls of this chamber slope inward, but since we are missing the stones of the upper part and the roof, we cannot tell exactly what it looked like. Nothing was found inside with the exception of four stones of various sizes.

One day while I was sitting and watching the excavations, I put my hand on a big limestone block. I looked down, and when I began to examine it more closely, I realized that it was the capstone of the pyramid, which Egyptologists call the pyramidion. This is one of the two oldest pyramidia ever found. We also found a trapezoidal block with three sloping sides from the third course down.

We recently discovered some very important blocks decorated with scenes showing the huge celebration that would have taken place when a royal pyramidion was installed at the top of its pyramid. We found these at the site of Abusir (a site about nine miles south of Giza), north of the causeway of the 5th Dynasty King Sahure (c. 2487–2475 B.C.). I had decided to prepare the site of Abusir for tourists by restoring the funerary temple of Sahure and an important Old Kingdom mastaba tomb. I asked Mohammed Moselhy, the driver of our front-loader at Giza, to clear an area that the German archaeologist Ludwig Borchardt, excavator of the complex of Sahure, had used as a dump, never imagining that we would discover anything of interest. But as Mohammed, an experienced worker whose father had also been part of my staff, was working, the loader hit a limestone block, and he stopped immediately. He got down from the truck to clean the stone off with his hand and saw wonderful scenes carved on it. He went home to Giza (he lives in an uninscribed tomb near the Great Sphinx) and got his camera. When he showed me his photographs, I was amazed, because these were very important scenes. We found three other inscribed blocks near the first one and managed to reconstruct their original context.

We determined that these blocks had originally lined the northern wall of Sahure's causeway corridor. They are decorated with scenes showing the completion of the pyramid: the trip to quarry stone for the pyramidion, the trip on the river to bring it back to the pyramid site, the

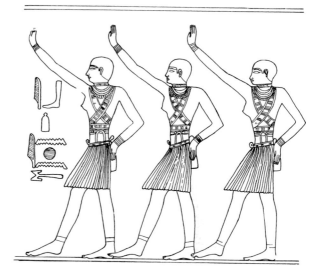

This line drawing shows a scene from one of the blocks that had originally lined the northern wall of Sahure's causeway corridor, these dancers would have performed as part of the installation ceremonies.

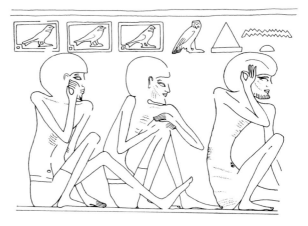

Another scene from the blocks shows starving Bedouins from the desolate land where the pyramidion was quarried, perhaps brought to Egypt to be put on trial.

dragging of the gold-covered pyramidion to the pyramid, the reporting of this event to the king, and the celebrations and offering ceremonies that marked this important occasion. These last scenes include dancers, wrestlers, archers, and men fighting with staves, as well as images of various groups of courtiers and officials bowing in the direction of the pyramid and of architects holding under their arms papyrus rolls that would have contained the plans for the pyramid complex itself. Unfortunately, none of the blocks join, although it is clear that they were once close to each other on the wall. The quality of the relief carving is exceptional, with such delicacy of line that they had to be photographed at night with artificial illumination. Tiny bits of green paint are all that remain of the original color.

The most fascinating scene depicts a group of squatting desert nomads, watched in amazement by a group of Egyptian courtiers and high officials. The nomads are emaciated, and most raise their hands in a gesture of supplication, although one of them is so weak from hunger that he cannot even lift his arms, and another is so far gone he cannot even squat! The inscription above this scene, in connection with the context in which it was found, proves that it is connected with the building of the pyramid. A fragment of a similar scene, discovered decades ago in the causeway of Unas, last king of the 5th Dynasty, has traditionally been interpreted as evidence for a widespread famine at the end of the third millennium B.C. that may have eventually brought about the end of the Old Kingdom. This new find suggests that both examples tell the story of the hunt for stone for the pyramidion. In order to get the best stone for this vital part of the king's eternal monument, the builders had to travel into the inhospitable mountains of the desert, where only the Bedouin could survive, and they only barely. The Bedouin depicted here may also be prisoners being brought to Egypt for trial.

Based on the relatively sloppy construction of the satellite pyramid's core and its small size, I believe that it was built in a hurry at the end of Khufu's reign. So that visitors

to the plateau can get a good idea of its original appearance, and to keep what remains from crumbling further, we have restored parts of the superstructure, replacing some of the fallen blocks, and using new masonry to fill in some of the holes.

SOUTH OF KHUFU'S PYRAMID

Two of the most essential items for pyramid building were a local quarry to supply limestone for the pyramid core and a supply ramp to allow the transport of this stone to the rising pyramid. Khufu's quarry lies to the south of his pyramid. As part of the Giza site-management program, we relocated the cables for the Sound and Light Show (a regular event put on for the tourists in which the pyramids are dramatically illuminated to musical and narrative accompaniment) south of the pyramid, and we were able to excavate along the paths of the new trenches. During this clearance work, north of the paved road and south of the pyramid, we found part of Khufu's supply ramp, which consists of two parallel retaining walls of stone rubble mixed with *tafla* (a claylike form of limestone used for construction ramps and the like); the area between the

In the foreground of this photograph you can see remains of the main supply ramp that once led from the quarry south of the pyramid of Khufu up to its southwest corner. What is left here are two parallel retaining walls of stone rubble mixed with soft limestone; the area between would have been filled with sand and gypsum.

Hag Ahmed Youssef with a scale model of the solar boat of Khufu. The original was found dismantled and placed inside a pit south of Khufu's pyramid by Kamal el-Mallakh in 1954. Hag Ahmed spent many years restoring this full-size royal vessel.

walls was filled with sand and gypsum. We excavated to the south of the modern paved road and found another part of this ramp lined up with the first. This ramp, most of which would have been removed after the pyramid was completed, must have led from the quarry directly to the southwest corner of the pyramid. There has been endless discussion and theorizing about how the pyramids were built, specifically whether there was one straight ramp against one side of the pyramid or a spiral ramp rising from each corner. The orientation of this ramp supports the theory of a single ramp running straight from the quarry to the southwest corner of the pyramid, then rising in a spiral around the pyramid.

In 1954 the Egyptian archaeologist Kamal el-Mallakh discovered two sealed rectangular boat pits south of the Great Pyramid. He excavated one and discovered the carefully dismantled remains of a full-size wooden boat. This was painstakingly restored by Hag Ahmed Youssef, who dedicated many years of his life to this extraordinary work. In 1988 the National Geographic Society installed a small camera in the second pit and took photographs of the dismantled boat that lies inside. The camera also

caught sight of an insect running along the wood, so we knew that the ancient plaster sealing of the pit had been damaged when it was uncovered and that air and moisture had been allowed to seep in. In 1993 we invited a team of Japanese Egyptologists working under my dear friend Sakugi Ushimura to come and study the problem. They devised a plan for killing the insects and built a shelter above the pit to protect it.

The restored boat of Khufu now sits inside a hideous museum over the site of the first pit. As part of our site-management plan, we will move the boat to a new location in the desert south of the plateau, dismantle this structure, and also restore the second boat. Ushimura is trying to raise funds from the Japanese government to complete this project, which will cost a great deal of money. In the meantime, I am proposing to set up a system whereby tourists can, for an extra fee, make a virtual visit to the second pit via a closed-circuit camera—a magical view into a sealed archaeological site. The money raised will go toward the construction of the new boat museum and the difficult and delicate task of moving the first boat.

NEW TOMBS IN THE WESTERN FIELD

West of the Great Pyramid is a vast cemetery, begun in the fifth year of Khufu's reign and continuing in use through to the end of the Old Kingdom, where many officials and priests are buried. The mastaba tombs were arranged in regularly laid-out streets, just like the city that the people buried here would have lived in during their lifetimes. Most of these tombs were identified and excavated by scholars working in the early part of the twentieth century, and many of the reliefs and statuary they once contained have been taken away to museums around the world. Over the last few decades, a number of Egyptologists, led by William Kelly Simpson of Yale University, have recorded and published these tombs, whose painted decoration and inscriptions provide valuable information about this period of Egyptian history.

When I returned to Giza from the University of Pennsylvania, I was interested in publishing the mastaba of Nesut-nefer, originally excavated by Reisner in the early part of the last century. I had become very interested in the administration of Khufu's cult while writing my dissertation, and the tomb contained some titles that intrigued me. To the east of Nesut-nefer lies the 5th Dynasty tomb, excavated by Hermann Junker, of a dwarf named Seneb who was a priest of both Khufu and Djedefre.

Reisner and Junker had both unloaded the debris from their excavations nearby. I appointed one of my archaeologists, Mahmoud Afifi, to begin clearing away this dump so that we could make a plan of Nesut-nefer's tomb; the architect Nevien el-Maghraby requested that she be assigned to this project, too. During the clearance, we found a limestone wall and discovered that the area under the dump had never been excavated! This is an important message for future excavators: when you see a big mound of debris, you should look underneath.

An overview of the cemetery west of the pyramid of Khufu, seen from the top of the Great Pyramid. This necropolis was started in the fifth year of Khufu's reign and used by priests and officials until the end of the Old Kingdom. We have found several important tombs in this area.

The eastern facade of the tomb of Perniankhu, with offering stands inscribed for the dwarf and his two wives in front.

Don't assume that previous archaeologists cleared an area before using it as a dump!

We continued our excavations, and the first new tomb we found was a big mastaba belonging to a dwarf named Perniankhu, who I believe may have been the father of Seneb. Over the course of our excavations, we found sixty-five more tombs of various sizes, mostly of mud brick, none of which had ever been recorded. We found many skeletons of handicapped people in this area, and I think that this part of the cemetery was specifically set aside for them. There are three particularly interesting tombs here: the first belongs to Perniankhu, and the second and third belong to the family of a high official named Kay.

The tomb of the dwarf Perniankhu lies west of the tomb of Nesut-nefer and north of Seneb's tomb. The superstructure is rectangular and built of limestone. We first uncovered the northern end of the tomb and on

January 11, 1990, we found a *serdab,* a small chamber used to hold statues of the deceased. When I looked at the inscription on the lintel above this serdab, I read: "The King's Acquaintance, the Dwarf of the Great Palace, Perniankhu." I peered into the eye slits in the wall of the serdab and was thrilled to find eyes looking back at me. The eyes were so beautifully carved and painted that I thought at first I was looking at a royal statue.

The head of the Antiquities Department at the time was the late Sayed Tawfik. I told him about this discovery and invited him to witness the opening of the serdab. He was very excited and invited the media to come. When everyone had arrived, I started taking out the ceiling of the serdab, stone by stone. I was assisted by Mahmoud Afifi, who could barely contain his excitement. As soon as I could, I reached in with my hand to get the statue, with television cameras whirring and clicking around me. This was a very important moment for me, the first major discovery I had made after my return from the University of Pennsylvania. Looking at this beautiful and unique statue and holding it for the first time was like holding my first child. The news was on the front page of all the newspapers in Cairo and all over the world, and it was good publicity for my country. I experienced the joy of discovery and was given encouragement to continue my work.

In this statue, which is made of basalt, Perniankhu is seated on a chair with his right hand resting flat on his thigh. He holds a short scepter in this hand and a long staff in the other. His short kilt has been painted white with a black belt, and his short curled wig bears traces of brown paint. His eyes look very lifelike, with a white iris and black pupil. The forehead also bears traces of paint, and the nose and the mouth were carefully carved. Perniankhu's arms, shoulders, and chest are normally proportioned and depict a strong and healthy young man, although his right shoulder is slightly higher than his right, as if he had a slight curvature of the spine.

Above: This is the moment when I looked into the serdab and saw the statue of Perniankhu for the first time.

Left: The serdab, *or enclosed niche, where I discovered a painted basalt statue of Perniankhu. The serdab has a window in the front wall, through which the statue of the deceased could look out. In front of the serdab are two offering stands and a burial shaft.*

Right: In this statue, now in the Cairo Museum, Perniankhu sits on a chair with a scepter in one hand and a staff in the other, both indicating that he is a government official. Although his upper body is normally proportioned, his legs are extremely short. An inscription on the statue reads: "The one who delights his lord every day, the King's Dwarf, Perniankhu of the Great Palace."

Opposite: The standing statuette of Perniankhu's wife Nyankh-Hathor, found inside a niche beside one of his false doors

His legs are abnormally short and slightly bowed outward. The left leg is different from the right, especially around the knee, and shows clear deformities on its upper part, as if he had once been badly injured. The lower part of this leg looks swollen or deformed, and I believe that he suffered from a mild case of elephantiasis, a disease in which parasites block the lymphatic system and cause swelling in parts of the body. If I am correct, this statue represents the earliest record of this disease.

A line of text runs vertically down each side of Perniankhu's backless chair, the hieroglyphs carved surprisingly badly, given the fact that the statue itself is an absolute masterpiece of Old Kingdom sculpture. I think that perhaps the text was added later by another artist with less talent. Together, the two lines read: "The one who delights his lord every day, the King's Dwarf, Perniankhu of the Great Palace." This suggests that Perniankhu was in charge of dancing before the king each day in order to please him, a traditional function of dwarves in the Old Kingdom. Dwarves also participated in funeral dances and were closely associated with the sun god.

In the eastern wall of the tomb are two false doors, solid limestone slabs carved to imitate a door through which the deceased was believed to magically exit the burial shaft and receive offerings; these slabs are inscribed for Perniankhu. Inside niches beside each of the false doors was a limestone statue of a woman: one, shown standing, is Perniankhu's wife Nyankh-Hathor, a priestess of Neith and Hathor; the other, portrayed seated, is his concubine or secondary wife. In front of this wall, we found six limestone stands, some inscribed with the name of Perniankhu and others with the names of his wives. Inside the mastaba are three shafts: in one was the skeleton of a dwarf, evidently Perniankhu himself; in each of the others were some artifacts and a female skeleton, almost certainly the women whose statues we found. I believe that this tomb dates to the reign of Khafre.

The most spectacular of the new tombs that we uncovered belongs to a man named Kay, whose titles include priest of the cults of Khufu, Djedefre, and Sneferu, senior

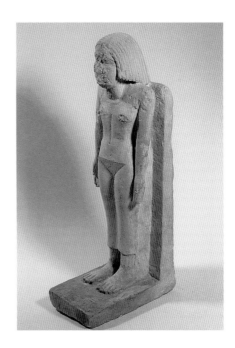

scribe of Anubis, and overseer of the *ka*-priests (priests responsible for the funerary cult). The beauty of the relief decoration shows that it was a product of the royal workshop, and the titles date it to the 4th Dynasty, perhaps to the reign of Djedefre, a date supported by the style of its architecture.

To the right of the entrance to the chapel is carved a unique inscription that reads: "It is the tomb makers, the draftsmen, the craftsmen, and the sculptors who made my tomb. I paid them with beer and bread. I made them take an oath that they were satisfied." Another remarkable detail is that the name of the artist who designed the decoration is inscribed on the south wall of the chapel. In ancient Egypt, art was not considered an expression of individuality, therefore artists were not in the habit of signing their work. This is a rare exception. Kay is shown with his wives and his various sons and daughters in many places in the tomb: on the doorjambs, entrances, and walls. One of his wives, named Hetka, is shown hugging her husband with both arms in an outpouring of affection. Both his wives were priestesses of Neith, and at least one daughter was a priestess of Hathor and held the high rank of "King's Acquaintance."

Inside the chapel are a number of scenes, mostly of offering bearers. On the east wall is a funerary menu— a list of the foods, drinks, oils, and other offerings that

would magically insure a prosperous and well-nourished afterlife for the people buried here. The tomb contains two false doors in the western wall, and offering tables were found in front of each of these.

Peering out from behind the southern false door were the strikingly beautiful eyes of a statue, a masterpiece of Old Kingdom art. It is carved of limestone and beautifully painted. Kay is shown sitting on a low-backed chair, wearing a white kilt and a short, curled wig. Next to his right leg stands one of his young sons, naked and with his finger in his mouth, the traditional pose of childhood. On the left, one of his daughters sits cross-legged. When we found the statue, Kay was wearing a lovely amulet drawn

Opposite: The most spectacular new tomb we found in the Western Cemetery was built for a priest and official named Kay. This is an overview of the tomb, looking southeast toward the pyramid of Khafre.

Above: The drum above the doorway into the tomb of Kay bears a hieroglyphic inscription announcing his name and titles, "King's Acquaintance, senior scribe."

Opposite: Kay with one of his wives, Nesytet, and a number of their children, from the north wall of the tomb.

Above: We had to do important restoration work in the tomb of Kay as soon as we found it to preserve the wonderfully carved and colored reliefs.

Left: Behind the southernmost false door of Kay's tomb was a handsome statue of painted limestone. Kay sits on a low-backed chair, with a daughter next to his left leg and a son next to his right one.

Above: North of this tomb was a second tomb belonging to Kay's family, probably to two of his daughters. It was built of mud brick, and the scenes were painted on plaster. The two false doors in the western wall, one of the two shafts (each of which held the skeleton of a woman), and a limestone column base inscribed with the names and titles of Kay are visible in this photograph.

Right: A detail of one of the false doors from the tomb of the family of Kay, painted with a scene of offering bearers.

in a turquoise color on his chest, but exposure to the air destroyed it immediately, before we had a chance to preserve it.

A burial shaft was cut into the rock behind this statue. Inside the shaft we found a wooden sarcophagus inscribed with Kay's name and titles; a beautiful headrest made of wood, also inscribed with his name and titles; and the skeleton of a pig. This was very strange. Pigs never appear on offering lists, and they seem to have been proscribed in some way as unclean. We know that workmen ate pigs, because pig bones were found at the settlement of Deir el-Medina on the west bank of Thebes, where the artisans who carved and painted the royal tombs of the New Kingdom pharaohs lived. We also found pig bones in the settlement of the Giza workers (see p. 130). But the burial of a pig in Kay's sarcophagus is a mystery.

North of Kay's mastaba, we found a fragile tomb of mud brick. We excavated it very carefully and found clear evidence that this tomb belonged to his daughters. This is perhaps the most delicately beautiful tomb in the cemetery. The chapel consists of a single square chamber, with entrances on the south and east and two false doors in the west wall. The interior walls of the chapel are covered with a thin layer of plaster on which scenes were beautifully drawn and then painted, with some areas left unfinished. The ceiling of the chapel is missing, and the top parts of all the walls have weathered away, so much of the decoration is gone. The scenes that remain include the lower portions of several large-scale images of a man and woman, figures of two daughters of Kay dressed in tight dresses held up by straps, offering bearers, and activities such as plowing, boat building, and traveling in the marshes. There are also some unfinished sketches that demonstrate clearly the skill of the ancient artists; the images are drawn perfectly, with no faulty lines and no corrections.

In the center of the chapel floor is an unusual round base with a hole where a wooden pillar once stood. The inscription on this base says: "the King's Acquaintance, senior scribe, inspector of the priests/cleaners of the seats of the royal children, Kay." This last is a unique title; it tells us that Kay was truly an intimate of the royal family. Into the floor of the tomb were cut two burial shafts, each of which contained the skeleton of a woman.

Noha Abdel Hafiz, who has a degree in conservation in addition to her artistic skills, asked me if she could take on the preservation of this tomb as a project for her master's degree. I readily agreed, and she did a wonderful job. The scenes drawn on the plaster were very delicate, especially the figures of the two daughters, the unfinished sketches, and the offering bearers. Noha carried out a painstaking treatment of the tomb and delivered an excellent paper at the Ninth International Congress of Egyptology in Cairo.

CLEARANCE AND RESTORATION

For a major project of the site-management program, I have a team, led by Abdel Hamid Kotb and his assistant, Nevien el-Maghraby, of Egyptian archaeologists, architects, conservators, and stonemasons engaged in the process of re-excavating and restoring many of the Old Kingdom tombs at Giza. These lie in several locations around the plateau: in the cemeteries around the pyramid of Khufu, south of the causeway of the pyramid of Khafre, and south of the causeway of Menkaure. Their job is to clear the tombs, conserve the scenes inside, and, in the case of the mastabas, reconstruct the superstructures by returning missing blocks that now lie scattered around to their original places and filling in missing blocks with freshly cut limestone. Where necessary, missing pillars are added and inscribed blocks are returned to the walls. Ceilings are put above the tombs, the floors are protected with wood, and electrical systems are installed. Each monument is then labeled with the original excavation number, and a sign is placed outside showing the plan of the interior, the name of the owner, and the location of major scenes and inscriptions. This is an enormous job and will take many years. But every journey begins with a single step, and we have made an excellent start. We have already cleared and restored more than one hundred of the mastaba and rock-cut tombs on the Giza Plateau.

Left: My team and I are carrying out a great deal of clearance and restoration work in the Western Cemetery. We clear each tomb, do conservation work on the scenes inside, and wherever necessary rebuild and reconstruct the superstructures. Each tomb is given a ceiling for protection, and we are installing electrical systems.

Below: Here is one of the restored mastabas, this one of an official named Imry. Outside the tomb you can see a new sign showing a plan of the interior and the location of major scenes and inscriptions.

Right: We have done important new work under the village of Nazlet es-Samman. As the population of Cairo exploded, this suburb grew until it is now at the foot of the Giza Plateau. An inadequate sewage system caused the water table to rise, threatening the ancient monuments, so the Sphinx Emergency Sewage Project was launched and successfully completed.

Below: This plan of the Giza Plateau shows the area as it might have looked in the time of Khufu.

Opposite: In this trench, which was dug for the new sewage system, we found limestone blocks from Khufu's causeway. We found that the causeway turned sharply to the north about 2,000 feet from the mortuary temple instead of running straight to the east.

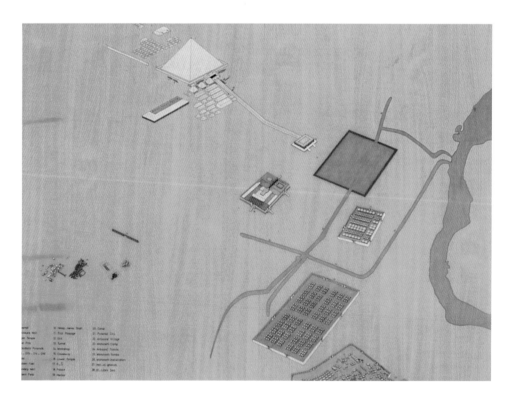

NEW DISCOVERIES AT THE FOOT OF THE PLATEAU

As our population explodes, the Cairo suburbs have been creeping closer and closer to the pyramids, threatening to overrun the plateau. In 1989, at my urging, immediate action was taken by the governor of Giza to stop any kind of new housing construction within the village of Nazlet es-Samman, which lies at the foot of the plateau, and in other surrounding villages. A decree established that new houses could be built in a different area, called the New Nazlet es-Samman, located on the Faiyum Road. At the same time, a new sewage system was installed as part of the Sphinx Emergency Sewage Project. The installation of this system, in addition to protecting the monuments by successfully lowering the salinity and the height of the water table, led directly to some very important finds.

An American company called AMBRIC was responsible for the sewage project. The project chief was Bob Kachinsky, who understands the importance of saving our monuments. The company also paid an archaeologist named Michael Jones to work as part of my team. Together, we recorded all of the archaeological evidence that came to light as the sewage trenches were being cut. It was a fascinating process and revealed clearly the stratigraphy underlying Cairo. In one trench, we found a Coptic inscription on top, with Middle Kingdom pottery on the next level, and Old Kingdom artifacts at the bottom.

While trenches were being dug to install the new pipes, remains of the causeway of Khufu were discovered in five locations, which has allowed us to trace its ancient path. About two thousand feet from the mortuary temple, we found quite a surprise: instead of running straight to the east, as most pyramid causeways do, Khufu's causeway turns sharply to the north before continuing for another 375 feet to the valley temple. The bend in the causeway is most likely an artifact of the change in plan of the mortuary temple associated with the change in Khufu's cult in the fifth year of his reign, when he took on the role of Re as the living king.

The valley temple itself lies under the village in the area of the Mansouria Canal, on the site of a large private villa. We were able to trace the north-south length of the basalt pavement that had once served as its floor, but we were not able to excavate its entire width because it ran underneath the villa. We were already having a lot of trouble with the villagers, and I did not want to ask that the villa be moved, so we collected the pieces of the pavement and put them nearby so that people can see the approximate location of the temple. Perhaps the next generation will be able to do what I have not and finish this important excavation.

All of these discoveries upset the people of Nazlet es-Samman because they were afraid that we were going to demolish their houses. They sent telegrams criticizing me, started rumors about me, and even encouraged people to pray against me. One day, I took my car to visit a part of the ancient causeway that lay inside the village, and while I was there, some of the villagers set my car on fire. I have never had any intention of moving villagers without their consent, or without proper compensation,

Above: We also found traces of the large harbor that was dug at the foot of the Giza Plateau. Boats from all over Egypt, carrying raw materials for the pyramids and food from the scattered royal estates, would have navigated from the river through a series of canals and into this harbor. Several limestone blocks from the harbor are visible in this photograph.

Right: In a number of the soundings made under the modern suburb of Nazlet es-Samman, we caught glimpses of a vast Old Kingdom settlement. This photograph shows two of the mud sealings—gobs of mud used to seal baskets or jars and impressed with a royal signet— found in this area. These bear the names of Khafre (on the left) and Menkaure (on the right).

and I am sorry they do not understand this. It is my hope that sometime in the future, if the government can afford to do so, we can build a modern village for these people that they will be happy to move into, and we can explore the rich archaeology underneath their current homes.

In 1993, while I was away from the pyramids, a construction company found an ancient wall during the construction of a new building. Instead of informing the Antiquities Department, as they were required to do by law, they tried to hide it quickly and even destroyed part of it. Fortunately, the police found out and informed the Antiquities Department, but the construction was allowed to continue while the wall was being excavated and recorded. When I came back to Giza, the wall was surrounded by new building, and I could not do anything except write a strong letter to the department expressing my belief that what had happened was a crime.

The ancient wall has a thirteen-foot-thick limestone foundation and inclined sides of basalt and limestone slabs encasing a core of packed limestone chips. In 1992 Michael Jones had recorded some east-west limestone

and basalt walls in a sewage trench along Zaghloul Street, one 820 feet south and the other 656 feet north of the 1993 wall. Taken together, these bits of wall can be extrapolated to form a large rectangular enclosure. The use of basalt is typical of Khufu's reign, and is found in both his mortuary and his valley temples. Basalt is black, but when the sun hits it, it looks green. These are the colors of Osiris, associated with fertility and the renewal of the land. I believe that these walls represent traces of a harbor that lay in front of Khufu's valley temple, a conclusion supported by an outer casing of limestone cut into steps that shows clear evidence of water wear, as noted by a French scholar named Goyon, east of where we found the valley temple.

During the Old Kingdom, the Nile lay farther west than it does now, and it was closer to the pyramid sites. It is therefore likely that a canal connected the river to the harbor. Pyramid harbors and canals were an important part of the pyramid complex, since they were needed during construction for the delivery of fine white limestone casing from Tura, granite from Aswan, alabaster from Hatnub, and workers and food from the agricultural estates that supported the pyramid builders and the royal administration. After the death of the king, the canals would have featured in the funeral procession, for the body of the king was delivered via the harbor to the foot of the valley temple. People coming to Giza to celebrate important religious feasts would have also come by river.

It used to be thought that the capital of Egypt during the Old Kingdom was always at Memphis. However, it has long been accepted that the administrative center of the country for each king was near the site of his pyramid. In the course of taking soundings for the new sewage system to serve the villages at the foot of the Giza Plateau in 1988–89, we were able to catch tantalizing glimpses of an Old Kingdom settlement that begins 150 feet south of Khufu's valley temple and stretches for an area of more than a square mile under the modern suburb. Of seventy-three soundings, forty-nine contained archaeological material dating from the Old Kingdom. We were also able

The buildings in Khufu's pyramid city were made of mud brick; in this picture, some of the ancient architecture is visible.

to clear several larger areas, which provided still more information.

These glimpses showed us that the inhabitants of this settlement had lived in groups of mud-brick buildings. In and around these buidings we found layers of ash and a good deal of other domestic rubbish, including sealings—gobs of clay with impressed seals that would have served to close storage pots, bags, or boxes, or the fasteners of doors—of Khufu and Khafre, and lots of Old Kingdom potsherds of all types: cooking pots, bread molds, beer jars, trays for sifting grain, and many red burnished bowls (thought to be only for members of the upper class), as

This statue of Khafre has long been considered one of the masterpieces of Old Kingdom art. It was found in the nineteenth century hidden in a pit inside Khafre's valley temple and shows the king seated on a throne, protected by the falcon god Horus.

well as pottery used for imported food from southern Egypt. There were also animal bones with butcher's marks on them and microscopic remains of pollen. This is an extremely rich area, but we are limited in our excavations by the modern dwellings that lie above.

In the area just to the south of Khufu's valley temple, as trenches were being dug for the sewage project, part of a monumental building, constructed of mud-brick walls faced with limestone, was uncovered. The building was more than three hundred feet long and had a limestone pavement. Although we were able to catch only a small glimpse of it, I suspect that this may be Khufu's palace.

I believe that the area directly south of Khufu's valley temple was his pyramid city, where the court, the administration, and the priesthood lived. From inscriptions found in officials' tombs at Giza, we know that it had the same name as the pyramid itself: "Akhet Khufu," the Horizon of Khufu. After the death of Khufu, the priests who maintained the cult of the glorified king would have continued to live here.

Discoveries in the Complex of Khafre

The pyramid of Khafre stands in the center of the plateau, easily recognizable by the remains of the original casing that still cling to its top. South of Khafre's pyramid is his satellite pyramid, and to the east lies his mortuary temple, five boat pits, and a causeway that leads to his valley temple, the Great Sphinx (which we have recently restored), and the Sphinx temple, all of which are part of his complex. We have carried out excavations in the area of Khafre's valley temple, clarifying some of its elements, and have also discovered evidence for a harbor that lay in front of this temple.

NEW WORK AT THE VALLEY TEMPLE OF KHAFRE
The valley temple of Khafre is one of the best-preserved temples of the Old Kingdom, and it attracts many visitors each day. It is built of limestone, cased with granite, and has a beautiful alabaster floor. The temple can be entered

Overview of the valley temple of Khafre looking northwest, with the Great Sphinx and the pyramid of Khufu in the background.

by one of two doors from a limestone-paved platform against the eastern face. The north door was associated with Bastet, a lion-headed goddess whose home was in the Delta, and the south door was sacred to Hathor, the principal goddess of Dendara in Upper Egypt and the focus of an important cult in the Memphite area as Lady of the Sycamore. Markings that show the emplacements for the doors can still be seen, and it is interesting to notice that the southern doorway would have been quite narrow, barely wide enough for one person to fit through.

There were once twenty-three statues of Khafre lining the interior walls of this temple, one of which was found in a deep cachette in the entrance hall. (This beautiful statue is now one of the centerpieces of the Egyptian Museum in Cairo.) This is a wonderful temple to visit; some of its walls still stand to their full height, so that the visitor can get a good sense of the ancient structure. From a passage at the back of the valley temple, one can enter the causeway that leads to the pyramid.

In 1960, the Antiquities Department built an amphitheater just east of the valley temple for a famous Egyptian singer, Om Kalthoum; this was later expanded into a Sound and Light Theater. Many artists have performed here over the years, including Frank Sinatra, Pearl Bailey, and the Grateful Dead.

This theater was a bad thing for Giza in many ways. While it was being built, two ramps and a tunnel were found in front of Khafre's valley temple. Unfortunately, this information was never recorded, and no site plans were made, so that the construction of the theater could proceed without delay. I blame the archaeologists in charge at the time for failing to insist that construction be halted so these important finds could be recorded properly. Only one plan of the archaeological features was drawn at the time, by Ahmed Fakhry, but it is not accurate.

As part of the site-management project, we are removing all modern structures from the site of Giza. We have already removed many workmen's houses that were in the area of the valley temple, and we started to remove the old theater in October 1995. After the large stones were taken away, we started to clean the site and found cement blocks about nineteen and a half inches thick. It was very difficult to remove those blocks and also to believe that such a building was ever built; we have had to leave parts of it in place for the time being. We even found that trenches had been dug into the actual pavement of the temple platform so that technicians could run cables for electricity. A new Sound and Light Theater was built farther to the east (see p. 89).

When we cleared the upper platform directly in front of the temple, we were able to distinguish some important features. On top of the platform, in a line from north to south, are large sunken rectangles, each about twenty-five feet in length, which were probably bases for sphinxes. There were four of these, two flanking each doorway. There were also emplacements for ancient flagpoles at each of the entrances. Other square holes, used to help with the temple construction, run in a line from north to south across the platform.

After very careful cleaning, we found a square depression surrounded by emplacements for the legs of a wood-framed kiosk in the center of the platform. This structure would have been used during Khafre's purification ceremonies. According to evidence from private tombs of the same period, the ceiling of this kiosk would have been made of reeds or papyrus. On either side of this central

Opposite: Many tourists enjoy coming to the plateau at night for the Sound and Light show.

Left: These trenches are not ancient remains, but gouges cut into the original platform of the valley temple of Khafre so that cables could be run for the Sound and Light show.

Below: This view shows the main features of the valley temple uncovered by the new clearance work.

area are square bases that once held alabaster flagstones on which priests would have stood to pour purifying substances onto the king's body, which would have laid on a mortuary table set in the middle of the tent. We also found evidence for what I believe would have been an entrance to this kiosk on the south side.

In the process of clearing the areas to the north and south, we found two ramps sloping up to narrow pathways that lead to the upper platform and the entrances to the temple. The ramps themselves are pockmarked, possibly by water erosion from the harbor that I believe once existed nearby. At the top of each ramp is the foundation for a small pylon (ceremonial entrance), which would have been entered through a series of two doors. Near the south ramp, we found an area cut into the paving stones

Left: This ramp and walkway lead to the northern entrance of the valley temple, associated with the goddess Bastet. In the foreground, markings in the stone show the emplacements for two doors and a small pylon, which would have formed part of the impressive entrance to Khafre's complex. Flanking the walkway are entrances to the tunnel that runs underneath it.

Above: A boat-shaped tunnel runs under each of the ramps; under the southern tunnel (in the foreground here as we face north) is an ancient well, still covered with a limestone slab. The purpose of these tunnels may have been to serve symbolically as boats for the king as ruler of Upper and Lower Egypt, or they may simply have provided access for the ancient workmen and priests to walk through the area without entering the sacred precinct.

where a statue might have been placed. We also found evidence that these ramps were originally roofed.

Under each ramp is a tunnel, partly dug into the bedrock and partly built of limestone blocks. Each tunnel slopes down from one side, flattens out under the ramp, and slopes up to emerge again on the other side. Under the south ramp, inside the tunnel, we found a shaft whose cross section measures about three feet square. Closing the shaft was a cover made of a polished block of limestone into which were cut four handles for ropes that would have allowed the cover to be raised and held upright. The cover is broken in places and is missing some pieces, so we can see that the shaft contains water. We have not yet taken out the cover and begun to excavate, but I think that this shaft was used to collect water to be used for the purification of the king's body.

Excavating is one thing, and interpreting what we find is another. These two tunnels are very mysterious and have no known parallels. My current theory is that as they are boat-shaped, they represented boats for the living king in his guise as Horus, the prototypical ruler of Egypt. Or they could simply be tunnels to enable workers to pass by the valley temple without entering the sacred space.

There was once a wall built of limestone between the two ramps that would have isolated the valley temple from the area to the east. This wall was destroyed during the construction of the first theater, but we were able to find parts of its base. In the course of our excavations, we also found pottery from the Old Kingdom, New Kingdom, and Roman Periods. We found the shattered remains of an alabaster statue (the pieces fill twenty-two baskets!) and some fine granite tools. Just north of the tunnel, we found a road cut into the rock of the plateau; this runs by a mud-brick platform, which was perhaps used by the queen and the royal children to watch the purification of the deceased king. Against the south side of the temple, we re-excavated a building that consists of six rectangular rooms of mud brick, entered from the east; these may have been rooms for the priests who were in charge of the royal ceremonies.

THE SPHINX CONSERVATION PROJECT

In 1977, when I was a young archaeologist, the Grateful Dead came to perform in the Sound and Light Theater in front of the Great Sphinx, and a huge crowd of ten thousand young people came to shout, scream, and drink beer. I hated to see this affront to the dignity and the safety of the site; the music was so loud that I could feel the stones of the pyramids trembling with the vibration and the delicate rock of the Sphinx crumbling. The next day, I felt that I could hear the Sphinx crying. Ten years later, in February 1988, a large chunk fell from the right shoulder of the Sphinx. I began to feel that this ancient statue was talking to me, weeping because of the damage that had been done to him, including poorly done restorations. As soon as possible, we began a major conservation project, on which I worked for almost ten years at the head of a group of well-trained archaeologists, architects, restorers, and conservators, as well as a geologist and an artist. After the completion of Phase I, we held a symposium that brought about ninety scholars to Egypt to discuss the restoration and future of the Sphinx.

We completed the conservation on December 25, 1997, and when they took the scaffolding away, I could feel that the Sphinx was smiling because of the good work we had done. Egypt hosted a celebration on May 25, 1998, to announce to the world that the Sphinx was safe. President Hosni Mubarak gave me the first and most important award I have ever received in my life, the First Class Award of Art and Science. We had a wonderful ceremony planned: the Cairo Symphony Orchestra was to play while the newly restored statue was unveiled. We had covered the Sphinx with an enormous silken scarf, which we planned to pull off at a dramatic moment. However, when the moment for the unveiling arrived, a strong wind suddenly rose up and blew the scarf off the Sphinx without any help from us!

Several years ago, a letter came to my office asking permission for Sting to sing in front of the Sphinx. I said no, and Dr. Gaballa Ali Gaballa, then secretary general of the Supreme Council of Antiquities, supported me. The

organizer of the concert decided to hold the show in front of the new Sound and Light Theater, which is not on Antiquities land, and he sold fifteen thousand tickets. But of course, the theater only holds three thousand people, so it was decided that the overflow would have to be accommodated on Antiquities land north of the theater. Negotiations went on for days. The Egyptian Tourist Authority wanted the concert; the Supreme Council of Antiquities continued to refuse until only a few hours before the concert, when they were forced to give in.

The concert was packed, and many of the fifteen thousand young people who came couldn't even get onto the plateau. There was no crowd control, and the spectators

The Great Sphinx, an image of King Khafre, with its associated temples. In the background is the valley temple; in the center of the photo is the Sphinx Temple, built during the 4th Dynasty; and in the foreground (set diagonally) is a small temple built by Amenhotep II in the New Kingdom, when worship of the Sphinx was renewed.

jumped around to the beat of the music that came from gigantic speakers and shook the ground. I was terribly upset and angry, and I worried about the safety of the monuments. I believe that Antiquities sites should be used only for cultural performances, such as *Aïda* or other classical works, which are in keeping with the dignity of the ancient monuments, and I have selected a site west of the pyramids for such events. What is done is done, but I will do everything in my power to prevent something like this from happening in the future. I am afraid that I will hear the Sphinx crying again, and I only hope that this time he will forgive us.

THE HARBOR AND PYRAMID CITY OF KHAFRE

In 1980, working with Mark Lehner, I found evidence for a harbor to the east of the valley temple of Khafre: a significant drop-off that occurs in the area to the east of this temple and the nearby Sphinx temple. Near these temples, sixty-three feet to the east, remains dating to the Old Kingdom lie just below the surface. Probes that Mark and I made only forty-five feet farther east show that the bedrock lies twenty feet below the surface. Core drillings made by the Ministry of Irrigation another sixty feet to the east hit granite at a depth of about forty-eight feet. The drop-off between our probes and the Ministry drilling suggests the existence of a harbor in this area. I believe that this is part of the pyramid harbor of Khafre, and that the granite hit by the probe may be from one of his temples, fallen there either during construction or as a result of later dismantling of the temples. Mark Lehner reconstructs a harbor here based on the Birket Habu, the harbor fronting the palace of Amenhotep III (c. 1390–1352) at Malkata, on the west bank of the Nile at Thebes.

This is a close-up view of the reconstruction work we did on the tail of the Great Sphinx. We worked on this project for almost ten years and finished our job in December of 1997.

The ramps and pathways that lead west to the valley temple of Khafre slope down sharply at their eastern ends, and I believe that they connected with the harbor here. This harbor may date to early in the Old Kingdom history of Giza, since it corresponds with a natural dip in the formation that underlies the plateau. Like the Khufu harbor, it would have connected the pyramid complex with the waterways that served as Egypt's lifeline. The pyramid city of Khafre bore the same name as the pyramid complex: "Khafre is Great." A stele found in the area of the valley temple was dedicated by the chief official of the city, called the "Overseer of Khafre is Great." I do not believe that Khafre had his own separate city, but that his city was an extension of his father's (see p. 44).

This beautiful pair statue, now in the Museum of Fine Arts, Boston, depicts Menkaure, son of Khafre and grandson of Khufu, with a queen, probably his chief queen, Khamerernebty II.

Discoveries in the Complex of Menkaure

The pyramid of Menkaure, which lies at the southern edge of the Mokkatam Formation that is the main plateau at Giza, is dwarfed by the monuments of Menkaure's father and grandfather. It would originally have been quite impressive in its own right, however, with a casing of gleaming white limestone and a thick band of red granite covering its lower third. To the east of Menkaure's pyramid are the remains of a beautiful mortuary temple, a causeway, and a valley temple, which was finished in mud brick by Menkaure's son and successor, Shepseskaf. Within the confines of this valley temple, George Reisner, one of the early excavators at Giza, found the remains of a city that housed the priests of Menkaure's cult through the end of the 6th Dynasty. The original pyramid city most likely lay farther to the east. As the number of people holding hereditary responsibility for Menkaure's cult grew, the city expanded to the west and into the courtyard of his valley temple at the foot of the plateau.

In June 1996, I began work on the south side of Menkaure's pyramid. I planned to clean the area as part of a larger campaign to make it more accessible and inviting, since many tourists never visit it. Much of this area is filled with fallen blocks and sand that had never

been cleared, despite earlier excavations. The stone robbers of the Middle Ages had done a great deal of damage: all of the fine limestone that cased the top has disappeared, and many of the casing blocks of red granite that once adorned the lower third of the pyramid lie strewn in the sand at its base. In addition to improving the appearance of the site by mapping and labeling the fallen granite casing, and with the eventual goal of restoring them to their original places, I hoped to discover evidence about the construction of this pyramid and perhaps its boat pits, which had never come to light. I also wanted to excavate the area near the causeway and to re-excavate a number of tombs that Reisner had explored but never published.

Our systematic excavations brought many Late Period burials to light, and we rediscovered many tombs recorded by Reisner. The question of Menkaure's boat pits is still up in the air: one possibility is that he never built them and that Shepseskaf didn't have the time or the funds to cut them into the rock, but simply carved some outlines in the rock near the base of the pyramid to act as substitutes. Another possibility is that they lie under the debris we are now clearing.

THE SATELLITE PYRAMID OF MENKAURE
South of Menkaure's pyramid are three smaller pyramids that were built for queens. The one at the east end was probably built for Queen Khamerernebty II (daughter of Khafre and sister-wife of Menkaure), but she may have

died before it was finished; in any case, it was never used for a burial. I believe it functioned instead as Menkaure's satellite pyramid. No one had entered this pyramid since Reisner's time. In 1998 Fox TV asked me to do a live show from Giza. I thought of this pyramid and decided that it could be very interesting for the public to see a living archaeologist enter a monument for the first time. I knew it would be difficult: the substructure is cut into the solid rock and consists of a nine-foot-wide corridor, left unfinished, which descends for more than sixty feet to the burial chamber. In front of the entrance, the ancient Egyptian workers had brought a boulder of granite to seal the pyramid, leaving only a small space between the block and the floor.

In the last segment of the Fox program, I entered the pyramid first, followed by Suzy Gilbert, one of the hosts. The crew had put a camera on my back, and Suzy had one on her head so she could record what I was doing. As I tried to crawl under the stone blocking the entrance, I got stuck because of the camera on my back. I couldn't move, and I have to admit that I started to panic. Suzy had to come and help me by taking the camera off so I could squeeze through. The small burial chamber, about eight

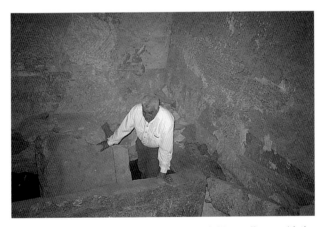

In 1998 Fox TV broadcast me live as I entered this small pyramid, the easternmost of the three small queens' pyramids near Menkaure's tomb. I got stuck halfway into the burial chamber under the huge granite plug that blocked the entrance, but I finally made it inside.

feet high, eleven feet wide, and twenty-three feet long, was filled with stone rubble, and it appears that the sarcophagus was never used. Leaving the pyramid was also very difficult.

I had thought it would be an exciting adventure that would encourage people to become interested in the reality of archaeology rather than the ridiculous stories the pyramidiots tell, about men from Atlantis and aliens from far-off galaxies. The pyramids were built by people like us, and it is much more interesting and exciting to explore the actual remains than to make up fantasies. This is what I hoped to share with millions of television viewers, and I think I succeeded. After the broadcast, I received many letters from young people all over the world, and continued media coverage of my work has helped encourage the interest of many people in archaeology.

THE PAIR STATUE OF RAMESSES II

A big surprise was waiting for us near this small pyramid, an important artifact that I never expected to find on the Giza Plateau. During the clearance on its north side, one of the workmen found the edge of a granite casing block that had been reworked in a later period. One of my inspectors carefully cleared a small area, where he saw part of the head of an unfinished statue, and he called me in immediately. When we cleared the rest of the block, we found a pair statue sketched out in the granite.

The ten-foot-high block lay face up, and two figures had been roughly carved into the upper surface, as if they were emerging from the stone. To the left is the kilted figure of a king, with the short, square beard of kingship and a *nemes* headdress (a striped cloth) with a uraeus cobra on his forehead and a sun-disk above his head. He holds a folded piece of linen in his right hand, and with his left he touches the figure next to him. This figure, also kilted and male, wears a long wig, uraeus, and sun-disk. However, his beard is longer, and although it has broken off at the end, enough remains to indicate that it was a divine beard—a long narrow beard with a curl at the end. A large diagonal crack runs across the block, across the

A general view of excavation to the north of the easternmost small pyramid of Menkaure, showing the fallen granite casing blocks of the small pyramid and the newly discovered pair statue of Ramesses II.

waists of the two figures. This must have happened while the statue was being carved, so it was abandoned, left unfinished and uninscribed. Nearby we found some of the diorite tools that were used to carve it, showing wear from contact with the hard granite.

As soon as I saw the statue, I remembered an inscription on the blocks of the second pyramid at Giza and several stelae of the Overseer of Works, Maya, under Ramesses II (c. 1279–1213 B.C.), and I wondered whether this could be a statue of that powerful king. We have a number of clues that tell us that this is a representation of Ramesses II accompanied by himself as the sun god Re. First, we have the style and the proportions of the figures, which are very like other statues of this king. There are even a number of examples of pair statues like this one that show Ramesses II with himself as a god. We also know that the Giza pyramids were used as convenient stone quarries during the New Kingdom: the Dream Stele of Tuthmosis IV that sits between the paws of the Sphinx was carved on a lintel from the mortuary temple of Khafre, and some of the stones used to repair the Sphinx in this period probably came from Khafre's causeway.

Evidence of this sort of activity during the reign of Ramesses II is found in the temple of Ptah at Memphis, where granite casing blocks from Giza were reused.

I believe that Ramesses II ordered Maya to make this statue for an addition that he made to the sanctuary of the sun god Re at Heliopolis. Rather than traveling all the way to the granite quarries at Aswan, Maya ordered his men to rework one of the granite blocks near Menkaure's pyramid. The stone was not in good condition, so it cracked before the statue was finished and the artisans left it there. This is a remarkable find, one that tells us a great deal about how the Old Kingdom monuments were treated in the New Kingdom.

We are continuing our work around the pyramid of Menkaure, and we hope to find part of the pyramid's construction ramp and boat pits. The most important thing that I want to do is to restore all the fallen granite blocks to their original positions casing the pyramid. We plan to do a photogrammetric map of the surface of the pyramid, document all the fallen bocks, and return them back to their places. We also plan to do significant restoration and conservation of the subsidiary pyramids.

Here I am holding a dolorite polishing stone, a tool used by the ancient sculptors to shape these statues. I am sitting next to a granite pair statue of Ramesses II that was discarded when it cracked all the way across. In this photograph, the image of the king, wearing the royal beard, is below, and the king as the sun god, with a divine beard, is above.

The monumental Wall of the Crow separates the sacred precinct of the royal pyramids from the world of the pyramid builders. It runs west to east from the edge of the Maadi formation south of the main plateau at Giza toward the floodplain. Just south of this wall lies a vast complex of the Old Kingdom, with remains of the living, where the pyramid builders were fed and housed, to the east and the tombs of these men and women to the west. In this view we are looking northwest toward the pyramid of Khafre.

In Search of the Pyramid Builders

Many people still believe that the pyramids at Giza were built by slaves forced to labor in the service of tyrants; they cannot imagine that people would voluntarily do the kind of work required to build these massive monuments. Hollywood has done its share to add to the confusion; many people have an indelible image, courtesy of Cecil B. DeMille, of lines of dusty slaves toiling in the hot sun under the lashes of harsh Egyptian overseers. This misconception persists; even now, I am often met with great surprise at my public lectures when I announce that the pyramids were built by native Egyptians who willingly offered their services to their god-king.

Egyptologists have long known this fact. We have a parallel example at the New Kingdom site of Deir el-Medina, where generations of artisans who carved and decorated the spectacular royal tombs in the Valley of the Kings lived with their families. These men and women lived comfortably, owned property (including slaves), and took pride in their work. But traces of the workmen respon-

Here I am removing one of the many exquisite sculptures found in the Cemetery of the Pyramid Builders from the niche where it had lain hidden for 4,500 years.

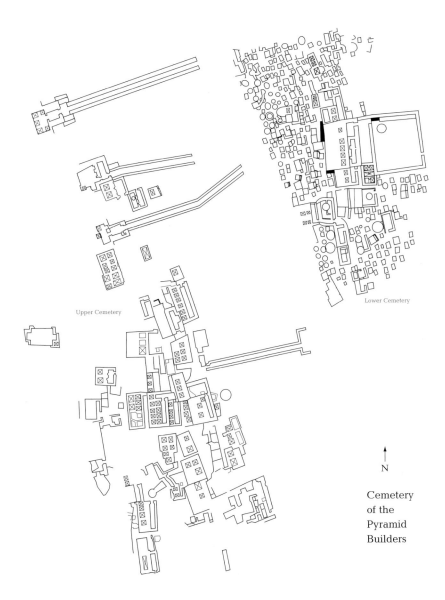

Upper Cemetery

Lower Cemetery

N

Cemetery
of the
Pyramid
Builders

sible for the building of the pyramids were, until recently, lacking in the archaeological record of the Old Kingdom.

While writing my dissertation at the University of Pennsylvania in the 1980s, I became fascinated by this issue. Although we knew a great deal about the kings, queens, and nobles of the 4th Dynasty, we knew almost nothing about the common people. But the incredible monuments of Giza could not have been built without them. The Giza pyramids were monumental projects that spanned three generations—at least sixty-seven years—and required the services of tens of thousands

of Egyptians: stonecutters to quarry, prepare, and move enormous blocks into place; artisans to carve and paint the reliefs and inscriptions for the walls of the temples, causeways, and tombs; sculptors to fashion the statues of the kings and their nobles; support staff in charge of food, drink, clothing, and equipment; and administrators to coordinate and record the various activities. A full quota of pyramid builders would have lived at Giza for three generations, and, since the cults of the kings were maintained and priests, nobles, and officials were buried there until the end of the Old Kingdom, a smaller permanent settlement must have existed for more than 350 years. All of these men and women (recent estimates of the number of workers needed to build the Great Pyramid stand at about twenty thousand) could hardly have disappeared without a trace, and I was certain that there were remains to be found if only we looked in the right place. The lack of direct evidence for the pyramid builders added fuel to the fire for those who insisted that the pyramids were built by slaves, or men from Atlantis, or even aliens, and I was determined that, when I returned to Giza with my doctorate, I would find the facts to prove these theorists wrong.

During the 1988–89 season, Mark Lehner and I began our search for the pyramid builders, a search that continues today. From the beginning, we have each had our own teams, but we have worked together closely and shared our discoveries. The reality that we are finding on the ground at Giza is that the pyramids were the national project of Egypt and that, as much as the Egyptians built the pyramids, the pyramids also built Egypt. For each king, building the pyramid and its surrounding temples and staffing the royal cult was an enormous undertaking that required the cooperation of the entire country. The administrative skills and nationwide participation necessary to carry out these projects effectively helped to create a centralized nation.

In my dissertation, I had devoted an entire section to the workmen, reviewing both archaeological and textual evidence for their existence. Through inscriptional evidence found at Giza, scholars had already been able to reconstruct the way in which the pyramid builders were organized. There were two classes of people working on the complexes: the artisans and administrators, and the workers who actually dragged the stones. It seemed most likely that the artisans and administrators were permanent employees of the royal court, while the workers were peasant farmers who came to Giza from the surrounding countryside and the provinces on a temporary basis, offering their labor to the king as a sort of national service in lieu of taxes.

A graffito from one of the five relieving chambers above the burial chamber of Khufu, showing the name "Friends of Khufu," one of the teams responsible for building the Great Pyramid. Through the evidence of this and similar graffiti combined with ancient texts, scholars had been able to reconstruct the way in which the pyramid builders were organized But it was only recently that we found the archaeological remains of this enormous labor force.

From inscriptional evidence, such as ancient graffiti found in the relieving chambers above the King's Chamber in the Great Pyramid, in several of Khufu's boat pits, and in Menkaure's complex, we knew that for each project, these workers were organized into four large gangs, or crews, with names such as "Friends of Khufu," and "Drunkards of Menkaure," each with its own overseer. These crews were each divided into five phyles, or smaller groups of about two hundred, and then into either ten units of twenty men or twenty units of ten men.

From my research, I had come to believe that there was one workmen's camp that housed the rotating workers from the provinces for the reigns of all three Giza kings. Through my review of the available evidence, I concluded that we should concentrate our search for this camp to the southeast of the Sphinx, where several earlier excavators had found tantalizing traces of the pyramid builders. There is a large limestone wall here, called the Wall of the Crow. This monumental structure stretches east for about six hundred feet from the northwest corner of the Maadi Plateau, the geological formation that lies directly south of the Mokkatam Formation on which the pyramids were built, separated from it by a large wadi, or dry stream bed. South of this wall is a thirty-nine-acre tract of undeveloped desert. I came to believe we should look for the pyramid builders south of the Wall of the Crow, which I theorized was built to isolate the royal precinct to the north from the area of the workmen to the south.

PREVIOUS EXCAVATIONS

Several earlier excavators had uncovered glimpses of some of the more mundane activities associated with the pyramid complexes, such as industrial areas and some tantalizing traces of settlements. As part of my investigation, I carefully reviewed all of this work, looking for clues. In 1880–82, Petrie had excavated a large area, almost 1,500 feet long and more than 250 feet wide, directly west of Khafre's pyramid. Walls of limestone rubble cased with mud plaster enclosed this space and divided it into narrow galleries (each about 9 feet wide

and at least 80 feet long), seventy-three galleries running east to west and eighteen oriented north-south. At least some of the rooms end to the east in wide limestone columns. Inside the galleries, Petrie found many chunks of granite, limestone, and basalt, as well as a number of statue fragments and many pottery sherds from the Old Kingdom. He concluded that this area was used as housing for the permanent workers who built Khafre's pyramid, which he estimated to be four thousand men; thus he called it the "Workmen's Barracks," and the name stuck for more than a hundred years.

I was not convinced that this area was really the living quarters for more than four thousand men. Mark Lehner and the British scholar Barry Kemp both believed that these galleries represented storage magazines, and I was convinced that they should be the workshops for Khafre's pyramid complex. Immediately after my return to Egypt in 1988, Mark and I, along with Nicholas Conard of the University of Tübingen, reexamined this area. From the remains on the surface, we could count almost one hun-

We carried out new excavations in the Workman's Barracks west of the pyramid of Khafre, an area explored earlier by Petrie. Our work demonstrated that the area was used in the Old Kingdom for workshops and storage magazines.

*This small limestone fig-
ure of a king in the white
crown of Upper Egypt
and the royal kilt was
found in the area of the
Workmen's Barracks; one
of the arms is missing
and the break looks
deliberate, perhaps indi-
cating that this was a
sculptor's model or trial
piece.*

dred galleries, and we decided to excavate several large, randomly selected squares. The galleries had been carefully cleaned out in antiquity (or else never fully used), but we were still able to recover bits of copper, unworked feldspar, malachite ore, and several small flints. Just when we were about to finish our season, we found several interesting deposits in front of two of the southernmost galleries. These contained potsherds, bones of domesticated animals, wood charcoal, barley, emmer wheat, and lentils. In the same deposits, we found fragments that suggested a royal sculptor's workshop: collections of basalt chips, unworked pieces of granite, a flint core with flakes nearby, and pieces of very small royal statuettes and limestone figurines.

Based on the physical evidence, and on later tomb models and New Kingdom parallels that show just this sort of layout for storage areas and workshops, Mark and I have reinterpreted this area as workshops and magazines for producing and storing certain of the materials associated with the cult of Khafre, including statues, food for the personnel who serviced the cult, and fresh offerings. It is possible that goods arriving by boat from the provincial estates that belonged to Khafre's cult were also stored here.

Several decades ago, the late Egyptian Egyptologist Abdel Aziz Saleh uncovered an industrial area about 230 feet south of the causeway of Menkaure, in the main wadi that runs between the Mokkatam and Maadi formations. This complex consists of two foundations made of stone rubble mixed with mortar, which Saleh identified as embankments connected with transport ramps. Fifteen buildings of various sizes were built against these embankments. The remains here—which include large ovens, some for baking bread, others for firing ceramics; a hearth for metallurgy; an area for working faience; and some large pieces of alabaster and granite, perhaps the remains of a royal statuary workshop—suggest that the entire area was most likely devoted to workshops connected with Menkaure's pyramid complex and cult, and probably functioned from the reign of Menkaure through the end of the Old Kingdom. This is a relatively small installation, but from the evidence seen here, I expected similar remains on a much larger scale in the area further south and east.

In the 1970s, Austrian archaeologist Karl Kromer carried out a series of excavations in a sandy basin enclosed by peaks and ridges about fifteen hundred feet south of Khafre's pyramid and east of Menkaure's pyramid. His work uncovered glimpses of a large deposit covering an area of twelve and a half acres filled with settlement material belonging to relatively poor people—pottery, fish hooks, bone, stone bowls, mud-brick debris, ashes, and a poorly carved sphinx. His finds also included clay sealings bearing the names of Khufu and Khafre. What he found was debris (which is what Egyptologists call garbage with no associated architecture) that seems to lie in several layers. A thick sandy deposit of limestone chips, the remnants of quarrying activities, lies on top of the settlement material to the east and south. Karl Butzer, an Egyptologist who specializes in geology, analyzed Kromer's data and concluded that the mound contained five strata, the first two separated from the last three by sterile material. The debris in "Kromer's Dump" probably came from the razing of several successive settlements or royal installations associated with the building of the pyramids, possibly mixed with material from the construction ramps.

A modern cemetery lies at the edge of the desert southeast of the Sphinx. In 1934 Selim Hassan did some test trenches within the confines of this cemetery and found mud-brick buildings, potsherds, and granite fragments. He decided to look for a new piece of land with no ancient remains buried beneath the surface, so that the cemetery could be moved and he could excavate underneath. He had gained the support of all the parties involved, including the village chiefs, and dug in an area south of the Wall of the Crow. He immediately hit mud-brick walls, flint fragments, and pottery, along with seal impressions of Khufu and Khafre, so he had to abandon his plans. Unfortunately, he only published one paragraph about this work, so we knew only that the area warranted further investigation.

THE GREAT DISCOVERY: THE TOMBS OF THE PYRAMID BUILDERS

In addition to re-excavating Petrie's "Workmen's Barracks," Mark Lehner and I investigated an area several hundred feet south of the Wall of the Crow, at the northwest corner of a modern soccer field. There, with Fiona Baker of Scotland, we found a rectangular building, measuring about twenty-nine by twenty-seven feet, with a wall running through the center that divides it into two halves. On either side of this wall are low rectangular pedestals, and the whole construction looks a great deal like Old Kingdom granaries that we find represented in tomb scenes, although some details call this interpretation into question. Several sealings found in a corridor adjacent to this building mention the *wabet,* or mortuary installation, of Menkaure.

We stopped the excavation to concentrate on other things, having no idea that hundreds upon hundreds of tombs and the remains of a vast worker's installation lay buried in the sand around us. Mark went back to the United States, and I stayed at Giza.

I was sitting alone in my office at Giza in April of 1990, already feeling the heat of summer, when the chief of the pyramid guards, Mohammed Abdel Razek, came to tell me that an American tourist had been thrown from her horse when it stumbled over a mud-brick wall in an area only about thirty feet from our earlier excavations. I went

The tomb chapel of Ptah-shepsesu, the first tomb to be found in the lower cemetery of the workers. In the west wall is the false door, on which the name of Ptah-shepsesu was crudely written. The arched ceiling is also of mud brick, modeled and painted to look like palm logs.

In the lower cemetery, each of the larger tombs, belonging to an overseer, was surrounded by smaller tombs, belonging to his workers or family members.

with Sheik Mohammed, and took Mansour with me. When I looked at the wall, I knew that we had found the tombs of the pyramid builders, just as I had predicted in my dissertation. Every year since, we have spent six to nine months excavating, and we have found extraordinary things. There are two parts to this necropolis: on the lower slopes lie the mud-brick and rubble tombs of the gang overseers, surrounded by the smaller monuments of the workers under their supervision; on the escarpment above them stand the larger, stone-built tombs of the skilled craftsmen and administrators. This cemetery is as important as the tomb of King Tut, because it opens a window into the lives of the workers—silent until now—who built the pyramids of the Old Kingdom, part of the 80 percent of the Egyptian population that has generally been neglected by archaeologists.

We began our excavations in 1990 and found that the wall exposed by the horse belonged to a tomb chapel built in the shape of a long vaulted chamber, with the mud brick of the inner ceiling shaped to look like palm logs and painted red to imitate wood. Two false doors were set into niches along the western wall. Crude hiero-

glyphs on one of the false doors identify the tomb owner as Ptah-shepsesu. Three shafts, each containing a skeleton (probably of Ptah-shepsesu, his wife, and his son) lay to the west of the vault, and as we continued to excavate, we found that a large courtyard fronted the tomb to the east. Pieces of granite, diorite, basalt, and limestone had been used for the low walls, which links the tomb clearly with the royal workshops, where such luxury materials were used.

Around this tomb were a number of much smaller mastabas of mud brick, with niches in the west face to serve as false doors, and even, in some cases, miniature courtyards. These mastabas cover single shafts, probably for people who worked under Ptah-shepsesu's supervision, and perhaps other members of his extended family. This entire area, which we call the lower cemetery, is arranged like this, with large tombs surrounded by smaller ones.

So far, we have excavated more than sixty large and six hundred smaller tombs in this portion of the necropolis, which sprawls across the lower slope of the Maadi formation. There are many remarkable and unique tombs in this cemetery, which dates to Dynasties 4 and 5. The small

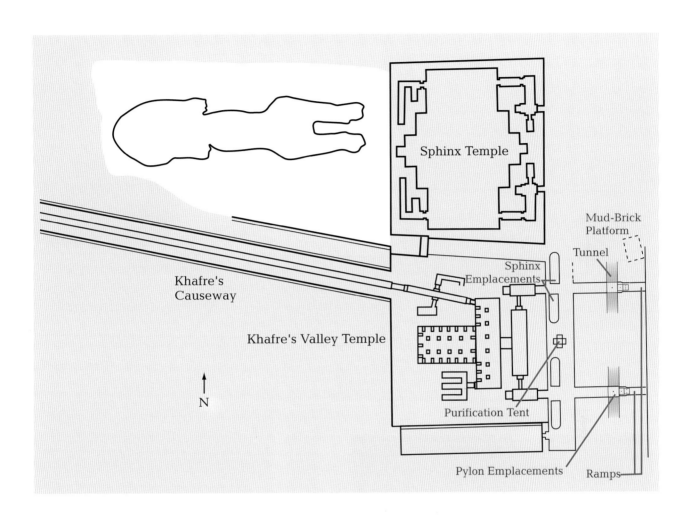

Sphinx Temple

Mud-Brick Platform

Tunnel

Sphinx Emplacements

Khafre's Causeway

Khafre's Valley Temple

N

Purification Tent

Pylon Emplacements

Ramps

tombs, from three to six feet high, come in many shapes: in addition to the mastabas, there are beehive tombs, an egg-shaped tomb, and even a stepped pyramid of mud brick; one small tomb had a miniature ramp spiraling around its dome, perhaps to represent the construction ramp of a royal pyramid. These tombs echo the symbolism of the pyramids themselves, showing us that pyramids were not just for kings and queens. One of the meanings that Egyptologists have ascribed to the pyramid shape, which can be traced back to 1st Dynasty mounds left inside elite tombs, is that they represent the earthen mound on which the primeval god stood to create the Egyptian cosmos. It is possible that the idea came from the lower classes and filtered up to the ruling elite, rather than spreading from the top down, as has traditionally been believed.

These are the tombs of the workers and overseers who built the pyramids, farmers sent from the provinces to serve their king for a set period of time, as today many nations have their young people serve temporary stints in the army. Some of the people buried here would thus be

This limestone "reserve head" was found discarded between the tombs in the lower cemetery. There are thirty-six other of these reserve heads, all dating from the 4th Dynasty. Scholars are still debating their function, but I believe they were substitutes left in the tombs in case the body was destroyed.

the ones who died while the pyramids were being built, before they could return to their homes in the provinces, and the wide variety of tomb styles may reflect their local traditions. There are also many women buried here, usually buried either with or next to their husbands.

The tombs had mud-brick or limestone false doors, most of them uninscribed. From the inscribed material that we did find scrawled on some of the false doors and stelae, and carved into several offering basins, we were able to recover the titles of "Inspector of Building Tombs" and "Director of Building Tombs"; women were usually priestesses of Hathor.

Two of the tombs that we have found so far belonged to single women, working at Giza alone, without husband or children. One, Repyt-Hathor, was buried in a simple shaft surmounted by a small mastaba. A small offering basin inscribed with her name and her title, priestess of Hathor, was found in front of her false door. The second woman, Nubi, was a priestess of Neith, the only woman in the cemetery so far with this title. Her very simple tomb is built of stone rubble. The entrance is to the east, with one burial shaft; inside we found an offering table bearing the tomb owner's name and titles: "The King's Acquaintance, the Honored One, the Priestess of Neith, Ninubi." This offering table acts as a substitute for a false door and as a place for the deceased to receive offerings. It is one of the most beautiful artifacts to be discovered in the cemetery.

Two of the tombs in the lower cemetery belonged to single women. Repyt-Hathor, a priestess of Hathor, was buried in a simple shaft sur- *mounted by a small mastaba. This small offering basin, inscribed with her name and title, was found in front of her false door.*

Several small but remarkable statuettes were found in this cemetery, demonstrating that the people buried here had access to skilled sculptors. One of the most interesting is an unfinished "reserve head" of limestone, which we found discarded between the tombs, not associated with any of them in particular. This is one of thirty-seven reserve heads (portrait heads that show the deceased only from the neck up) that have been found to date. All come from the 4th Dynasty, and their function is a bit of a mystery. There are many theories, but I think the mostly likely explanation is that they acted as substitutes for the body in the event that it was destroyed or damaged. This head does not seem to have been used and was perhaps discarded because of mistakes that the artist made and could not correct. This head shows a man with close-cropped hair, the hairline marked by a straight line across the forehead. He has high cheekbones and a straight nose, and he wears a faint smile.

We found this beautiful limestone statuette representing an overseer in his tomb in the lower cemetery of the workers. It was stolen in 1993 during the visit of some VIPs to Giza, and, although we know that it is now in Germany, it has not yet been returned.

In a small limestone box formed of three upright stone slabs placed against the west face of a small mud-brick mastaba (Tomb 7) were three limestone statuettes, the tallest fifteen inches high, and a limestone vessel. The sculptures are of a man named Kaihep, standing and striding forward; a woman, Hepnykawes, seated on a backless chair; and an unidentified woman kneeling to grind grain. This last sculpture is very realistic and conveys the sense of a woman hard at work, with strong shoulders and long, muscular arms. Her clothing consists only of a short kilt, since the work that she was doing would have been hot and difficult.

It is thought that the purpose of figures such as the kneeling woman was to provide the deceased with food in the afterlife and to help them with work that they might want done there. Since this statuette is as well carved and painted as the others and indicates a wig and a bead collar, I believe it represents the lady of the house, Hepnykawes herself. As the wife of a workman, it is unlikely that Hepnykawes could afford to hire someone else to do this work.

Tomb 1914 was built mainly of mud brick, except for an eastern wall of limestone, basalt, and granite chunks, that was covered with white plaster. The tomb is entered from the north through a passage that leads to an open court. In the middle of this court is a rectangular building whose east wall contained three false-door niches. In the southernmost niche was a wonderful statuette of lime-

These three limestone statues were found in a small limestone box made from three stone slabs that were set against the west face of a small mastaba (Tomb 7). The standing man is Kaihep, and the seated woman is his spouse, Hepnykawes. The third statue depicts a woman grinding grain and may also represent Hepnykawes.

stone, painted mostly black, with traces of red and yellow. It shows a man with a mustache in a short flaring wig and a kilt striding forward energetically. Judging from the size and complexity of his tomb, this man was clearly an overseer. In a shaft to the west of the main shaft was found the skeleton of a young woman about fifteen years old, holding in her right hand an oyster shell filled with kohl, a material used to line the eyes and associated with ritual purity. Around her neck was a beautiful necklace of semi-precious stones.

The overseer statuette is a superb example of Old Kingdom sculpture. It is only about eight inches high, but the details are carefully and accurately modeled in a remarkable manner for a statuette of this size. Around his neck, the overseer wears a broad collar, called a *wesekh,* which could be worn as jewelry during life and as a funerary ornament. The pendant, which is only partially preserved, seems to be the *ib,* the hieroglyph for heart. In the New Kingdom, the *ib* means that the deceased is innocent and can pass safely to the netherworld; it may also represent a special award from the king.

This statuette has special significance for me, because it represents a difficult but important period of my life. From the moment it was found, it was one of my favorite pieces from the workers' cemetery, but it got me into a bit of trouble. The discovery of the tombs of the pyramid builders was international news, and many important visitors came to see our excavations. In January 1993, a group of VIPs, including Minister of Culture Farouk Hosni, came to see the new cemetery and the beautiful sculptures we had found there. The woman who was in charge of the magazine where the statuettes were stored was on vacation because of a Coptic feast, but she came anyway just to open the storeroom. My guests enjoyed the visit enormously, and all the media broadcast the event.

At 4 o'clock that afternoon, the chief of police informed me that the overseer statuette was missing. I was devastated and furious. The man who was head of the Antiquities Department at the time did not like me, and he had been looking for an excuse to get rid of me. He told the

media, and everyone else, that he needed to review security at the storage area, and he transferred me from Giza to the Cairo Monuments section of the department. He also transferred all my good archaeologists away from Giza. I did not argue, because I couldn't explain to the public what the head of the Antiquities Department knew very well, that I had no direct control over this storeroom. I didn't waste my time retaliating, or even defending myself, because I knew that the truth would eventually come out. Instead, I resigned and left Egypt to teach at the University of California at Los Angeles for six months. Another highly placed official made things worse by giving the media a picture of movie star Omar Sharif holding the statue, something I had allowed him to do on one of his visits to the site. He made it seem as if Sharif and I had stolen it, and some people spread the rumor that I had been transferred because I was involved in the theft.

When I came back from Los Angeles, I kept myself busy writing my book about women in ancient Egypt, *Silent Images.* One day I was sitting at the Nile Hilton café, writing my book and smoking my water pipe, when a man came to my table. He introduced himself as the chief of police at the airport, and he told me that they had just discovered what had happened to the statue. While they were transferring the statues from the storage magazine to the area of the Sphinx, one of the security guards, in cooperation with two Egyptian archaeologists from Saqqara, had taken the statue and sold it to an Egyptian, who then took it to Germany. The next day, this news was all over the papers.

The head of the Antiquities Department was already in trouble with Parliament for many illegal activities; he was subsequently fired, and a new head was appointed. I came back to Giza after a year, but the beautiful statuette never came back from Germany. The case is still in court, and the archaeologists from Saqqara are in jail. But this taught me that when people attack you, you cannot always defend yourself; sometimes you just have to keep quiet and trust that the truth will eventually come out.

This view of the lower cemetery of the workers, looking west, shows the first ramp we found leading to the upper cemetery of the artisans. The wooden staircase was built for modern visitors to the site.

CEMETERY OF THE ARTISANS

One day, as we were working in the workers' cemetery, we stumbled across the beginnings of a ramp outlined with low walls of limestone rubble. This ramp led directly to the upper part of the escarpment, where we found additional tombs, larger and more elaborate than those in the lower cemetery, looking out over the valley below. So far, we have excavated seventy tombs in this upper cemetery. Many are completely rock-cut or have a stone facade in front of a low cliff face; others are freestanding mastabas of limestone and mud brick. The artifacts and statuary in these tombs are of higher quality than those

from the lower cemetery, and the inscriptions tell us that the people buried here were of higher status than those below, holding titles such as "Inspector of Dragging Stones," "Inspector of the Craftsmen," "Inspector of the Sculptors," "Chief of the Estates," "Overseer of the Linen," "Overseer of the Tomb Makers," "Overseer of the Harbor," and even "Overseer of the Side of the Pyramid." The most important title found here was "Director of the King's Work." I believe these are the tombs of the artisans who designed and decorated the pyramid complexes and the administrators who oversaw their construction. Based on the pottery, names, and titles found in this cemetery,

my conclusion is that it was begun as early as the reign of Khufu and continued in use through the end of Dynasty 5, from about 2589 to 2345 B.C.

Some of the tombs were robbed in antiquity, and intrusive Late Period shafts have destroyed or damaged others. However, we have still found many amazing artifacts. Many tombs contained false doors or stelae inscribed with requests for offerings, as well as the name and titles of the tomb owner and his family. Other tombs contained statues, usually within a serdab. As in the lower cemetery, the majority of the tomb shafts still protected skeletons, many in wooden coffins, but all lying so that the head faced north and the face east.

The first ramp we found did not lead directly to a tomb but was flanked on each side by important monuments. At the end of the ramp were two children's graves without offerings. Just to the south was the limestone mastaba of a man named Inty-shedu, built in the style of the 4th Dynasty. This tomb had six burial shafts and two false doors.

To the southwest of the mastaba, attached to it but cut into the bedrock, was a roughly cut chamber in whose west wall was a niche sealed with limestone, mud bricks, and mortar, with one small hole left uncovered. This looked like it could be a serdab that might hold a statue, but I was not prepared for what awaited me inside. When I peered inside the hole, I could see the eyes of a beautiful limestone face staring back at me. I began to remove the

Above: Detail of a limestone relief from the upper cemetery of the artisans. The visible title is "Overseer of the Side of the Pyramid."

Right: View of the tomb of Inty-shedu, "Overseer of the Boat of Neith," one of the first tombs we found in the upper cemetery.

mud-brick walls to the north and south, until I could see the head of the statue clearly. But when I took down the wall of limestone, I found not one, but four exquisite statues: a large seated figure in the center, flanked by two figures (one seated and one standing) to its right and a standing figure to its left. I thought that this was very unusual. The ancient Egyptians would normally have made a symmetrical arrangement, with two statues on each side—and when I looked more closely, I saw the disintegrated remains of a wooden statue that had stood to the left.

Inscriptions on the statues identify the owner as Inty-shedu, an overseer of the boat of Neith. The largest statue also bears the title "King's Acquaintance," suggesting that he was promoted to this rank later in life, after the other statues had been made. All of the images are beautifully carved of limestone and then painted; the largest is about thirty inches tall. All four statues wear knee-length kilts and broad beaded collars, which may have religious

significance. In the three seated statues, Inty-Shedu's skin has been painted a dark reddish-brown, and he wears a short, flaring black wig. The standing statue has much lighter skin and wears a short, curled wig.

These sculptures all represent Inty-shedu at different stages of his life: the statues on the left and right show him in various stages of his youth, and the central statue depicts him at the time of his death. Inty-shedu's moustache is unusual, as this is a feature rarely seen in Old Kingdom statuary, with some important exceptions. However, many of the sculptures we have found in our new cemeteries have moustaches, which perhaps reflect class differences. It is the same in Egypt today: the majority of the men who live in the villages wear moustaches, while most city-dwellers are clean-shaven.

We have no parallels for Inty-shedu's primary title, "Overseer of the Boat of Neith." Neith was an important goddess, a daughter of the sun god Re, and she seems to have had a minor cult at Giza. We have evidence for

In this, one of the four statues of Inty-shedu, the large expressive eyes of the man who served as an overseer of the boat of the goddess Neith and gained, by the end of his life, the title of "King's Acquaintance," seem to speak to us over a distance of 4,500 years.

many more people bearing titles associated with her sister Hathor, but we do know of others at Giza who served as priests or priestesses of Neith. Inty-shedu's title, however, is unique, and suggests that there was a temple of Neith at Giza.

The discovery of the statues of Inty-shedu was also the occasion of another brush with the so-called Curse of the Pharaohs. The excavations at the tombs of the pyramid builders were in the news every day, and people were fascinated to learn that the pyramids were built by Egyptians and not by slaves.

My dear friend Anis Mansour, who may be the best writer in Egypt (he has written many wonderful books that should be translated into English, and I believe he should receive the Nobel Prize) writes a daily column in the *el-Ahram* newspaper. He came to visit the excavations and began to write every day about the discoveries,

emphasizing how important they could be for promoting tourism to Egypt. He even invited President Mubarak to come to the site, because he knew that the president liked to visit archaeological excavations.

When we discovered the tomb of Inty-shedu and the wonderful statues that were hidden inside, I called Farouk Hosni, minister of culture, to tell him about this important discovery—the first time so many statues had been found inside a niche for one person. He set a date to come to the excavations and to bring the newspaper reporters with him. That day, October 12, 1992, I was sitting in my office at Giza when I felt a big earthquake. I ran down to make sure that the Sphinx and the new tombs were safe, and I was relieved to find that they were all still standing.

We postponed the announcement and set a new date. But the new date was when I had my heart attack, so the discovery was never announced. In early 2002, I took the statues to the Cairo Museum, and because they are near to my heart, I go every Friday to the café at the Hilton Hotel and say hello to them.

There are many other fascinating tombs in this cemetery, of which I will describe only a few. One of my favorites lies near the tomb of Inty-shedu and is built in the shape of a large beehive. It was constructed in three stages. In the first stage, the burial chamber was cut into the rock, with steps leading down to an entrance on the east side. This chamber was then covered with a limestone ceiling, and the twelve-foot-high domed pyramid was then built above. We have covered this unique tomb with a roof to protect it from the elements.

One of the most beautifully decorated tombs in the Upper Cemetery belongs to a man named Nefertheith. It lies just north of the tomb of Inty-shedu. The plan of the tomb is simple: a long chamber with three beautifully carved false doors along the west wall. The northernmost false door is for Nefertheith himself, whose titles include: "King's Acquaintance" and "Overseer of the House." Some unique scenes at the bottom of this door show people grinding grain and baking bread, which suggests that Nefertheith may have been in charge of the bakeries that

Above: The tombs in the cemetery of the pyramid builders come in many different sizes and shapes. This beehive-shaped tomb is one of my favorites. The burial chamber was cut into the rock and roofed with limestone, and a twelve-foot high dome was built above it.

Right: The tomb of Nefertheith is one of the most beautifully decorated of the tombs in the cemetery of the artisans. Here I am examining an inscription located between two of the false doors.

Left: In this close-up of one of the three false doors in the tomb of Nefertheith, men are shown brewing beer, working with the mash, then pouring the liquid into jars.

Below: This detail of one of the three false doors in the tomb of Nefertheith indicates that it is dedicated to the tomb owner and his second wife, Neferhetepes, whose title was "midwife." Since there are eighteen children represented in this tomb, she certainly would have had plenty of experience with childbirth!

Mark Lehner and his team found in the Workmen's Installation in the plain below (see p. 121).

Between this false door and the central one is a carved menu listing the various breads, beers, clothing, oils, and other items that were needed for the funerary cult. The false door in the middle is dedicated to Nefertheith and his first wife, Nyankh-Hathor. An inscription on the door tells us that he made the false door for his beloved first wife, who had died and gone to the necropolis. The third false door is for Nefertheith and his second wife, Neferhetepes, who bore a unique title that Henry G. Fischer, one of the greatest living interpreters of ancient Egyptian titles, first translated as "weaver," although he later suggested that it meant "midwife." She would certainly have had lots of practice at home: eighteen children are represented in the tomb. Below a standing figure of Nefertheith on this door is one man making beer while another stores it in four jars, which may indicate that he was in charge of both bread baking and beer brewing.

Another important monument is the rock-cut tomb of Nyankh-Ptah, which is fronted by a second ramp. This tomb complex seems to have been designed to follow the example of the royal pyramid complex, with a lower courtyard containing an offering basin, (corresponding to the valley temple), a ramp (for the causeway), an upper

The rock-cut tomb chapel of Nyankh-Ptah in the cemetery of the artisans is approached by a ramp, corresponding to the royal causeway. Notice that the ramp does not run straight, but, like the causeway of Khufu, bends partway up. At its foot is an offering basin (the "valley temple").

enclosed courtyard and upper tomb chapel with false doors (mortuary temple), and tomb shafts. It is particularly interesting to note that Nyankh-Ptah's "causeway," like Khufu's, has a distinct change in angle part of the way up.

The design of this tomb is very unusual. It is built of limestone and consists of a narrow antechamber and a small square inner chamber. From the end of the ramp, several stairs lead down to the antechamber, which has small windows high up in the north wall and another on the south wall. These are features designed for the comfort of living, since the family of Nyankh-Ptah who would have come at festival time to make offerings and celebrate his cult. From the south wall of this chamber, stairs lead to the roof, where the family may have cooked their feast before coming inside to eat.

The inner offering chapel is very roughly carved from the living rock. The only inscribed artifacts found here were a very small false door, found propped in a corner of the inner chapel, and an offering table, roughly incised with the name of Nyankh-Ptah and his title, "Overseer of the Desserts," found in the antechamber. Five skeletons were found in the burial shafts of this tomb, and we also found a large bread loaf inside the tomb.

Another tomb that provides a window into the tomb chapels as functioning places of worship is the tomb of Weser-Ptah, also approached by a ramp. This is relatively steep, and was built over some older mastabas of mud brick. A stele in the north doorjamb of the entrance shows the tomb owner wearing a kilt and holding a scepter and staff, with an inscription which reads: "The Inspector of the Officials, who is Behind the Officials, Weser-Ptah." I think that this title means that Weser-Ptah was in charge of counting the officials who worked at the pyramid complex. Set into the walls of the roughly cut chapel are two false doors. One of these, for Weser-Ptah himself, is inscribed with offering formulae and a long list of feasts. To the south is a small false door inscribed for his son, who was an "Inspector of the Doorkeepers of the Palace." What is odd about this false door is that someone deliberately covered the son's name with mud.

Above: The tomb complex of Weser-Ptah is also approached by a ramp. This is quite steep and was built on top of some older mastabas of mud brick.

Right: The entrance to the tomb chapel of Weser-Ptah is decorated with a relief depicting the tomb owner holding a scepter and staff. He is given a very unusual title: "The Inspector of the Officials, who is Behind the Officials, Weser-Ptah." A unique feature of the roughly-finished interior of this tomb is the dome carved into the ceiling so that visitors could stand upright in front of the false door.

Opposite, top: Mansour Boriak with an unfinished pair statue discovered by the ramp of Weser-Ptah. The figure of the woman is finished, but the man was left incomplete, perhaps because he was mistakenly depicted striding with the right leg instead of the customary left leg. When the mistake was noticed, the sculpture was evidently abandoned.

Opposite, bottom: This small painted limestone statue depicts an Overseer of Craftsmen named Neferefnesutef seated next to his wife, Neferefmenkhetes. It was found in a serdab attached to their tomb.

An interesting feature of this tomb is that the ceiling is very low, perhaps because the rock was not of good quality and was difficult to cut successfully. However, just in front of the false door of Weser-Ptah, a dome was roughly hewn into the ceiling so that there is a place where it is possible to stand upright. This is a wonderful glimpse into the use of the chapel: it was important to provide a place for family members to stand in order to make offerings to the deceased, so this dome was cut out for them. There are three burial shafts here, cut into the rock under the chapel.

Tomb 1948 is very small, but inside a serdab at the south end of the eastern face of the chapel was a beautiful pair statue of painted Tura limestone. The statue, which is only about ten inches tall, shows a man named Neferefnesutef, who was an "Overseer of Craftsmen," seated next to his wife, Neferefmenkhetes. The faces of this couple are very distinctive, different from the royal and noble portraits of the Old Kingdom. There were three burial shafts associated with this tomb, each containing a skeleton; one shaft contained the body of a woman buried in a wooden coffin and dressed in robes that suggest she held some important position.

One of the masterpieces found in the upper cemetery is a small limestone statue of a tenant farmer ("Overseer

of the Gardens"), Wenemniut. This was discovered in a serdab high in the east wall of his small limestone mastaba. The deceased is shown striding forward, wearing a short kilt and a shoulder-length wig. The features of his face are finely modeled and very distinctive, and the figure reminded me of one of our current overseers.

Another very interesting tomb was built for the family of an official named Petety, a "Royal Acquaintance" who held the unique title of "Inspector of the Small Ones." This tomb was built in three phases and displays a rather complex plan, with many courtyards and several interior chambers. The main burial chamber is rock-cut, but the rest is mostly of mud brick, with some walls of limestone plastered with mud. Door sockets in front of several doors suggest that some of the entrances into the tomb were closed with wooden doors. There are nine burial shafts associated with this mastaba.

Five inscribed stelae were included in the first phase of the tomb's construction, and emplacements suggest that there were others, which were removed in antiquity. In one of the courtyards, we found a limestone block covered with white plaster surrounded by a large quantity of charcoal that was perhaps used to burn incense. To the west of this is an unusual structure of mud brick, plastered in mud. Inside a niche on top of this was the top part of a strange anthropoid (human-shaped) statuette of unbaked clay that seems to be of a monkey. This perhaps served a protective function, to ward off unwanted spirits or visitors.

One of Petety's titles, in addition to his high rank as "Royal Acquaintance," is "the Eldest/Inspector of the Small Ones, of Good Reputation." This title, like many of those found in this cemetery, is unique and suggests that Petety was a teacher of some sort. Two stelae face each other on the jambs the doorway leading to the innermost court of the tomb. The southern stele was dedicated to Petety, and the northern one was for his wife, Nesyher, "beloved of Neith, Priestess of Hathor, Mistress of the Sycamore." These are unique stelae, as they both bear "curse" inscriptions warning against desecration of the tomb.

Listen all of you!
The priest of Hathor will beat twice any one of you who
*   enters this tomb or does harm to it.*
The gods will confront him because I am honored by his
*   Lord.*
The gods will not allow anything to happen to me.
Anyone who does anything bad to my tomb, then the
*   crocodile, the hippopotamus, and the lion will eat him.*

Many of the burial shafts in the cemetery of the pyramid builders contained skeletons with their heads to the north and their faces to the east, as we see here.

Nesyher's curse is similar, but she threatens the evil-doer with a crocodile, snake, hippo, and scorpion.

An open courtyard was later added to the eastern side of the tomb, where nine shafts were dug, each covered with a rectangular superstructure. Four more-or-less complete skeletons were found in these shafts: one male, aged twenty-five to thirty years; one female, aged forty to forty-five; and two children under the age of one year. The female was found in a wooden coffin, with her head facing west rather than east, as is usual in this cemetery. This skeleton is very odd in other ways: the head is large, with a full set of teeth, but the body is comparatively small. She may have been a dwarf, or a person with some disability. An unusual patch in the skull may also point to some pathology. The other burials were fragmentary. Also found in the shafts were pottery from the 4th Dynasty, charcoal, and one cylindrical faience bead.

This is one of the finest and most elaborate tombs in the upper cemetery, but I am not convinced that Petety himself was buried here, at least in one of the nine shafts in the added courtyard. The burials all look very rushed and do not conform to the usual position in which we find the bodies, with the head to the north and the face to the east. This tomb, and its enigmatic owner, will benefit from further study.

Many of the burial shafts in the upper and lower cemeteries contained skeletons curled in the fetal position, usually lying with their head to the north and their face to the east. Occasionally (more often in the upper cemetery), there would be a coffin of sycamore wood, associated with Hathor as "Lady of the Sycamore," in one of the shafts. Males and females are equally represented in the burials.

We are fortunate to have an excellent lab at Giza, and an X-ray machine with which to study the skeletons. Our principal forensic anthropologist is Dr. Azza Sarry el-Din, an excellent scientist who has helped us shed light on the lives and deaths of these men and women. The bones, especially the spines, of a majority of the skeletons showed the effects of stress, probably from hard physical labor. Excellent medical care was available; there is evi-

Our forensic anthropologist, Dr. Azza Sarry el-Din, studied the skeletons from the cemetery and found that many of the vertebrae showed signs of chronic stress from hard physical labor.

dence of broken bones that had been set; the leg of one worker had been amputated successfully (the worker lived for approximately fourteen years after the operation), showing that they had emergency medical care on site; and one skull showed evidence of brain surgery. We also found the skeleton of two female dwarves, one of whom had died in childbirth; the skeleton of her baby was found within her remains. Dr. Azza also found traces of a disease similar to syphilis. The average height was between five and six feet, and the typical life span was thirty-five to forty years (as opposed to fifty to sixty years for nobles at this time). Women under thirty had a higher mortality rate, probably a result of the dangers of childbirth.

Simple and multiple limb fractures are found in skeletons from both the upper and lower cemeteries. Most frequent were fractures of the bones of the upper arm and of the more delicate of the lower leg bones. Most had healed completely, and had clearly been set. Depressed fractures of the frontal or parietal skull bones were found in both male and female skulls, mostly on the left side, which may indicate that these injuries are from face-to-face assault by right-handed attackers.

Anyone visiting the site today can see immediately that there must be hundreds or even thousands of tombs left to uncover. We are working simultaneously in several areas. The terrain suggests strongly that we will find more tombs in the stretches between our excavations and probably all the way north to the Wall of the Crow. We must work slowly and carefully so that we recover all of the information that is left for us to find. We have also done several sections, going down below the level of these tombs, and it is clear that there is some sort of building activity below, perhaps remains of an older cemetery. It will be the work of many years to excavate this cemetery and interpret our results, but as we go, we are building a fascinating picture of the lives and families of the men who built the pyramids.

I am sitting in the lower cemetery of the workers, with the upper cemetery of the artisans visible behind me.

The Old Kingdom settlement revealed by the soundings taken for the sewage project under the modern villages at Giza extended for over a mile south of a boundary formed by extending the line of the Wall of the Crow to the east. In fact, the bulk of the soundings came from this area. I believe that the land to the north belonged to the pyramid city, where the court and administration lived, and that the area to the south was reserved for the artisans and workmen responsible for building the pyramids, the men and women buried in the upper and lower cemeteries. Artifacts found in this area included, as I have mentioned, sealings of Khufu and Khafre and many Old Kingdom potsherds of all types, including some clearly imported from Upper Egypt that probably arrived in Giza carrying food. The animal bones included cattle, sheep, and pigs; this last animal was eaten only by the lower classes.

I believe that the remains south of the Wall of the Crow belong to two settlements. The first one, directly south of the boundary wall, would have been a village for the corps of artisans and their families who were permanent employees of the royal house. The second, farther south, would have been a workmen's camp for temporary conscripts from all over Egypt and their overseers. The build-ings here would have been primarily huts, with larger houses for the overseers, much like those for the artisans. The average population living in these settlements would have been about fifteen thousand, a figure that includes about five thousand artisans. In addition, as many as seven thousand workmen would have come daily from sites nearby, such as Memphis, Saqqara, Meidum, and Heliopolis. Thus, the total number of workmen actually involved in building the pyramids would have averaged about twenty-two thousand, at a time when the total population of Egypt was approximately one million.

THE ROYAL INSTALLATION

Archaeology often both suffers and benefits from accidents. In 1991 a backhoe was digging up sand to use in a construction project when it hit some ancient remains that lay south of the Wall of the Crow, near the edge of the low desert. Unfortunately, it cut through walls, floors, and layers of potsherds, completely destroying the southeast corner of a massive building complex. My assistant Mansour Boriak was working nearby, supervising excavations in the cemetery of the pyramid builders, and he noticed what was happening. He came down to investigate, saw

large amounts of Old Kingdom pottery in the exposed trenches, and told me about it right away. We stopped the work immediately so that no more damage would be done and we could salvage what was left.

When Mark Lehner returned to Giza that year, he asked Mansour where he should start. Mansour pointed to the backhoe trenches and said, "Right there!" Mark and his team opened a new area near the trenches and made a remarkable discovery. They found a series of rooms that they were able to identify as Old Kingdom bakeries. Each room was seventeen feet long and eight feet wide; along the east wall of each were two lines of holes set into a shallow trench. Pots containing bread dough would have been set into the holes, and hot coals would have been heaped in the trenches to bake the

Above: The National Geographic Society sponsored a reconstruction of this bakery, and Mark and his master baker actually baked bread according to an ancient recipe.

Opposite: When Mark Lehner first began excavating in the area south of the Wall of the Crow at Giza, where a backhoe had cut through an ancient site, he immediately found an Old Kingdom bakery.

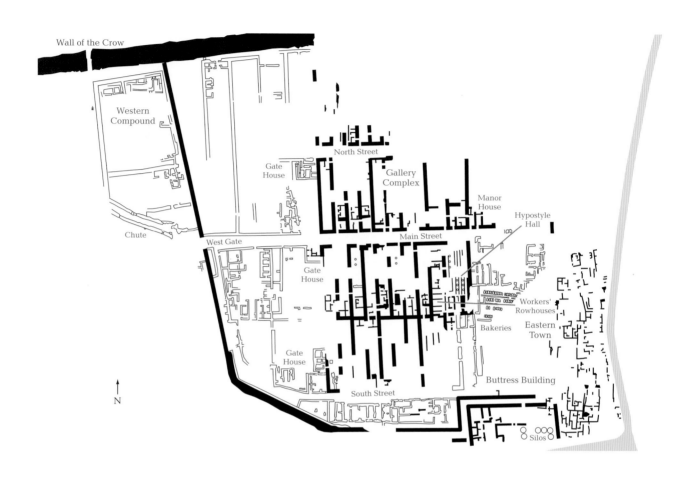

Wall of the Crow

Western
Compound

Chute

West Gate

North Street

Gate
House

Gallery
Complex

Manor
House

Hypostyle
Hall

Main Street

Gate
House

Workers'
Rowhouses

Bakeries

Eastern
Town

Gate
House

Buttress Building

South Street

N

Silos

The area of the royal installation southeast of the Great Sphinx (map courtesy of Mark Lehner). In the center are the galleries; to the north is the massive Wall of the Crow; to the east are houses; to the south is what may be a palace of some sort; and scattered throughout the site are bakeries and workshops.

bread. There was also a hearth in the southeastern corner where lids to put on the pots were heated, and low counters of stone and mud along the walls. Piles of broken bread pots—small and large bell-shaped pots and flat trays—lay on the floors of these rooms, where they had been discarded when the bakeries were abandoned. In the debris associated with these bakeries was found a potsherd inscribed with the term "per shena." This term appears in an important Old Kingdom tomb at Saqqara, the tomb of Ti, in which bakeries are labeled "per shena." My friend Rainer Stadelmann has suggested that this phrase means "workmen's installation." Mark and I think it may refer to the entire area connected with the workers, which would also have included breweries, where beer,

Top: One of the major roads
inside the royal installation
leads through a wall of limestone rubble and directly to
the monumental gateway
through the Wall of the Crow.
I believe that the workers
laboring on the pyramid site
passed through the installation,
collecting rations and tools, on
their way to work each morning
and their way home at night.

Bottom: Here is an overview
of the royal installation being
excavated by Mark Lehner.
The modern soccer field is to
the left and the cemetery of
the pyramid builders is in the
background.

the other staple of the Egyptian diet, was made. This area
would have been under the supervision of the state and
used to feed the artisans and workers who lived at Giza
and worked on the pyramids. With the help of the
National Geographic Society, Mark was able to build a
reconstruction of the bakery and to bake, more or less
successfully, several loaves of bread.

After a hiatus of several years, Mark returned once
again to Giza and began a major salvage project, which
continues today. Since 1998 he has, with my permission,
been using the services of expert front-loader handler
Mohammed Moselhy, and since 1999, he has been working almost year-round, with generous financial support
from a group of donors, including Ann Lurie, Bruce

Ludwig, and Peter Norton. Through careful use of the front
loader, he has been able to uncover the ground plan of an
enormous area, more than seven football fields in size.

Mark's excavation area lies just to the west of the horse
stables in Nazlet es-Samman. For years, the stable owners
have been taking the sand from this area, using it in their
stalls, and then bringing it back, creating a layer of what
Mark likes to call "horseshit sand." The owners have also
been hosing down their animals here and liquefying the
remains of the mud-brick walls that lie just below the surface, creating "mud-melt," which then solidifies in an
undifferentiated mass. So Mark's work is in part a salvage
operation, since the ancient remains would not have survived for much longer under these circumstances. The

Inside the installation is a unique complex of long, narrow galleries. These face onto long streets that run east-west. Each gallery is about 15 feet wide and 103 feet long. In this completely excavated example, the long porch or colonnade in the front and the living area in the back are visible. Mark Lehner now thinks that these may have been dormitories.

architecture that remains is only the lowest level of the original site, the stumps of ancient walls. But Mark is recovering every possible particle of information, mapping and numbering every artifact and feature, sieving everything, doing flotation to recover plant traces—in short, using all the methods known to modern archaeology.

The ground plan of this huge area, combined with in-depth excavation of selected areas, provides a detailed picture of an ancient royal installation dedicated to the construction of the pyramid complex of Menkaure. The monumental Wall of the Crow, which stretches for six hundred feet east from the foot of the Maadi Plateau, constitutes its northern boundary. This wall clearly acted as a mechanism for controlling traffic in and out of the area of the pyramid complexes, and it also may have served as a barrier for flash floods that occasionally roared down the great wadi between the main plateau and the Maadi formation to the south.

Mark has found the remains of a smaller wall of limestone rubble running south from this great wall and then curving around to the east to form a boundary for the main part of the site. A roadway runs south from the monumental tunnel-gate that pierces the Wall of the Crow, then turns east to pass through a gate in the north-south boundary wall and become what we call "Main Street," a wide paved road graced by an ancient drain that runs directly to the east. Two other streets, North Street and South Street, run parallel to Main Street. Between them lies a unique complex of long, narrow galleries.

Along the street that runs through the boundary wall are two large and relatively elaborate houses, which are nicknamed the Manor House (to the east) and the Gate House (to the west). These look like control posts, and the entire setup looks very much as if it was designed to keep track of people passing through the Wall of the Crow.

The galleries inside the boundary wall face onto the long streets, and run all the way to the Wall of the Crow to the north, where they link up with its eastern end. These galleries are each about 15 feet wide (east-west), and 103 feet long (north-south). They are arranged in blocks of eight, with thick mud-brick walls defining their outer boundaries and thinner walls marking off internal divisions. The northern portions of at least eight or nine of the galleries contain low benches with column bases embedded in them; these appear to be colonnaded areas that would have been partially roofed. In the southern parts are what look like typical living areas, as well as areas where activities such as copper working, cooking, and baking seem to have taken place. A likely reconstruction for these galleries is that they were simultaneously workshops and dwellings for some of the support staff responsible for supplying the pyramid builders.

In the easternmost of the galleries that open onto Main Street is a series of simplified houses whose chambers are defined by rough fieldstone walls. Mark has dubbed these Worker's Rowhouses. West of the entire gallery complex are more fieldstone ruins, which include small chambers arranged around an open courtyard; these may have been storerooms.

The bakeries that Mark found first lie to the east of the galleries, and other, similar bakeries have been found on the site. Near the original bakeries, at the east side of the gallery containing the Worker's Rowhouses, is a hypostyle, or columned, hall. This is a large structure, enclosed by a five-foot-thick wall. Inside were found low partition walls and two sets of low benches separated by troughs that held complete jar stands and lids, but no jars. When the team explored further, they found a broad court filled with sets of long parallel troughs and mud-brick benches. They were able to recover bits of fish gills, fins, and bones and also an assortment of flint blades and flakes. It is likely that this was some sort of fish-processing plant, although it could also have been a communal dining hall of some sort.

Farther east Mark's team is exploring an area that may be a faience workshop. The part of the site farthest to the east, which almost certainly continues under the houses of the nearby village, is occupied by buildings that look like houses, which may be part of the living area for the artisans and workers, perhaps an extension of the settlement glimpsed to the east.

To the east of the gallery complex is one of the first examples known of a hypostyle, or columned, hall. A broad court was filled with sets of long parallel troughs and mud-brick benches, visible here. Mark Lehner's team recovered bits of fish gills, fins, and bones as well as an assortment of flint blades and flakes; the most likely reconstruction of this area is that it was some sort of fish-processing plant; alternatively, it may have been a sort of cafeteria.

Connected with the boundary wall and the galleries at the southern end of the site is a very large building with rounded corners, which Mark calls the Buttress Building. He is just beginning to excavate this area, which he believes may be an administrative center or perhaps even a palace. The floral and faunal remains show a high incidence of cattle bones (an expensive meat) and cereal grains that seem to have been processed elsewhere, both of which suggest that an elite population may have been fed here. Stretching to the west is a series of what look like storage areas.

The many seal impressions found so far date this level primarily to the reign of Menkaure. It would appear that the main area of the site represents a royal installation, where rations and tools were produced, perhaps for the workers responsible for Menkaure's pyramid. We know from the New Kingdom site of Deir el-Medina that the workers who carved the tombs in the Valley of the King were supplied with carefully monitored food rations and tools; it looks as if we have a similar situation here. One can imagine that the artisans and workers lived to the east, and each morning, rose with the sun and passed through the royal installation, collecting what they would need for the workday. The purpose of the huge Buttress Building remains to be revealed, but it seems likely that it served some sort of administrative or even palatial function, in which case at least some of the production activity carried out here would have been for the benefit of the court.

It is clear that remains from an earlier period lie underneath the level that Mark is now excavating. From the glimpses he has gotten of these remains, it does not appear to be as organized or as massive, but it seems that similar functions were being served.

THE WORLD OF THE PYRAMID BUILDERS

The entire complex here, with the town to the east and the cemetery to the west, is very much like the New Kingdom site of Deir el-Medina, where the artisans responsible for the royal tombs in the Valley of the Kings lived over a thousand years later. There, as here, the village lies east, at the foot of an escarpment, and the tombs lie to the west. The Deir el-Medina tombs are separated from the Valley of the Kings by a natural mound; here, the Wall of the Crow and a natural wadi divide the artisans and workers from their royal and noble patrons.

The small houses of the artisans would have been built of mud-brick and stone rubble and designed to suit the climate, with domed ceilings to keep them cool in summer and warm in winter. The house of Chief Baker Nefertheith, who had a household of twenty-one, would probably have had two rooms plus a hall, which would have acted as the

Opposite: These are some of the bronze tools, including a fishing hook, found in the royal installation.

Below: Some of Old Kingdom pottery from the cemetery of the pyramid builders. This type of jar was the most common pottery find; most of these were found in the areas between the tombs rather than inside them.

reception, meeting, and eating area. The furniture would have been mainly of stone; kitchens were equipped with pottery vessels for cooking and storing food, serving trays, water jars, and cups for beer and wine. The mud huts of the workmen would have been similar to the houses of farmers in the villages of modern Egypt. A typical village house includes a small court surrounded by rooms, with a staircase leading to the roof. There would have been few furnishings, probably just sleeping mats and large vessels to cool water.

In addition to keeping their own houses and raising their children, women living at Giza often worked with their husbands at the construction site or acted as support staff, grinding grain, mixing dough, making beer, and perhaps assisting in the distribution of food. Some women held their own titles; the second wife of Chief Baker Nefertheith, Neferhetepes, was a midwife. Many women were priestesses of Hathor (whose cult was also important later at Deir el-Medina), and several were also priestesses of Neith. Hathor was the patron goddess of workmen and artisans; in addition to serving as priestesses, which involved duties such as performing offering rituals and sacred dances, many women compounded their names with Hathor.

Personal artifacts found in our excavations include razors, tweezers, and combs. The wives of the artisans used perfumes and cosmetics of all types, including both green and black kohl. The wives of the workmen probably could not afford these luxuries; they wore simple earrings and necklaces with amulets in the form of deities and other protective symbols. The standard costume for workmen and artisans was a short kilt; they would wear longer kilts, sandals, and wigs on feast days.

This tomb scene, from the 5th Dynasty funerary chapel of Nefer at Saqqara, depicts men fishing with scoop nets. This simple technique would almost certainly have been used by the workmen at Giza.

The ancient Egyptians liked large families, and every Egyptian was encouraged to get married. An Old Kingdom text states: "Take a wife while you are young, that she may make a son for you. . . . Happy is the man whose people are many." From the scenes in the tombs and the statuary, we can see that the relationship between married couples was one of affection. Sons were preferred to daughters, since only a son could follow in the footsteps of his father. This was important, since it offered the only reliable method of family advancement.

Like the rest of Egyptian society, including royalty, the workmen's daily diet consisted of bread, garlic, figs, and beer. (It is interesting to note that Egyptian beer had a higher alcoholic content than modern-day beer.) They also drank fruit juice and milk when available. Of the fourteen types of bread recorded in ancient tombs, at least three are still made by Egyptian farmers today. The pyramid builders liked aged wine, and they also ate pork, like the workmen at Deir el-Medina. Fish, often caught after the workday was over, was a favorite dish, and on feast days, they might have roasted goose, pigeon, duck, beef, or mutton.

Despite their healthy diet, the workmen's physical health was poor because of their strenuous occupation. As we have seen, bone analysis of some six hundred skeletons from the cemetery of the pyramid builders shows that the workmen and their wives had some degree of spinal stress from moving heavy objects. The average life span was between thirty and thirty-five years. By comparison, the workmen at Deir el Medina lived longer, to between forty and forty-five years. The work at Giza was hazardous: six skeletons showed signs of traumatic death, and we discovered separate burials for severed legs and hands. In addition to physical stress, workers were exposed to fatal diseases such as bilharzias, which is still prevalent in Egypt and much of tropical Africa. One workman suffered from cancer in his skull and ribs; this is the earliest example we have of cancer in Egypt.

From ancient texts (especially those from Deir el-Medina) and tomb scenes, coupled with the archaeological evidence we have recently uncovered, we can reconstruct a typical workday at the pyramids as follows: a workman living in the Giza settlement would probably have gotten up before sunrise, washed, and dressed in a short kilt. He may have prayed to his local god, the god of his village, to Hathor, and to the sun god, Re, and then eaten a breakfast of bread with garlic washed down by beer mixed with water. His walk to work, which took about twenty minutes, would take him through the workers' installation, where he would sign out any tools that he might need; then he would pass through the gate in the Wall of the Crow and head up to the plateau. Workmen who lived in the Memphite area would travel either by foot or by boat to the pyramid site; we estimate that they would put in a ten-hour workday before returning home at sunset.

If a workman's job were in the quarry, he would cut the stone, using tools of diorite and flint and following the lines made in the living rock by the chief stonecutters. After cutting into the rock from the top on all four sides, the artisans would come and hammer wood into the holes and then pour water on top. The wood would expand, fracturing the rock along the scored lines. Once freed, the block would be shaped and then smoothed. Another group of workmen would transport the stones on sledges, using water to decrease friction, to a point at the southwest corner of the pyramid. I believe that it took eight to ten men to move a one- to two-ton block of stone. When I was an inspector at Tuna el-Gebel in Middle Egypt, it took only fifteen workmen and one overseer to move a statue of Thoth weighing about six tons.

At the construction site, other workmen would take charge of the stone as it was assigned to a particular side of the pyramid and to a specific level. Across the river at Tura, other workers would be shaping fine white limestone for the pyramid casing, and up the river, at Aswan, granite and diorite would be cut. All of these materials would be brought to Giza via the Nile, through a connecting canal, and into the Giza harbor.

Some workmen functioned as support staff, bringing water for drinking and for use in the construction. Other workmen would sing for their gangs, to take the crew's mind off the labor and to organize the rhythm of the work. One can imagine a workman with a gift for comedy making jokes for his fellow workers.

Workmen who arrived late were reported by the phyle overseer to the workmen's scribe, who would deduct a small share of his salary. If a worker felt he was wrongfully penalized, he could go to a higher authority and lodge a complaint. If a worker got sick, he would be taken to the clinic or sent home. There was emergency medical care available in case of accidents. After work each day, every overseer had to report to the appropriate scribe about the progress that had been made and whether or not the work was on schedule. The scribes then reported to the overseer of all the work, who reported in turn to the overseer of all the king's work. Finally, a report would be made to the king, who kept a close eye on the progress of his complex from his palace nearby.

The drudgery of the work was broken by the many feasts celebrated by the workmen, such as the feasts of Thoth, god of Wisdom; Sokar, patron god of Saqqara; the Feast of Burning; and the national feast of the New Year. For these feasts, the workmen and their families would dress in new clothes, including sandals if they could afford them. Feast days were a time for visiting both neighbors and family, for preparing special food and cakes, and for making offerings at the tombs of their ancestors. Judging from the tomb scenes that depict these festivals, there was much singing and dancing, as well as boat rides on the Nile.

The pyramid projects must have been a tremendous socializing and nationalizing force in the early days of the Egyptian state, as young conscripts left hamlets and villages far and wide for Giza, where they worked for their king and learned the habits and manners of the capital. The elaborate and sophisticated administration that arose to facilitate the national projects of pyramid building, which were carried out almost continuously throughout the Old Kingdom, had a profound influence on the development of the Egyptian nation. Over the course of the Old Kingdom, the bureaucracy of the country became more and more complex. In the earlier part of the 4th Dynasty, the highest administrative titles, such as vizier and overseer of all the king's work were held by members of the royal family; in the late 4th Dynasty and the 5th and 6th Dynasties, these titles were held by nonroyal individuals. The skills and organizational sophistication required for the construction of the giant pyramids of the 4th Dynasty and the elaboration of the state cult provided the impetus for the development of a stable, highly centralized state.

Left: In the foreground is the reconstructed chapel of Tetiankhkem, looking southwest. In the background are the mortuary temples of Iput I and Khuit.

Chapter III. New Explorations at Saqqara and Heliopolis

Saqqara, which has long been one of my favorite sites in Egypt, is vast, stretching for more than two miles along the desert plateau directly west of the ancient site of Memphis. It lies in the barren land where the sun sets each night just west of the line of green that marks the edge of the fertile Nile Valley. During my tenure as inspector of antiquities for Imbaba (see p. 29), I lived in an apartment in Cairo with several friends who also worked for the Antiquities Department. One of my roommates was Loutfi Sherief, whom I met when I was asked to train him at the site of Edfu; he also worked with me at Kom Abu Billo, and we have been friends ever since.

Loutfi was later made an inspector at Saqqara, where he lived in a beautiful rest house located at the eastern edge of the site, above an area known as the Doors of the Cats because of the many Late Period mummified cats found there. During my time at Imbaba, I would come to Saqqara every Thursday and stay until Saturday morning. On Friday, our day off, Loutfi and I spent our time wandering around the site, visiting the monuments and breathing in the magic of this ancient place, which is dominated by the Step Pyramid of Djoser (c. 2667–2648 B.C.), the first large-scale stone monument ever built.

Since those early days, this site has been near to my heart, and when I returned from the United States with my Ph.D. in 1987, Saqqara was one of the sites added to my jurisdiction. I have had two important goals for Saqqara since my time there with Loutfi. The first has been to protect the site from the local thieves who break into tombs and storerooms to steal artifacts, and the second has been to protect the monuments from the ravages of tourism and environ- mental hazards by doing site management. I started my work near the pyramid of Teti, where I made several major discoveries, including the pyramid of Khuit, principal queen of Teti; the tomb of their son Tetiankhkem; a wonderful group of Old Kingdom statues; a number of New Kingdom tomb chapels and artifacts; and many Late Period burials. The sand of Saqqara has also yielded the 6th Dynasty tomb of the royal physician Qar, who was buried with his copper surgical tools, and a wonderful cache of Late Period bronze statuettes, all found west of the pyramid of Unas.

A Brief History of Saqqara

Saqqara has been used as a burial ground since the 1st Dynasty, when Memphis, located in the floodplain to the east, became the capital city of a newly unified Egypt. The Early Dynastic settlement of Ineb-hedj (White Wall) has recently been excavated by David Jeffreys at the base of the plateau where the Early Dynastic tombs lie. Although the administrative center of the country moved with each successive king, who had a palace and royal city near his pyramid complex, Memphis remained important as the cult center of the god Ptah.

The earliest tombs at Saqqara, fourteen enormous mastabas of mud brick, belong to high nobles of the 1st Dynasty, and two large underground complexes of galleries are thought to be what remains of the tombs of the first two kings of the 2nd Dynasty. The early kings of the 3rd Dynasty also had tombs at Saqqara. The first and most impressive of these is the Step Pyramid of King Djoser, which rises in six stages to a height of thirty-five stories and dominates the plateau. The Step Pyramid is surrounded by a great rectangular enclosure with models of courtyards and reed-and-wooden shrines that echo in stone the actual structures that would have been built at and around the king's palace and used for ceremonies, rit-

uals, and administration. These structures are symbolic rather than functional; the interiors are solid and the entrances end in blank walls.

In November 1953, the Egyptian archaeologist Zakaria Ghoneim found the corner of a new pyramid near the Step Pyramid at Saqqara, which he named the Buried Pyramid. This pyramid belonged to the 3rd Dynasty King Sekhemkhet and was left unfinished, but in a burial chamber underneath, Ghoneim found a sealed alabaster sarcophagus, complete with a decayed funerary wreath on top. Thinking that he had found an intact Old Kingdom royal burial, he invited the head of the Antiquities Department and other dignitaries to witness the opening of the sarcophagus on June 26, 1954. To his dismay, and everyone else's, it was empty, leaving us with one of the great mysteries of Old Kingdom archaeology.

At that time, Gamal Abdel Nasser, then prime minister of Egypt, had been planning to visit the site. When he heard that the sarcophagus was empty, he decided to come anyway, in order to give encouragement to Egyptian archaeologists. In the same year, the solar boat of Khufu was discovered by Kamal el-Mallakh, and these two major discoveries were in the newspapers everywhere. Ghoneim and Mallakh went to America and Europe to gave lectures about their discoveries.

Upper left: The 3rd Dynasty step pyramid of Djoser (Netjerykhet) at Saqqara, seen from the cultivation to the east.

Right: This painted limestone statue of Djoser-Netjerykhet in the nemes headdress and royal beard is dressed in the cloak worn at the Sed Festival, during which the king celebrated the achievements of his reign and renewed his rule. The piece was found in the serdab against the north face of his step pyramid at Saqqara.

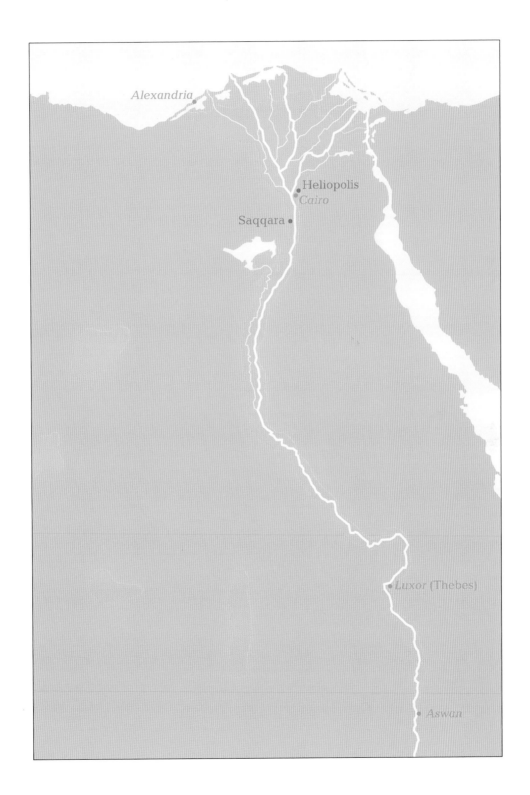

Alexandria

Heliopolis
Cairo

Saqqara •

Luxor (Thebes)

• *Aswan*

135

But Seth was jealous of Ghoneim and would not leave him alone. Ghoneim came back from the States after he had finished his lecture tour and went back to his job as chief inspector of antiquities at Saqqara. Some of his colleagues were counting the artifacts in one of the storerooms under his jurisdiction and reported that one artifact was missing. According to the law, Ghoneim was responsible for this, and jealous people spread rumors that he was stealing objects. Ghoneim could not stand this. He knew that he was innocent, but he could not prove it, and he could not stop the talk. So one night he went to a casino along the Nile and drowned himself in the river. This was a terrible tragedy for everyone, made more ironic by the fact that they later found the artifact he was accused of stealing. The discovery of the Buried Pyramid cost Ghoneim his life. Mallakh was also treated badly, so he resigned from the Antiquities Department and became a newspaper reporter.

Two other large 3rd Dynasty enclosures, whose outlines are barely discernable through the overlying sand, remain to be investigated. After they were built, Saqqara was abandoned for other sites, until the last king of Dynasty 4, Shepseskaf, came back to be buried here in a huge mastaba; the first and last two kings of the 5th Dynasty

were buried here as well. All of the 6th Dynasty kings, as well as their queens, constructed their pyramid complexes near the complex of Djoser. Throughout the Old Kingdom, the king's family and officials of the court were buried near their ruler's pyramid in tombs that became larger and more and more elaborately decorated over time. Some of the most spectacular Old Kingdom private tombs ever found are at Saqqara.

The ancient city of Memphis, center of the cult of the god Ptah, and its associated necropolis at Saqqara were revived in the 18th Dynasty. Alan Zivie has found several fascinating tombs from this period in the crumbling cliffs below the rest house, including the labyrinthine tomb of Aperia, prime minister of Egypt during the reigns of Amenhotep III and his son Akhenaten; the tomb of Maya, wet nurse to King Tutankhamun; and the tomb of the ambassador who signed the peace treaty between Ramesses II and the Hittites. It is amazing to think that these treasures lay hidden below our bedrooms! Recently, a Dutch team, working in the New Kingdom cemetery south of the causeway of King Unas, has rediscovered several important New Kingdom tombs. These include the tomb of the 18th Dynasty king Horemheb, constructed while he was a general under Tutankhamun; the tomb of Meryt-Neith, who was associated with the cult of the Aten, the sun disk worshiped by Akhenaten; and the tomb of Maya, treasurer under Tutankhamun. In the 1980s, Sayed Tawfik excavated tombs from the Ramesside Period belonging to some of the officials who were in charge of Lower Egypt. The site became important again during the 26th Dynasty, so there are also many Late Period remains here.

Upper left: Abdel Nasser (center) at the entrance of the Buried Pyramid of Sekhemkhet. This monument was discovered by Zakaria Ghoneim in 1953. Inside the burial chamber was a sealed sarcophagus; it looked intact, but it was empty.

Opposite: A Dutch team working at Saqqara recently discovered this beautiful painted limestone statue of Meryt-Neith, an 18th Dynasty official who lived during the Amarna period, and his wife.

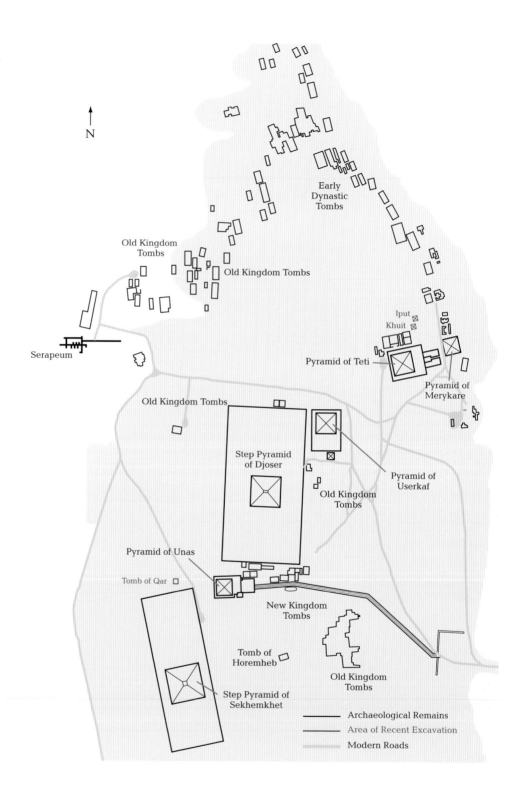

An overview of the Saqqara plateau showing the major monuments. My recent excavations are highlighted in red.

N

Early Dynastic Tombs

Old Kingdom Tombs

Old Kingdom Tombs

Serapeum

Iput

Khuit

Pyramid of Teti

Pyramid of Merykare

Old Kingdom Tombs

Step Pyramid of Djoser

Pyramid of Userkaf

Old Kingdom Tombs

Pyramid of Unas

Tomb of Qar

New Kingdom Tombs

Tomb of Horemheb

Old Kingdom Tombs

Step Pyramid of Sekhemkhet

Archaeological Remains

Area of Recent Excavation

Modern Roads

My Excavations in the Complex of Teti

Since 1992 I have been carrying out excavations in the pyramid complex of Teti, first king of the 6th Dynasty (c. 2345 B.C.). This area had previously been explored in the late nineteenth and early twentieth centuries, but Teti's causeway and valley temple have never been found, and most of the excavated areas had long since disappeared again beneath the rapidly drifting sands. The early 6th Dynasty is poorly understood, and I hoped to shed light on this period of Egyptian history. We have made a number of interesting discoveries in this area. My colleagues and I re-excavated the pyramid complex of one of Teti's queens, Iput I, and uncovered the complete plan of her funerary temple. While excavating here, we found a remarkable

carved doorjamb bearing one of the names of the king, Djoser-Netjerykhet (c. 2667 B.C.), who built the Step Pyramid. We discovered the pyramid of Teti's principal queen, Khuit, and re-excavated her mortuary temple. Another exciting discovery was the tomb of Tetiankhkem, Teti's crown prince. I plan to carry out more excavations

This photograph shows our recent excavations in the complex of Teti, first king of the 6th Dynasty. We are looking south; the ruined pyramid of the king is in the background. In the foreground are the tomb of Tetiankhkem, crown prince of Teti; the pyramid and mortuary temple of Iput I, secondary wife of Teti and mother of Pepi I; and the pyramid and mortuary temple of Khuit, principal wife of Teti.

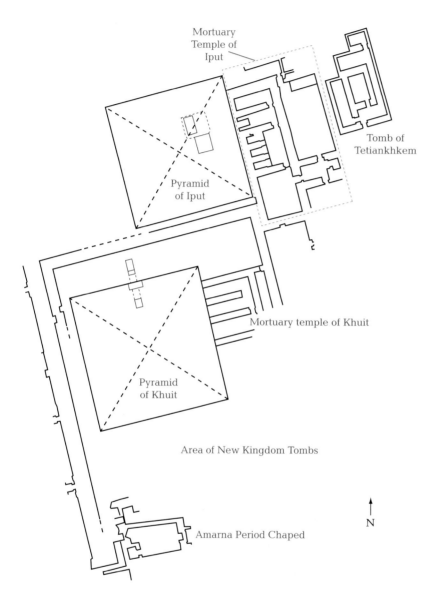

Mortuary
Temple of
Iput

Tomb of
Tetiankhkem

Pyramid
of Iput

Mortuary temple of Khuit

Pyramid
of Khuit

Area of New Kingdom Tombs

N

Amarna Period Chaped

*A sketch map of the Teti complex
excavations, showing the pyramids of Iput I and Khuit, the tomb
of Tetiankhkem, and the area
where the New Kingdom tombs
were excavated.*

around the pyramid of Teti, and I hope to
locate his causeway and valley temple.
There was a shadowy king named
Userkare who ruled after Teti, and I
think that his tomb may also be somewhere near here.

This is a very rich area, and we made
a number of other remarkable discoveries during our excavations. Near the area
of Iput I's pyramid, we found some wonderful Old Kingdom statues made of
wood. South of Khuit's pyramid are a
number of New Kingdom tombs in and
around which we found some beautiful
reliefs and other artifacts. In this area, we
rediscovered the location of an important
New Kingdom tomb that was built for
a man named Mose. Reliefs from this
tomb in the Cairo Museum include one
long inscription telling the story of a
court case that spanned almost three
hundred years.

At the beginning of our excavations in
the complex of Teti, we found the tomb
of the crown prince of Teti, Tetiankhkem,
which lies just east of the mortuary temple of Iput I. The tomb is relatively small
and was left unfinished. A much later
mastaba, perhaps from the 26th Dynasty
(664–525 B.C.) lies directly to the east,
covering part of the tomb chapel. In sub-
sequent seasons, we will excavate, map,
and remove this Late Period mastaba so
that we can finish the clearance of Tetiankhkem's tomb.

The plan of the tomb is simple. An entrance to the
south leads to a small hall. To the west of this is a long
north-south hall; to the east a long north-south corridor
leads first to the offering chapel and then to a storage
room; to the north is the entrance to the burial chamber.
We found beautiful decoration on many of the preserved

blocks of this tomb. On one side of the entrance is the lower part of a standing figure of a man, Tetiankhkem himself, accompanied by the smaller figure of a woman named Merut, probably his wife. On another part of the entrance is the lower part of a man (again, presumably Tetiankhkem) with Queen Khuit, his mother. In the tomb chapel are scenes of offering bearers and animal sacrifice, and in the corridors are more offering bearers and the tomb owner inspecting his funerary furniture. The colors in these scenes are distinctive, and the style is characteristic of the tombs of Saqqara during the Old Kingdom.

On the west wall of the tomb chapel, we found the false door intact, with much of its original red paint. It is a large, well-prepared slab of limestone, but the inscriptions are roughly carved, as if they were done quickly, and do not come up to the standard of excellence set by the scenes on the walls. Here are the name and titles of the tomb owner, which include: "Eldest Son of the King, Hereditary Prince, Lector Priest, Overseer of Upper Egypt, Overseer of the Two Granaries, Keeper of Nekhen, Tetiankh." These titles tell us that Tetiankhkem was crown prince and second in command to his father, King Teti.

The burial shaft, which was about fifty feet deep, was completely filled with debris, and the burial chamber had been robbed in antiquity. Tetiankhkem's uninscribed sarcophagus of unpolished limestone lay directly under the false door. The lid had been raised just enough for a small child to slip through and steal the amulets and jewelry from the body.

The Saqqara Inspectorate boasts two experts who are known for their ability to move heavy stones and open sarcophagi, using the same methods as the ancients.

Above: At the entrance to the tomb chapel of Tetiankhkem were the remains of some painted limestone reliefs. This fragment shows the feet of Tetiankhem himself.

Here is the false door of Tetiankhkem before the reconstruction work was started. The false door was carved from a single slab of fine limestone, but the text carved on it was evidently done in a hurry, as the hieroglyphs are roughly carved. The false door was then painted red.

These two men are Reis (overseer) Talal el-Kriety and his brother Ahmed, who work with me frequently. I recognized their skill and intelligence during the discovery by the Czech expedition at Abusir of an intact tomb from the 26th Dynasty, belonging to an official named Iuf-aa. The shaft of this tomb was about sixty feet deep, and inside was a limestone sarcophagus weighing sixty tons. Ahmed and Talal have worked for many years with the Czech expedition, and the director, Miroslav Verner, thinks very highly of them. I witnessed their work in the successful opening of Iuf-aa's intact sarcophagus. When we found the burial of Tetiankhkem, I asked them to come and help. They have also worked with me in the tomb of the Governor (Djed-Khonsu-efankh) at the Bahariya Oasis (see p. 227).

Ahmed and Talal are polite, gentle, and very strong. They know the business of moving heavy blocks and stones without modern machinery better than anyone in the world, and I have complete faith in their methods. Once they arrived, they rigged up a sort of windlass machine to bring people in and out of the deep shaft. I have no fear of heights, but it was still very disconcerting to ride in their rickety machine. Once we all reached the bottom of the shaft, Ahmed and Talal set up their system of levers and pulleys. For them, this particular sarcophagus was fairly simple, especially when compared to some of the huge Late Period sarcophagi they have had to deal with. When they moved the lid, I peered inside and saw the mummy of the prince. I asked Dr. Azza to come and bring the portable X-ray machine from Giza. She found that the body was of a man who died between the ages of eighteen and twenty-five, with no obvious diseases or injuries. However, the mummy was in very poor condition, and we could not see clearly whether or not the body bore any wounds.

Inside the burial chamber were two lovely artifacts—an alabaster headrest and an excellent example of a tablet for the seven sacred oils used in the funerary rituals. The headrest, a sort of pillow for the mummy, is among the most beautiful ever recovered. It stands on a base that

This detail of the limestone false door shown opposite shows a roughly carved figure of the prince.

was inscribed with the name and titles of the prince: "the Eldest Son of the King of his Body, the Sole Friend, Honored before the Great God, Tetiankh." The tablet for the seven oils is also of alabaster and is divided into seven sections, one for each of the oils: festival scent, the *sefet* and *heknu* oils used in rituals, union oil, anointing oil, the best of cedar oil, and the best of Libyan oil. Under the names of each of the oils is a circular depression for the oil itself, which would have been used to anoint the mummy before it was wrapped in linen, as well as in the rite of the Opening of the Mouth, a ceremony that served to revitalize the spirit of the deceased.

The period at the end of the reign of Teti is a dark age in Egyptian history. In the standard chronologies, there is a gap between the end of Teti's reign and the beginning of the reign of his son Pepy I. The Egyptian historian Manetho (c. 250 B.C.) tells us that Teti was murdered in a palace conspiracy; a king named Userkare, who appears only in some later king-lists, seems to have taken over the throne. The relatively small size and simple architecture of Tetiankhkem's tomb and the crudeness of the hieroglyphs on his false door, combined with his age at death, makes it tempting to suggest that he too might have been a victim of this palace coup.

West of the tomb of Tetiankhkem, about three hundred feet north of the mortuary temple of Teti, lies the pyramid complex of Iput I, wife of Teti and mother of Pepy I. Our plan was to clean the area and re-excavate the funerary temple of this queen. It had previously been uncovered in the late nineteenth century by Victor Loret and again in the early twentieth century by the British team of Firth and Gunn, but the publication on the site was sketchy and there were no good maps. As we cleared the huge overlay of sand (up to forty-five feet deep) that lay to the east side of the pyramid, the mortuary temple began to emerge from the sand, and in 1996, we discovered the monumental entrance that leads to the funerary temple, missed by previous excavators. In 1996–97, we re-excavated the shaft in the body of the pyramid that leads to the burial chamber of the queen.

Inscriptions found in her complex tells us that Iput I was the daughter of a king (probably Unas, the last king of the 5th Dynasty), the wife of a king (Teti), and the mother of a king (Pepy I). The original plan of Iput's pyramid was a mastaba, whose burial chamber was reached through a shaft. When her son came to the throne, he honored his mother by changing her mastaba into a pyramid and adding a funerary temple to the east. By honoring his mother, Pepy I also insured his position: only the mother of a living Horus (who could be a ruling king or an heir to the throne) was entitled to a pyramid, as the incarnation of Hathor-Isis.

The previous excavators had never completely cleared Iput I's mortuary temple, so we excavated it completely and restored some fallen blocks so that we could understand the temple plan and the program of the wall reliefs. The monumental entrance to the temple, which we uncovered for the first time, is made of granite and bears Iput I's name and titles "Mother of the King of Upper and Lower Egypt; Daughter of the God; King's Wife, his beloved; the honored one, Iput." The inscriptions, followed by images of the queen, are carved in sunk relief.

The entrance, which lies at the southern end of the temple, leads into a small pillared hall and then through a passage to an open court. On the west side of this court is a small hall; on the north wall, the remains of an inscription naming Pepy I; and on the west wall; a fragmentary scene of priests. West of this hall is another room, where we found the remains of two limestone blocks on a square base in the center. On the north wall is a procession of offering bearers; on the south more offering bearers before the queen, of whom only feet and ankles remain. The queen's feet appear again on the west wall, where she is probably supervising the slaughtering of animals; to the left of this scene are the remains of two military groups. In the middle of the west wall is a doorway, now blocked, that leads to the area around the pyramid.

From the north wall of this room, a door leads to the temple sanctuary, which takes the form of a hall with three niches, probably for statues; beyond this is a small

Here is the burial shaft of Tetiankhkem, photographed during excavation. We had to travel up and down a sheer drop of fifty feet, using a rather rickety sort of windlass—a somewhat nerve-racking experience!

Above: The unfinished burial chamber of Tetiankhkem with his limestone sarcophagus, which was also left unfinished.

Right: When we opened the sarcophagus of the prince, we found the mummy inside. It had been disturbed, but our anthropologist, Dr. Azza, was able to determine that the body was of a young man who had died between the ages of eighteen and twenty-five.

Opposite: We found a fine alabaster headrest in the burial chamber of Tetiankhkem. Headrests were used as pillows for the mummy, and this example is among the most exquisite ever found. The base was inscribed with the names and titles of the prince: "Eldest Son of the King of his Body, the Sole Friend, Honored before the Great God, Tetiankh."

146

offering chamber. We have reconstructed the decoration of the north wall of this chamber from fragments of relief as a scene showing Iput I seated in front of an offering table. Hieroglyphs on a fragmentary false door in the west wall of this chamber read: "An offering that the king gives, and Anubis, he who is on his hill, gives. May an invocation offering come forth of bread and beer from 'Pepy's Splendor is Enduring' [the name of the pyramid complex of Pepy I] to the mother of the king, Iput," and "The king's mother, Iput, wife of the king, Iput." These inscriptions tell us a great deal: they confirm that Iput was both a royal wife and a royal mother, and they tell us that the offerings for her cult came from the offerings presented to her son Pepy in his pyramid complex. In front of the false door was a granite offering table in the shape of a *hetep* (the sign for offering). Beyond the sanctuary is a storage room.

On a block near the entrance to the temple, we found a relief showing the sun disk, cobra, and a goddess in a vulture headdress. Below this scene are seven lines of hieroglyphs, which include the important title of "Hereditary Princess." During our excavations, we also rediscovered two pyramidions (capstones) that had been noted but not published by previous scholars. The burial shaft that leads to the substructure is thirty-six feet deep and ends in a small burial chamber cut into the bedrock. A limestone sarcophagus, which was breached but not completely robbed in the Late Period, fills this chamber. Inside, Firth and Gunn found a coffin of cedar wood that contained the bones of the queen, who had died in middle age. Her mummy still wore some jewelry, and inside the burial chamber was also a group of alabaster vessels, copper tools covered with thin layers of gold, a group of gold-covered vessels bearing the name of the queen, and two rectangular tablets made of alabaster bearing the names of the seven sacred oils. Behind the sarcophagus were five canopic jars of rough red pottery. The usual number of canopic jars is four; it is possible that the thieves who opened a hole in the sarcophagus left a fifth jar behind, or that the person who made the vessels got the number

wrong. During the Late Period, a tomb was built in the body of the pyramid, in the mouth of the burial shaft. The walls and the vaulted ceiling were made of mud brick. The tomb was removed by Firth, but remains can still be seen today.

In the process of clearing one of the storage magazines north of the offering hall in Iput I's mortuary temple, we found two pieces of limestone that had been reused in the pavement. When we put them together, we found that they formed an extraordinary doorjamb from the 3rd Dynasty Step Pyramid complex of Djoser (c. 2667 B.C.). It was carved of fine white limestone and is in relatively good condition, although no traces of color remain.

The relief, which was meant to be placed upright, is decorated only on the front and two sides. The back and the top were left rough, as if it were meant to be attached to other blocks, and it is the right shape and size for a doorjamb. The decoration is very interesting and quite

Above: The mortuary temple of Iput I lies to the west of the tomb of Tetiankhkem. When we cleared the area, which had been excavated before, we discovered for the first time a granite portal carved with figures of the queen and her name and titles. In this view, we are looking to the northwest, and Iput's ruined pyramid is to the left.

Opposite: Iput I was originally granted a mastaba tomb for her burial. When her son, Pepi I, succeeded to the throne (after the short reign of a usurper named Userkare), he turned her funerary monument into a pyramid and added decoration to her temple. This fragmentary limestone relief shows the legs of the queen, her name, and her title of "Mother of the King."

unique. On the two sides of the jamb are the undulating images of snakes, stretched out with their heads pointing up. There are two snakes on each side, one atop the other. The snakes are carved in low relief, and the bodies are crosshatched to give a tactile impression of snakeskin. The hood and the eyes of each snake are clearly defined, and the tongues protrude as if the snakes were going to attack.

The front has been divided horizontally into two large sections that are further subdivided into twenty compartments (thirteen in the first section and seven in the second). At the top is a *serekh*, a rectangular enclosure with niches at the bottom that represents a palace, with the Horus falcon perched on the top. Inside the enclosure is written the name of the king. This image goes back to the 1st Dynasty, when pairs of stelae, each carved with a serekh containing the royal name, were set up in front of the royal tomb. Inside this serekh is the name Netjerykhet, one of the names of Djoser. The falcon, wearing the double crown that symbolizes the union of Upper and Lower Egypt, is the divine icon of kingship. The entire image represents the king as ruler of Upper and Lower Egypt within his palace—both his palace in life and his funerary palace—protected by the royal god Horus.

In the twelve compartments beneath the serekh are alternating images of a jackal and a lion or lioness. A new section begins with a repetition of the king's name in the serekh, and the six remaining compartments again contain alternating jackals and lions/lionesses. This section is not complete; given the Egyptians' penchant for symmetry, it is most likely that there were six more compartments so that the lower section would have looked like the upper one. This theory is supported by the length of the top snake, which is complete; if the lower snake, which breaks off partway down, were the same length, there would be just room for six more compartments. There may even have been a third identical section below, in which case the completed height of the monument would have been about twelve feet.

The jackal is a representation of Anubis, the god of embalming, associated with the world of the dead from early in Egyptian history. If the second animal shown here were a lion, which its shaggy mane suggests, it would represent the power and might of the king. However,

lions' tails are tufted and are usually shown curled around their bodies, and the tails here extend out from the body in a U shape and lack a tuft. The lioness is connected in Egyptian mythology with the protective goddesses Hathor, Sekhmet, and Bastet and is known to be fiercely protective of her young. One passage from the Pyramid Texts, a collection of magical spells found inscribed in the burial chambers of kings of the later Old Kingdom, mentions the lioness goddesses Sekhmet and Shesmetet as the nurse and mother of the king. Therefore, on this relief, the lioness may represent both the mother who nurses and protects the king and, through association with Hathor, the guardian of the sky. This would be the earliest representation of this creature found in Egyptian art (except for a hieroglyph found in a private tomb of the 3rd Dynasty). The alternating jackals and lionesses could represent the guardians of the netherworld and the sky respectively, protecting the king who sits inside his palace (represented by the serekh) and providing for his eternal rebirth through association with the sun god, who travels through the sky during the day, dies at sunset, travels through the netherworld during the night, and is reborn each morning. The attacking snakes on the sides also act as protectors of the king.

It is possible that this monument might have been matched by an identical jamb, with the inscription facing in the opposite direction, that would have stood on the other side of the doorway; alternatively, a complementary doorjamb might have had the same decoration on the front, but the sides might have been decorated with vultures, symbols of Nekhbet, the goddess of Upper Egypt, corresponding to the snake as the symbol of Wadjet, goddess of Lower Egypt.

The style of the reliefs and the writing of the king's name are very similar to the reliefs that were found inside the Step Pyramid complex. The serekh here is an exact parallel to ones found in passages under the Step Pyramid itself, in the South Tomb (a dummy tomb for the king), and on the base of the famous statue of Djoser found in the Step Pyramid complex (now in the Cairo Museum).

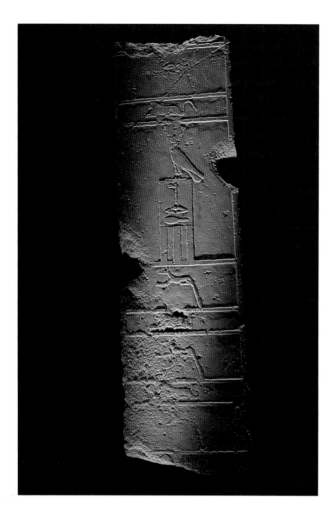

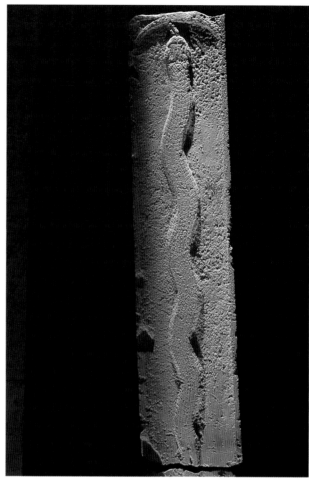

In the pavement of Iput I's mortuary temple, we found two reused slabs of limestone, which came from a doorjamb inscribed with the name Netjerykhet (one of the names of Djoser, builder of the Step Pyramid). The name was written inside a serekh, a rectangular panel representing the palace of the king—both his palace in life and his funerary palace—surmounted by an image of the falcon god Horus, protector of the royal house. Below the serekh are alternating jackals and lions or lionesses. There were probably three identical sections, of which most of two are preserved.

On the sides of the door-jamb of Djoser are undulating snakes, whose outthrust tongues make them look as if they are going to attack. I believe that this monument was once part of a ceremonial entrance to the pyramid complex of Djoser.

He is also called Netjerykhet in all of these locations (the name Djoser does not appear in the historical record until later), and the snakes here are also very similar to others found in Djoser's pyramid complex. The piece clearly dates from the reign of King Djoser, and I believe that this relief was taken from someplace in his pyramid complex.

The Step Pyramid sits within a wall which encloses thirty-seven acres of ground filled with an elaborate complex of subsidiary buildings, parts of which have not been completely excavated and other parts of which have been reconstructed, so the question of exactly where this doorjamb might originally have stood is not an easy one to answer. One day, Jean Philip Lauer (who has spent many years working in the Djoser complex and is responsible for much of its reconstruction) came to my office, and I asked him where this might have stood. He did not answer me, simply shrugging that he did not know.

There are a number of possible ways in which the original location of this doorjamb can be reconstructed: it may have stood in the court associated with Djoser's Sed Festival (see p. 60 for a discussion of this important royal festival), bordered to the east and west by dummy buildings that imitate the state shrines of the north and south, or on the northern side of Djoser's pyramid, where there is a large area that has not yet been fully cleared. I personally lean toward yet another interpretation, one that would link this complex to pyramid complexes from later in the Old Kingdom. I believe that it might have formed part of a ceremonial entryway into the enclosure. During the Old Kingdom, as we have seen at Giza, the pyramids are only one part of an elaborate complex, which included a causeway leading to the pyramid and, at the lower end of the causeway, a ceremonial entrance, which took the form of a valley temple. The layout of the Djoser complex is very different from that of the later pyramids, but most of the later elements can be traced back to structures here. I think it might be part of a ceremonial entrance for the Step Pyramid that has not yet been found. There are several possible locations for this, but the most likely reconstruction is that there was a ceremonial way leading to the complex from the northeast, past where the Teti complex now lies, in which case this doorjamb would have formed part of a gateway which would have been easily accessible to the builders of Iput I's temple. This may have been to connect Djoser with the tombs of Dynasty 1, and perhaps his capital was near the Early Dynastic capital of Ineb-hedj, at the foot of the plateau to the northeast of his complex. In any event, this is a fascinating find, one that opens another window into the development of the Old Kingdom pyramid complex and may change our understanding of the complex of King Djoser.

While we were working in the area just west of the outer wall of the pyramid of Iput I, we found three exquisite wooden statues under thirty feet of debris on the level of the temple floor. None is inscribed but all can be dated stylistically to the late Old Kingdom. All of the statues are of wood coated with plaster and painted (the skin reddish brown, the hair black, and the clothing white); the workmanship is good, although somewhat uneven. One of the statues, measuring about twenty-four inches high (including its base), represents a naked male, standing and striding forward with the traditional left leg in front. It is most likely that this statue was once dressed in a simple kilt of real linen that disintegrated or was separated from the figure long ago. The hair has been painted black and hugs the head like a skullcap, and the arms hang by the sides. The way in which the face of the statue was drawn gives him a silent, dreamy look, as if this young man were searching for the eternal, already a part of the spirit world for which the sculpture was made.

The second statue is smaller, only nine and a half inches high, and represents a man in a short white kilt kneeling and extending his body to the front, with his arms below him as if he were leaning on something. This is the least well made of the sculptures: the features of the face were hastily modeled in the mortar with which the statue is covered. The head is rounded and painted black to indicate his short hair. The two arms were carved separately and attached with wooden pins; they are actually too long for the body and look out of proportion, perhaps because the statue is kneeling. Much of the left arm has been lost. The two legs were carved from a separate wooden block. The figure is clearly engaged in some task, and may be a servant statue, similar in function to the female grinding grain that we found in the workmen's cemetery at Giza.

The third statue is of an official, striding forward with his right arm alongside his body, fist clenched, and his left arm extended to the front, holding a long stick that is fitted into a hole in the base on which he stands. The height of the figure with its base is about twenty-five inches. He wears a short belted kilt and a short black wig that covers his head and ears but does not reach his shoulders. This wig was carved from a separate piece of wood, and, in a technique unusual for this period, the artist has added thick black wax, some of which has now fallen, to deepen the modeling.

We cannot say here that these statues represent the same person: the features of the two standing statues, representing officials, are dissimilar, so they may represent different people, and the kneeling statue is of a servant. Since wooden statues are extremely delicate there may even have been more statues originally included with this group. The style of the short wig that covers the ears in addition to the simple, short kilt on one figure and the added kilt of linen on another suggests that these three statues date to Dynasty 6.

The Discovery of the Pyramid of Khuit

In 1996 we began to re-excavate the mortuary temple of Queen Khuit, the principal queen of Teti I. Her mortuary temple had been partially explored before, and we knew that her tomb must be nearby, but it had never before been found, and there was even some debate as to whether she had been buried in a pyramid or a mastaba. Within the first few days, on top of the mound that I thought would contain the monument of Khuit, we found the blocks that had once topped what had clearly been a pyramid, which had originally been sixty feet high. Later

we found several blocks of the pyramid casing. The entrance to the burial chamber is on the north side, and the passage was closed with blocks of limestone. A shaft had been cut by tomb robbers above the pyramid entrance. When we explored this, we found a short passage leading to a beautifully built burial chamber of limestone, undecorated but carefully constructed. Inside was an uninscribed granite sarcophagus that had been opened in antiquity. This sarcophagus was carefully placed so that it was in line with the sanctuary of Khuit's mortuary temple; the peak of the pyramid lies directly above the center of the east-west length of the chamber and the north-south axis of the passage. To the east of the sarcophagus, we found a hole for the canopic jars; on the eastern side of the burial chamber, a door leads to a square storeroom.

Scattered in the burial chamber, we found the remains of bones and a mummified skull. Dr. Azza did an X-ray examination of these bones and determined that they belonged to a woman who died when she was forty to forty-five years old. Her teeth were worn (she may have been in some pain from a dental abscess), and her leg bones showed evidence of either malnutrition or disease when she was about fourteen or fifteen. It would be very exciting to be able to report that these bones were the queen's, but the skull dates to the New Kingdom.

A wall surrounds the mortuary temple, separating it from the complex of Iput I. The entrance to Khuit's mortuary temple is on the south and leads to a rectangular east-west hall. In the north wall of this hall is a door that leads to a narrow north-south corridor that in turn leads to a large open court running along the north face of the pyramid. From the west wall of the entrance hall, a door leads to a storage room; relief fragments from this area represent offering bearers and part of a large royal chair in which the queen would have been seated. To the north of this room is the chapel: relief fragments here indicate that this wall would have looked much like the reconstructed north wall of Iput I's offering chapel, with the queen seated at an offering table. Offering bearers also decorated the south wall, and set into the west wall was a false door and

an L-shaped table made of limestone. A door in the north wall of the chapel leads to two more storage rooms. We also found a fragment showing the queen on a boat in the marshes, which links the queen with the goddess Hathor, mythological wife of the living king and mother of the coming king; a partial inscription on this block also identifies her as the daughter of a king.

The archaeology makes it clear that Khuit's pyramid complex was built before Iput's, since Iput used part of the north wall of Khuit's complex as the south wall of her own complex. This tells us that Khuit was the principal queen of Teti. These complexes were also interesting to explore because we were able to see that the standard measurement was the rod (2.3 feet, or 0.7 of a meter), rather than the royal cubit. The relief fragments we were able to recover also help us to reconstruct the program for Old Kingdom queens: the principal themes are the relationships of the queens to the kings with whom they were associated; their offering cults; and, at least in the case of Khuit, of her activities in the afterlife, in the marshes as Hathor.

Just west of the outer wall of the pyramid of Iput I, we found these three wooden statues, each coated with plaster and then painted. The largest (far right) is twenty-five inches tall, and the smallest is only nine inches high. The two standing statues represent officials, and the kneeling man is a servant in the process of carrying out some task. These statues can be dated stylistically to the 6th Dynasty.

Our recent excavations in the Teti complex shed new light on the chronology of the early 6th Dynasty. Tetiankhkem, the oldest son of Teti, and his principal queen, Khuit, herself the daughter of a previous king, died during the reign of his father at the age of about twenty-five, either before his father or perhaps even in the conspiracy thought by Manetho to be responsible for Teti's death. The almost completely unknown King Userkare, for whom no monuments have yet been found, then took over the throne and ruled until Queen Iput I, another of Teti's wives, was able to reclaim the throne for her son Pepy.

Directly above the Old Kingdom level is a New Kingdom layer (c. 1550–1069 B.C.), where we discovered many wonderful artifacts. This stratum had been ignored by earlier archaeologists, although treasure seekers and museum collectors had done a great deal of damage in the area. Nonetheless, we found a number of beautiful stelae, dating mostly to the late 18th and early 19th Dynasties, which were associated with a series of mudbrick tomb chapels and burial shafts that lie to the south of Khuit's pyramid. The chapels are of varying sizes, but most are oriented east-west, with an open court to the east and an enclosed chamber containing a statue niche to the west. The chapels were paved with limestone, and limestone column bases are often found in between the courtyard and the enclosed chamber. One chapel belongs to a royal scribe named Djehutyemhep, and in 2001 we

found the lower part of a statue of this man in the debris south of Khuit's mortuary temple. Reliefs found in the area of his chapel depict him with his wife, whose name is no longer legible.

The largest of the New Kingdom tombs in this area is anonymous but can be dated to the Amarna Period (late 18th Dynasty, c. 1352–1323 B.C.) by virtue of a fragmentary relief that shows a throne in the Amarna style, similar to those found in reliefs from Akhenaten's capital at Amarna and from Tutankhamun's tomb in the Valley of the Kings. Oddly, the entrance to this chapel is to the west, and a deep shaft from the center of the courtyard leads to six empty burial chambers.

One of the most important New Kingdom tombs in this area belonged to a man named Mose. Reliefs from this tomb were taken away from Saqqara long ago and deposited in the Cairo Museum. A long inscription from this tomb tells the story of a court case in which Mose was forced to sue a close relative who had taken away his inheritance. The documents for the case stretched back over hundreds of years, and the lawsuit, which was stud-

Above: A narrow court runs along the north face of the pyramid of Khuit, principal wife of Teti. There were two entrances to the interior of her tomb, both of which can be seen in this photograph.

Right: One of the inspectors at Saqqara enters under the granite plug that blocked the entrance to the burial chamber of Khuit. The chamber was beautifully lined with granite blocks; the queen's well-carved but undecorated sarcophagus can be seen to the left.

ied in depth by Gaballa Ali Gaballa, provides a fascinating glimpse into the legal system and the history of ancient Egypt. The tale unfolds thus: A man named Neshi received a piece of land for military service in the reign of Ahmose, founder of the New Kingdom (c. 1550–1525). The land was passed down to Neshi's children, who chose to administer it jointly. There were no problems for about three hundred years, until a woman named Wernero, a descendant of Neshi's, won a court case to become manager of the land during the reign of Horemheb (c. 1323-1295 B.C.). Her position was contested by her sister, who initially won but later lost on appeal to Wernero and her son Huy. Unfortunately, Huy died, leaving a wife, Nubnofret, and small son, Mose, as his heirs. A new figure, Khay, stepped in to contest Nubnofret's claim, and he won by supporting his case with forged documents and letters. Nubnofret and Mose were expelled from the land, and it was not until Mose had grown up that he was able to bring a fifth case before the council and reclaim his heritage.

Unfortunately, the location of Mose's tomb was lost long ago, but during our excavations of the temple of Khuit, to the south of the sanctuary, we found three limestone blocks bearing his name. We also found Mose's four canopic jars, part of a pillar, and eleven limestone relief fragments. These finds have enabled us to reidentify his tomb chapel and put him into his proper archaeological context.

We found many other New Kingdom artifacts scattered around the area: a beautiful sarcophagus of painted wood; a wonderful bit of relief depicting officials beating a man for failure to pay his taxes; a small piece of faience bearing the cartouche of Seti I, second king of the 19th Dynasty (c. 1294–1279 B.C.); and a number of amulets. To my dismay, thieves broke into one of our storage magazines and took many of the New Kingdom artifacts, but fortunately, we got all of them back except for several gold amulets.

The area around the pyramids of Iput and Khuit was also very popular in the 26th Dynasty (664–525 B.C.), and we found many intrusive shafts. For example, in the open courtyard to the north of the pyramid of Khuit, we found a

Top: The sanctuary of Khuit's mortuary temple contained a limestone false door, only the lowest portion of which remains. In front of this is an offering table of granite carved with a hetep sign, the hieroglyph for offerings.

Bottom: This fragmentary relief from the mortuary temple of Khuit shows the queen playing the role of the goddess Hathor as she sails through the papyrus marshes in a reed boat.

Right: Directly above the Old Kingdom level in the Teti complex were many New Kingdom remains. Here I am speaking with one of my inspectors in front of an 18th Dynasty tomb chapel south of the pyramid of Khuit. One of my favorite photographers, Ken Garrett, who took many of the photographs in this book, is in the background holding his camera.

Opposite: In our work south of the pyramid of Khuit, we found the tomb of a man named Mose, which had been discovered years ago and then lost again. Many of the reliefs that adorned the tomb's walls had been removed and taken to the Cairo Museum. The tomb bore inscriptions telling the story of Mose's long court battle to regain his inheritance, which had been stolen by a relative. In this painted limestone relief from the Cairo Museum (not from the recent excavations), Mose and his wife are offering thanks to the god Amon (not pictured) after Mose's success in court.

A New Kingdom relief of painted limestone found in the area south of the temple of Khuit.

large 26th Dynasty shaft, which drops forty-eight feet to a series of burial chambers. Inside we found two uninscribed limestone sarcophagi, and beside them were *shawabtis* (small statuettes that accompanied the deceased into the afterlife to work in his place), several skeletons, and some pottery vessels. There were two wooden coffins, one of which was painted with religious scenes, as well as amulets and jewelry, including a necklace of amethyst. We also found an enormous, beautifully carved and inscribed anthropoid coffin of the Late Period. We excavated a number of other Late Period and Greco-Roman shafts and found several more empty sarcophagi. In one we found pottery vessels and lamps from the Roman Period. In the area of the open court of Khuit's temple, we found nine skeletons of men, women, and children of the Late Period.

We are continuing to excavate around the pyramid of Khuit and in the area of the New Kingdom tomb chapels. We have found the casing blocks at the southwest corner of Khuit's pyramid and more remains of her complex around its base, and we look forward to more exciting discoveries in the months to come.

Above: The mat roll I am holding here contained a well-preserved mummy of the Roman Period.

Left: This massive and beautifully carved anthropoid coffin of the Late Period was found in the area of the temple of Khuit.

Dancing with Tomb Robbers

When Saqqara first came under my jurisdiction, a good friend of mine named Holail Ghali was the chief inspector under me. He got his doctorate in Vienna and did good work, but he had problems with Sayed Tawfik, the head of the Antiquities Department at the time. Before he held that position, Tawfik had done some excavating at Saqqara and found many important New Kingdom tombs. During this work, he and Ghali had many disagreements, which I believe were completely unnecessary, and when Tawfik became head, he wanted to move Ghali away from Saqqara. He told me so many times, and I would tell him that Ghali was a good archaeologist and an honest man, but Tawfik insisted he should be moved.

One day the police informed Tawfik that a storeroom where a German expedition was keeping their artifacts had been robbed. This gave Tawfik an excuse to remove Ghali and put in someone to whom I objected, a man whose reputation was not very good. I told Tawfik that this person was not honest and that I did not want him at Saqqara, but he did not listen. While the new man was in charge, thieves broke into various storage areas and removed hieroglyphic reliefs, gold jewelry, amulets, statues, and even some papyri.

In September 2001, I gave a lecture at the British Museum in London. Afterwards, I met with Vivian Davies, head of the Egyptian department at the museum, and his wife, Renée. Vivian told me the story known as the "Big Antiquities Theft": an Englishman had come to see him with a copy of a papyrus he wanted the museum to identify. The team at the British Museum recognized this at once as one of the items recently stolen from a storeroom at Saqqara, so Vivian told the man that he needed to see the original in order to give him a scientific opinion. The Englishman came with the papyrus and was caught red-handed by Scotland Yard, who immediately informed the Supreme Council of Antiquities. An international police operation found that several corrupt archaeologists and five British art dealers were involved in stealing the papyrus and other artifacts from the storage magazines at

Saqqara, and a court sentenced them to jail. I thanked God that those people were caught and that most of the stolen artifacts were returned to Egypt. Later, we found an honest man, Mohammed Hagras, to put in charge of the site; he has been succeeded by another good archaeologist, Adel Hussein.

But the tomb robbers keep dancing. In the summer of 2001, a woman from the office of the U.S. Attorney for the Southern District of New York called me and said she needed a legal officer or a lawyer from the Supreme Council of Antiquities to explain to her Antiquities Law 117 of 1983. She said that she had been trying for a long time to contact the appropriate Egyptian authority for a particular case. I referred her to Gaballa A. Gaballa, then general secretary of the Supreme Council of Antiquities, who in turn asked Hesham Saria, the legal consultant for the Supreme Council, to answer her questions. Apparently, the U. S. Attorney, Mary Jo White, had arrested Frederick Schultz, who ran a New York art gallery, and charged him in a Manhattan federal court for participating in a conspiracy to receive and possess stolen property, specifically four masterpieces of ancient Egyptian art. In October 2001, Gaballa asked the Federal Bureau of Investigations and Mahmoud Allam, the Egyptian consul general in New York, to invite me to look at the stolen Egyptian antiquities, which had been seized by the FBI.

At that time, I was in Los Angeles giving lectures about my recent discoveries in the Valley of the Golden Mummies, so I stopped in New York on my way back to Egypt. I invited David Silverman, head of the Egyptology Department at the University of Pennsylvania, to come with me to the FBI offices in Queens. We entered the building with an agent, who took us down long corridors to where the antiquities were being stored. I was shocked at the treasures we found there.

The first piece that we examined was the black granite head of a king, about nine inches high. I identified it as a head of King Amenhotep III, one of the great kings of the New Kingdom, known to us as "the Pasha of Ancient Egypt." I looked at the Egyptian vice consul who accompanied us, Tarek Abu Sena, and both of us had the same question: How could something like this leave Egypt? I told him that artifacts are stolen everywhere, but our Egyptian monuments have a magic and mystery that make them particularly desirable to museums and private collectors. Antiquities thieves try to fill this market demand. As I stood in front of this masterpiece of ancient art, the FBI agent said to me, "How much do you think this piece can sell for?" I said to her that antiquities are priceless and that I never assign a dollar amount to any artifact. She told me that the head had been sold for about $2 million, because it was very rare to see a royal piece leave Egypt these days, and because it was so beautifully carved. The king wears a royal headdress, and the right eye is preserved, with a finely detailed cosmetic line and a well-defined eyebrow. The remnants of a false beard are evident below the area of the now-destroyed chin. The right ear is complete and appears to have a depression in the lobe, indicating a pierced ear.

When David Silverman and I finished examining this first piece and turned to the second stolen item seized by the FBI, we found ourselves looking at a very large limestone fragment from an Old Kingdom tomb. A hundred questions raced through my head. How could such a huge piece have left Egypt? How did the robbers enter the tomb in the presence of guards, police, and antiquities inspectors? How could this large limestone piece go through the Cairo airport? I was so distressed by this case that I was on the verge of tears.

The fragment is carved in raised relief and shows the tomb owner on the left, grasping a staff in his left hand and holding an official's scepter in his right hand. Facing him on the right is a woman, perhaps his wife, who has a lotus in her right hand that she holds up to her nose; in her other hand, she grasps the necks of five ducks. Behind the man is a child, carved on a smaller scale. I could tell that this fragment was cut from an Old Kingdom tomb, specifically dating to Dynasty 6, and that it was from Saqqara.

The third piece seized was a standing bronze statue of the falcon deity, Horus. It is about fourteen inches high and has many finely incised lines indicating the pattern of the feathers. Heavily sculpted areas occur around the eyes to mimic the markings of the falcon. We believe that the statue came from the Western Delta and dates to the Late Period. The fourth and last piece we examined was another relief fragment showing agricultural scenes, with inscriptions that read "the Overseer of the Palace." It was claimed that local farmers and builders found these artifacts in Egypt.

The media reported that Schultz, the man caught with the artifacts, had been representing the United States in the protection of the monuments during the administration of former President Clinton. How could this man, supposedly devoted to protecting antiquities, become a dealer in stolen artifacts? We do not know the answer to this vexing question, but I am happy to report that he was recently tried and convicted for his crimes.

I was highly impressed with the care that the FBI devoted to these artifacts, storing them carefully in a humidity-controlled environment. But what really impressed me was the way that the U. S. Attorney and the FBI officers cared for the monuments of Egypt. The two cases in England and America prove that the international community cares a great deal about our common Egyptian heritage. They believe, as I do, that the Egyptian monuments do not belong to Egypt alone but to everyone, and to that end, they must be returned to Egypt. We are the guardians of these monuments. For my part, I now have built a new storage magazine, which is beside the offices of the Antiquities police, near the museum of the French expedition, so that the artifacts will be well guarded.

Excavations West of the Pyramid of Unas

West of the pyramid of Unas is an area still virtually untouched by archaeologists, and it has therefore become a magnet for antiquities thieves. Several years ago, modern tomb robbers working in the dead of night found the entrance of a 6th Dynasty tomb belonging to a man named Nyankh-nesut. Fortunately, the antiquities police of Saqqara discovered the thieves and arrested them. After this, I insisted that the only way to keep the site safe was to guard it night and day. It is clear to me and the rest of the Supreme Council of Antiquities (as it is also clear to thieves) that this part of the Saqqara necropolis is full of tombs, probably dating mostly from the 5th and 6th Dynasties.

The new excavations were supervised first by Mohamed Hagras, and other archaeologists from Saqqara continued the work; I would come twice a week to observe their progress. At the beginning of the excavations, something unique began to appear: a wall built of big chunks of limestone, about five feet high. The team at Saqqara called me and told me that they had found a new pyramid. When I got to the site and looked for myself, I saw that it was typical Dynasty 3 construction, and when I studied the map and saw where it was located, I realized that it was not a pyramid but part of a wall that I believe belongs to the complex of Sekhemkhet.

Our biggest surprise lay north of this wall, where we found a large square mastaba. Early in our excavations, we uncovered a limestone slab on the south side of the mastaba inscribed with the name and title of the tomb owner: "The Palace Physician, Qar." The tomb of Qar was originally a large mud-brick mastaba surrounded by an enclosure wall, with a false door set into a niche in the eastern face. After the mastaba was built, the architects

We recently found the tomb of a royal physician named Qar dating to the 6th Dynasty in the area west of the pyramid of Unas. In this photograph, we are looking southeast; the square mastaba tomb of Qar is in the middle ground and the step pyramid of Djoser is in the background.

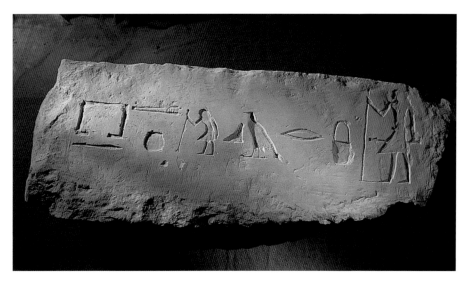

menu, such as we found in the tomb of Kay at Giza (see p. 69). rather than a simple and more general request for offerings. Based on the style of the carving, I believe that this tomb dates to the end of Dynasty 5 or the beginning of Dynasty 6.

Fragments of decoration can still be seen on the side walls of the tomb chapel: on the north are offering bearers; on the south, an interesting series of vignettes that show a bull mounting a cow, the birth of a calf, and some men in the papyrus marshes. The scenes were painted in dark colors on a very thin layer of white gypsum. North of the eastern chapel is a small open court, with a small niche in the eastern side. I believe that a statue of Qar stood here and that the court served to protect the statue.

made some changes in the plan and added a chapel on the eastern face of the tomb. This chapel takes the form of a narrow hallway topped by a vaulted ceiling of mud brick, with the original false door at the western end. The mastaba was then enlarged around this chapel and cased with mortar. An open court was left to the north of the chapel.

The false door in the west wall of the chapel is beautifully carved out of a single slab of limestone. This is an unusual piece in that it is inscribed with a complete list of items the deceased wanted for his afterlife, a funerary

The main body of the tomb is built of mud brick. The base is square, and the walls slope in to form a very trun-

Above: This limestone slab was set into the south outer wall of Qar's mastaba. It reads: "The Palace Physician, Qar."

Right: The tomb chapel set into the eastern wall of the mastaba is long and narrow, with an elaborately carved false door at the west end. The walls were plastered and painted with lively scenes, but little remains of this decoration.

Opposite, top: This close-up of the painted plaster decoration on the south wall of the tomb chapel of Qar shows cattle and men in the papyrus marshes.

Opposite, bottom: We made a remarkable discovery inside Qar's sarcophagus: a set of copper surgical tools, the oldest tools of this type ever found.

cated pyramid. It is nearly forty feet on each side and stands to a height of more than ten feet. This is the only tomb at Saqqara built in this shape. Another unique feature is that niches were built in the middle of the outside north and south walls for the placement of stelae. Only the stele in the southern niche (the one we found first) is preserved in situ. These niches remind me of the so-called airshafts inside the Great Pyramid that carry the soul of the king to the northern stars and the solar boats to the south. As the royal doctor, Qar must have had a close relationship with the king, which may be why he was permitted to build his tomb here in such an unusual shape and with these two niches.

The burial shaft was built right through the center of the tomb. The top part, where it passes through the body of the mastaba, was built of stone rubble and mud brick; the rest of the shaft, which is sixty feet deep, is cut into the bedrock. Each time I find a new tomb, I am amazed again at how deep the ancients dug their burial shafts and how, despite this, almost all tombs, including this one, were robbed in antiquity. At the bottom of the shaft, a passageway with stairs cut into the solid rock leads to the east, end-

ing in a burial chamber directly below the false door. We found that the shaft and the passage had been entered in the Late or Greco-Roman Period.

The finely carved burial chamber was rectangular, measuring eighteen feet from east to west and nine feet north to south. South of the stairs leading down was a large sarcophagus of fine white limestone, and written on the top of the lid in black ink were Qar's name and title. Thieves had cut a hole in the body of the sarcophagus at the point that gave them the best access to the chest, where they would have found the best amulets and jewelry. When we opened the sarcophagus, we found the body of Qar in good shape, but the robbers had taken all the amulets that had been wrapped with the mummy. Dr. Azza came to Saqqara and took the bones away to the lab; she is currently in the process of analyzing them.

Inside the sarcophagus, west of Qar's head, were the most important artifacts found in the tomb: a group of surgical tools made of copper. This is a truly unique discovery, as the tools represent the oldest surgical tools ever found. They are small, delicate, and quite beautiful. We can identify some as scalpels, others as suturing instru-

ments, and some have a small hole in the center, perhaps to fit them into a box that the doctor would have carried—the ancient Egyptian version of a little black bag. It is remarkable to find these tools and intriguing to think that perhaps they once were used to treat a king or a queen.

Inside the burial chamber, we also found a large group of pottery vessels, all of which were inscribed in black ink with the name and title of Qar; one of them, a very nice globular jar, is labeled "food for the Palace Physician, Qar." We also found a large pottery vessel that was still sealed; we have not yet looked inside. In addition, there was a group of alabaster vessels: an offering table inscribed with offerings and the name and title of

Qar, a tablet for the seven sacred oils, and another large alabaster vessel, inscribed with the name and title of the tomb owner, which is also still sealed.

Surrounding the tomb at a distance of about fifteen feet are the remains of a large wall, which may date to the Late Period, judging from the mortar that was used. We are now in the process of excavating this to determine the relationship between this wall and the 3rd Dynasty wall nearby. It is interesting to note that this tomb of a royal physician was built near the complex of Djoser, which was designed by the architect Imhotep, later revered as a healer and associated with Asculepius, the Greek god of medicine.

Around Qar's tomb were a number of wooden coffins and burials dating to the Late Period. One of these contained a mummy in good condition, and was inscribed on the outside with religious scenes in 26th Dynasty style.

To the east of Qar's tomb, we found a cache of bronze statuettes from the 26th Dynasty. Here are several examples (clockwise, starting at upper left): the goddess Isis nursing her son Horus; King Psametik; Harpokrates (Horus the Child); the goddess Nephthys; Imhotep, Djoser's chief architect and the patron saint of medicine; and the Memphite god Ptah.

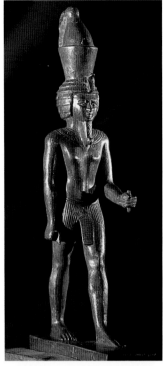

When we found the beginning of another hole in the sand to the east of the tomb, we were expecting to find another Late Period burial, but instead, we found a fantastic surprise—a cache of twenty-two beautiful bronze statuettes of gods and goddesses, also dating from the 26th Dynasty.

Most of these statuettes are beautifully detailed, and several are partly or fully gilded. They represent various gods and goddesses, such as Isis seated on a throne nursing her son Horus (seven examples!); Ptah, the Memphite god of artisans, dressed in a long robe that envelops his body and from which only his hands emerge to hold his staff of office; Osiris standing, wearing his Atef crown (the white crown of Upper Egypt with the feathers of Ma'at, the Egyptian concept of truth and justice, on each side) and holding the crook and flail of kingship; the Apis bull, sacred to Ptah; Horus in the shape of a falcon wearing the double crown; Bastet and Sekhmet (lion-headed goddesses with human bodies); Nephthys; and Anubis. Two statuettes depict Harpokrates, Horus the child standing, naked, with one finger to his mouth in the pose of childhood; one of the statues is inscribed with the name of the person who offered it, Sheben-hor. A beautifully detailed statuette shows a scribe dressed in a long robe, sitting and reading a papyrus that he holds in his hands. Another figure represents a king wearing the double crown and a wig, the false beard of kingship, and a kilt. The staff he once held in his hand is gone. He stands on a base inscribed with an offering formula and the name of Psammetik, one of the kings of the 26th Dynasty. And the most wonderful find of all is a very small statuette of the vizier and architect of Djoser, Imhotep, who became the patron saint of medicine. This was perhaps put into this cache because of its location near to the tomb of the physician Qar.

Heliopolis: The City of the Sun

Heliopolis was one of the most important religious centers in ancient Egypt and is now part of my responsibility as director of Giza and Cairo. The city was called Iunu by the ancient Egyptians and Heliopolis, "City of the Sun" by the Greeks. The ancient remains lie under suburbs of Cairo known as Ain Shams and Matariya. Some scholars believe that this was a sacred site as early as the Predynastic Period; it was certainly a major religious center by the time of the Old Kingdom and retained its importance until the end of the pharaonic period. There are innumerable references to the city and its gods in sacred texts from throughout Egyptian history, and many important officials bore titles connected with Heliopolis. Unfortunately, the site has been almost completely neglected by archaeologists, and little of what must have been a vast, gleaming city of temples remains to us today.

Iunu was the center of the sun cult, with the sun god Re (often fused with other gods, such as Re-Atum and Amon-Re, among others) as its chief god. It is here that Egyptian priest-philosophers first wrestled with the questions of creation, fashioning an elaborate myth whose prime players were nine gods of the Ennead. These scholars were known all over Egypt, indeed all over the Mediterranean world, as superior astronomers and careful observers of natural events such as the annual flooding of the Nile. One of the most important titles connected with Iunu was "Greatest Seer," often interpreted to mean "chief astronomer."

Iunu was intimately linked with the mythology of kingship, as expressed in religious texts and tomb and temple reliefs. The prototypical solar symbol, the pyramid-shaped ben-ben, was housed in one of the temples here. In a series of tales composed in the Middle Kingdom (c. 2055–1650 B.C.) King Khufu, builder of the Great Pyramid at Giza, wanted to find some esoteric information to help him with the proper design for his pyramid; a 110-year-old magician, who demonstrated his abilities by reattaching the severed heads of several animals, told him that the information he sought was hidden in Heliopolis.

The obelisk of Senwosret I, which now stands in a public park in the center of what was once ancient Heliopolis.

According to another of these stories, the wife of a priest of Iunu gave birth to the first three kings of the 5th Dynasty, all of whom were actually the sons of the Heliopolitan god Re. In fact, one of the most important and consistent royal epithets, borne by all kings beginning with Djedefre (son of Khufu), is "Son of Re." Many of the great thinkers of ancient Egypt were trained at Iunu, and some of the great Greek philosophers also studied here. The Bible tells us that Joseph married the daughter of the high priest of Iunu (On) and then went on to become vizier of Egypt.

Despite the enormous importance of this site, archaeological discoveries have been few, and a coherent picture of the site has yet to emerge. There are two major problems. First, because the site lies so close to Cairo, vast amounts of stone were taken from the ancient temples and reused in the building of the medieval and then modern cities. And second, excavation in Heliopolis is extremely difficult, because the area is now choked with modern houses; most ancient remains are now buried under modern construction. Much more was visible in the late 1800s, when Ahmed Kamal mapped a number of antiquities, and even in 1915, when William Flinders Petrie made a plan of the ancient city.

In general, because of the geography of the area, tombs lie in the eastern (drier) part of Heliopolis, while temples lie to the west. The earliest remains are Predynastic and consist of a cemetery containing a total of about two hundred burials, discovered during the construction of an

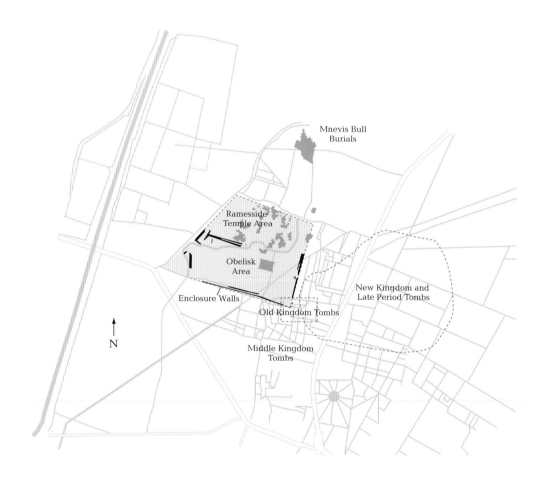

The open-air museum near the obelisk of Senwosret I is now filled with water from the rising water table. If action is not taken soon, the remains of this important center of the sun cult, much of which has never been excavated, will be lost forever.

apartment building in the 1950s. Scattered monuments have been found here which date from the reign of King Djoser of Dynasty 3 (c. 2667-2648 B.C.) through the Ptolemaic Period (332–330 B.C.). Massive mud-brick walls once enclosed a large trapezoidal area, about 3,300 feet east-west by 1,425 feet north-south, which contained the main temple area and perhaps the town.

One of the most impressive of the ancient remains is an obelisk dedicated by Senwosret I, second king of the 12th Dynasty (c. 1956–1911 B.C.). The obelisk is now in the middle of a public park, and near it, within the confines of the park, some mud-brick foundations were discovered

several feet below ground level, along with a number of New Kingdom stelae. This area was walled off, and some of the stelae were put into wooden display cases to create a small open-air museum. Several other miscellaneous antiquities found in Heliopolis have been set up on higher ground nearby.

Some 6th Dynasty tombs belonging to the high priests of Iunu were found southeast of the obelisk of Senwosret I, and the tombs of some of the Mnevis bulls sacred to the sun god Re have been discovered to the northeast. Adjacent to the obelisk park lies a large unde-veloped tract, owned by the Ministry of the Interior and

now used as a soccer field. We would love to excavate this area; we know there are extensive archaeological remains here that are certain to add to our knowledge of this enormously important site, but we have not yet been granted permission. It is frightening to note that over the last few years, the water table has risen so rapidly that the open-air museum is filling with water. On my last visit, I found that the area is now inaccessible to anyone without serious boots. This water will destroy the foundations and damage other remains that certainly lie nearby.

Recent excavations, including several seasons in the 1970s by Abdel Aziz Saleh of Cairo University, have uncovered tantalizing glimpses of a large and complex temple area with monuments dating to the reigns of various New Kingdom kings, including Amenhotep III, Seti I, Ramesses II, Merenptah, Ramesses IV, and Ramesses IX. The excavations lie in the midst of an area called Arab el-Hisn, a charming town of wide, shady, unpaved streets, green fields and large old houses, many of them built on ancient mud-brick foundations. Most of the residents own

Opposite: An overview of the vast Ramesside temple complex at Arab el-Hisn, where various kings of the 19th and 20th Dynasties left monuments.

Left: A detail of the granite column of Merenptah commemorating his victory over Libyan nomads in the fifth year of his reign. The column was found not far from the Ramesside temple area.

donkeys and horses rather than cars, and a visit here provides a moment of relaxation after the hustle and bustle of Cairo. Unfortunately, as an archaeologist, I quickly lose my sense of tranquility as soon as I realize what incredible riches lie buried in this area. This is where some of the most important Egyptian texts—on scientific, religious, and historical subjects—must once have been stored; information that could tell us so much about the ancient culture may yet await us, if we can only rescue it before it is gone forever.

There are many fascinating architectural elements still to be seen scattered about the site, which have been interpreted as belonging mostly to temples of Ramesses II (c. 1279–1213 B.C.) and Ramesses IV (c. 1153–1147 B.C.). One of the most interesting features still visible at the site is a chapel dedicated by a son of Ramesses IV named Nebmaatre who held the title "Greatest Seer." Near the temple remains, at a slightly higher level, are a series of mud-brick foundations of rectangular houses and circular granaries. These remains extend for about three miles, all the way to the oil refineries, but only a small section has been excavated.

Five minutes by foot from the main temple area is a gorgeous granite column of Merenptah, decorated primarily with six large images of the king making offerings to various gods as well as figures of bound and humiliated enemies. Inscriptions on the sides of the capital tell us that the column commemorates a victory over the Libyans. This column represents an important historical document and also gives us some sense of the vast expanse of temple buildings that must lie beneath the surface of this quiet village.

An important Antiquities Law of 1983 places the entire site of Heliopolis under the supervision of the Supreme Council of Antiquities, and we have an office in Ain Shams. Whenever someone wants to build a new house or renovate an old one, they are required by law to report this to the Antiquities Department so that we can examine the foundations. If artifacts are found and can be removed without damage, we let the people build their houses, but

Top: The burial chamber of a 26th Dynasty official named Panehsy ("the Nubian") was found about fifteen years ago when the villa built over it was torn down to make way for new construction. The beautifully carved and painted reliefs depict religious subjects. On the vaulted ceiling is an image of the sky goddess Nut, as it looked when the tomb was first excavated.

Above: When I got back to Egypt after my studies in the United States, Heliopolis was added to my concession, and I went to see the tomb again. I found that the rising water table was destroying the beautiful reliefs. This photograph shows what the interior of the tomb looked like before we started restoration work.

if something important is found that needs to remain in place, we buy the land from them at a fair price. This new law has led directly to some wonderful discoveries over the past decades.

About fifteen years ago, the Lawyers' Association of Cairo decided to tear down a villa that they owned in Ain Shams in order to build some apartment houses. As required by law, they carried out their work under the supervision of the Antiquities Department. When they removed the villa and began to dig the new foundations, they stumbled across some ancient foundations, and the Antiquities Department took over the site. The most spectacular find was a jewel-like tomb from the 26th Dynasty belonging to a man named Panehsy, a name that means "the Nubian."

The mud-brick chapel that once lay on the surface had disappeared, but the burial chamber was preserved intact. It is a small vaulted room of limestone with a figure of the sky goddess Nut on the ceiling, and beautiful vignettes and spells from the Book of the Dead adorning the walls. The Antiquities Department paid the lawyers eight million Egyptian pounds for the land so that the tomb could be left in situ.

At the time of this discovery, I was not in charge of Cairo, but I went to see the tomb. When I came back from my studies in the United States, Heliopolis was added to my concession, and I went to see the tomb again. To my dismay, I found that the rising water table and the leaking sewage from nearby houses were destroying the beautiful inscriptions and scenes that covered the walls. I put together a team of well-trained young professionals, and they have done an amazing job with the salvage, conservation, and restoration of this tomb. With the help of the Cairo Governate, we are in the process of designing a project to solve the problem of the rising water table.

In order to preserve and restore the tomb, my team— headed by Abdel Hamid Kotb and Nevien el-Maghraby as chief architects and Moustafa Abdel Kader as chief restorer—numbered all the blocks in the tomb and moved them temporarily to a higher, completely dry area in

A painted pottery mask from the lid of a Greco-Roman coffin, found in the area of the lawyers' villa at Ain Shams

another part of the site. They built a concrete base where the tomb had been, so that when it was restored to its original place, the tomb would be kept above the water table and protected from further damage. The team is now conserving the blocks, by cleaning them and removing the salt, and then moving them to their new places on top of the concrete base. This process has already taken us more than six years, but it is the most important work we have done at Heliopolis and is almost complete as I write this.

The entire area where the lawyers' villa stood is a rich archaeological site, covered with tombs from the Late and Greco-Roman Periods. The site is covered with limestone sarcophagi from the Late Period, and my team there recently found an anthropoid clay coffin decorated with black and red paint from the Roman Period. We have also found some gold and faience amulets.

We are certain that other tomb chapels from the 26th Dynasty lie buried beneath the surface. I am planning to make this whole area into an open-air museum. A colossal statue of Ramesses II, found in an area called Gebel el-Ahmar (the Red Mountain), has already been moved here. During pharaonic times, Gebel el-Ahmar was the location of a sandstone quarry; it is now in the middle of the Cairo suburbs. While the ancient sculptors were carving the left leg of this statue, they found a major flaw in the stone and abandoned it where it stood.

We plan to continue the excavations of this area and build a wall around the entire site to protect it. Soon visitors to Heliopolis can make a tour, stopping at the nearby

This colossal sandstone statue of Ramesses II, now in the area where Panehsy's tomb was discovered, was found abandoned near the ancient quarry of Gebel el-Ahmar. There was a flaw in the stone between the legs, so the ancient sculptors left it where it stood.

Tree of Mary (one of the stations on the Flight from Egypt), the obelisk area, the temple area, and the new open-air museum.

A little over a mile from the place where the open-air museum will be built once stood a villa owned by a man named Hassan Abu el-Fotouh. During the summer of 2001, he decided to demolish this villa and build a new six-floor building. As required by law, he went to the Antiquities Department to ask for permission, and I sent inspectors from the Heliopolis office to dig on the site. The archaeologists that I put in charge were Adel Abdel Haleim and Ibrahim Abdel Rahman, both very good workers. In December of the same year, about twelve feet below the surface, they found some limestone vaults, which were clearly the top of a tomb. I was telephoned immediately by Mohammed Abdel Galil, the director of Antiquities for Heliopolis.

I went to the tomb to examine it, and when I arrived at the site, I found thousands of people gathered around. There is a legend among the public that any pharaonic tomb will contain treasure, so they were waiting for me to come, open the tomb, and find gold. But most tombs have been robbed in antiquity, and few of them contained much of what most people consider treasure to begin with, only the treasure of information.

I had to decide how to excavate this tomb despite the crowds of people hovering nearby. When I went down into the excavation area, I was excited to see that the tomb looked intact: the mortar casing looked untouched. I could also see from the style of the architecture that it most likely dated to the 26th Dynasty. I was bothered by the crowd, which I could hear murmuring that Zahi Hawass was discovering treasure. I asked for my assistant Mansour Boriak and put him in charge. When I came the next day, I saw that it would be impossible to clear the entrance, because it was under a three-story building. If we were to try to uncover this entrance, the modern building would fall down.

I asked Abdel Hamid to do some preliminary work so that we could proceed safely, and he set up sandbags to

In the summer of 2001, a villa was demolished about a mile from the tomb of Panehsy, and another 26th Dynasty tomb, this one belonging to a man named Wadj-Hor, was discovered. This tomb consists of three chambers and a corridor, all roofed with limestone vaults.

The entrance to the tomb was blocked by a neighboring house, so we had to enter and leave the tomb through the vaulted ceiling of one of the burial chambers. This is my assistant Brook Myers, an American who works with me in my office at Giza.

Left: The central burial chamber has a sunken emplacement for the sarcophagus of Wadj-Hor. My colleague Janice Kamrin is standing inside, examining an inscription roughly carved into the wall which reads: "He made the house of his lord and he put himself under his feet for eternity."

Below: A selection of shawabtis and a djed-pillar amulet rescued from the debris inside the tomb of Wadj-Hor.

support the sides of the tomb. After two weeks of work, we found that the only way to enter the tomb was to take a block from the top of one of the vaults. I always like to enter any tomb first, and of course the news of this discovery was very big. The day that I entered, every newspaper, magazine, and television station in town came to witness the opening. I squeezed through the hole in the ceiling and found the first room filled with sand. I crawled through on my stomach and dug a hole with my hand so that I could see into the next room. I could see two sarcophagi of limestone, and I could also see, to my disappointment, that the tomb had been opened and reused in the Roman Period.

Mansour continued the excavation under my supervision and began to clear the sand from the tomb. I was afraid that the walls would fall, so we worked very carefully. The work was very exciting, but all the people standing around to watch us were very distracting. The owner of the land was also very worried and came often to ask us whether or not we were going to take his land.

There are two parts to the tomb. A small mud-brick chapel, where the relatives of the tomb owner would have come to leave offerings, was built above ground; this part of the tomb is poorly preserved, and we need to do further excavations extending under the nearby houses before

we can understand it properly. We found additional walls of mud-brick near the tomb, which may represent a later building erected above this tomb, or it may be a second chapel for this tomb. Our tomb was surrounded by a mud-brick wall, perhaps to set it off from other tombs nearby. The substructure—the vaulted chambers—lay below, partly cut into the rock and partly built of stone. This level was well preserved and contained a large rectangular hall oriented north-south and three east-west burial chambers. It is clear that this was a family tomb of the 26th Dynasty.

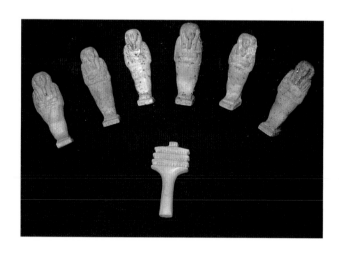

The tomb was built of blocks of fine Tura limestone, with vaulted ceilings above all of the chambers. The entrance was from the west, but we cannot explore this enough to understand it properly because of the house above. We can see that it was closed by five blocks of unfinished limestone, and nearby we found Roman amphorae, confirming that the tomb had been entered during the Roman Period.

Inside the entrance hall, which stretches for the entire width of the tomb, we found two sarcophagi of Tura limestone, both of which had been opened in antiquity. Inside the second were the remains of human bones dating from the Roman Period and some broken pottery. East of this large hall are the three burial chambers. The first and largest is at the south and contained three large limestone sarcophagi, again opened and robbed in the Roman Period. Inside the first were some bones, and inside the second were the remains of a mummy covered with linen, with the upper part and the head lost. Dr. Azza is in the process of examining these bones. The third sarcophagus must have been put into the room last, since it blocks the entrance to the room. In this room, we found a beautiful heart scarab of amethyst. I believe that this chamber was used for the burials of the children of the tomb owner.

The second burial chamber belonged to the tomb owner himself. The floor level is about five feet lower than the rest of the tomb, and the single sarcophagus found here had been opened and robbed. The south wall of this chamber is inscribed with religious spells, followed by name of the tomb owner, Wadj-Hor, and the information that: "he made the house of his lord and he put himself under his feet for eternity." Because of sewage leaking from the houses above, these inscriptions are not in good condition and are already encrusted with salt in some places.

Inside this chamber we found 149 beautifully made shawabtis of the 26th Dynasty, inscribed with the name of Wadj-Hor, son of Nesyre. We know from the recent find of the intact 26th Dynasty tomb of Iuf-aa, found by the Czech Expedition at Abusir, that the number of shawabtis in tombs of this period could reach 405: one shawabti for each of the 365 days of the year, and 40 overseer shawabtis to make sure that they did their work. Also found here were four pottery dishes dating to the 26th Dynasty.

The third burial chamber, through which we first entered the tomb, is the smallest one and may have been for the wife of Wadj-Hor. There was no sarcophagus here; perhaps the one that was left blocking the entrance to the southernmost chamber once stood here. Entering and excavating this room was extremely difficult, and it remains incompletely understood.

Our task is now is to move this tomb, since if we leave it in place it will be rapidly destroyed by the rising ground water. We will number the blocks carefully and move them to the open-air museum, near the tomb of Panehsy. I am sure that there are more tombs around it, but what can we do? Many people live in the houses around the site, too many houses to demolish, so we must try to preserve what we can and wait for chance to give us more opportunities to salvage the past.

An overview of the Bahariya Oasis.

Chapter IV. Spectacular Discoveries in the Bahariya Oasis

In 1996 my attention was focused on Giza, where we were deep in our excavations of the tombs of the pyramid builders. On the afternoon of March 2, Mansour Boriak came running into my office, yelling, "Doctor! Doctor! Ashry Shaker is here. Something very important has been discovered in Bahariya Oasis!" At first, I was sure this was one of Mansour's pranks; he is very fond of jokes and frequently tries to fool me into believing his wild stories. That very day I had caught him doing an imitation of me for some of our excavation team, and I was sure this was his revenge.

Mansour insisted that there was exciting news from Bahariya, but I refused to believe him until Ashry Shaker, whom I appointed director of the Antiquities Department for the Oasis, was standing in front of me. Ashry is a very polite, serious man who never makes jokes, and I trust him completely. He told me that the donkey of one of his guards at the Temple of Alexander the Great had found a hole in the desert. The guard went to get Ashry, who followed him back to the hole and peered into it. To his amazement, he saw part of the face of a mummy peering back up at him out of the sand. Even more extraordinary was the fact that the face was shiny and appeared to be made of gold!

Without wasting a moment, Ashry had set a guard on the site and rushed to Giza to get me. I was very busy at the time, supervising digs at Giza and Saqqara, so I told Ashry to appoint an inspector to begin surveying the site, and two archaeologists from Bahariya, Mohammed el-Tayieb and Mohammed Aiady, did some preliminary excavations. A week later, I made the three-hour trip by jeep to see the site for myself. When I arrived, Ashry introduced me to Abdel Maugoud, the guard whose donkey had found the tomb. Maugoud is a very serious and straightforward man in his forties, with a tanned, weather-beaten face and a big black moustache. I asked him to tell me the story of the discovery.

Keeping his eyes down as a sign of respect, he told me how he had discovered the tomb. On the afternoon of March 1, the guard who usually replaced him at the temple of Alexander the Great had been late. As he waited by the temple door, he saw that his donkey was running away, with one end of its lead rope in its mouth. This was very unusual for several reasons: donkeys don't like to run, and they don't like the ropes that are used to steer them; they certainly never voluntary take them into their mouths. He couldn't leave the temple to follow the donkey, but fortunately, the animal stopped within his line of sight almost a mile away. The next guard finally showed up an hour and a half late, apologizing profusely. In the meantime, the donkey had started back and arrived at the temple with the rope still in its mouth. Abdel Maugoud got on and tried to turn for home, but the donkey refused and insisted on heading back into the desert instead of taking the road that they had taken together for ten years. Finally Maugoud gave up and let the donkey have its head.

To his astonishment, the donkey took him back to the spot where he had stopped before and dropped the rope in front of a hole in the ground. Maugoud got off, looked into the hole, and saw gold shining beneath the sand. He went immediately to Ashry Shaker to report what he had seen, and Ashry came to tell me. To help keep the site safe from treasure seekers and to avoid premature media attention, I delayed announcing the find until June of 1999, when I had secured the funding and cleared the time to begin excavations.

The Valley of the Golden Mummies is the site of the most exciting and spectacular discovery since the tomb of Tutankhamun and has captured the imagination of the world. We have now spent three seasons excavating there, and have discovered wonderful things. The seventeen intact tombs we have unearthed so far have yielded burials whose sparkling gold and untouched contexts will reveal much about the civilization of the oases during the Greco-Roman Period. Nothing can prepare you for a discovery of this magnitude. It is the largest undisturbed burial site ever found, containing probably more than ten thousand mummies, and it represents an enormous accumulation of wealth. We have only scratched the surface of this site. It will take decades to excavate and conserve, and it will provide vast quantities of data for scholars to contemplate.

At the end of our first season at the Valley of the Golden Mummies, prompted by reports of some tomb robbery, we also began to excavate at another Bahariya site, in a neighborhood of the town of el-Bawiti, named for Sheikh Soby, a local religious leader. We first rediscovered three tombs that had originally been excavated by Ahmed Fakhry in 1938; these tombs belonged to members of a wealthy and powerful family who lived during the 26th Dynasty. In the course of clearing these chambers, we unearthed the entrance to the lost tomb of one of the most important members of the family, Djed-Khonsu-efankh, a governor of Bahariya during this period. Over the past seasons, we have found the burials of four more members of this family. These tombs were robbed during the Roman Period and have also sustained a great deal of damage from houses that were built above them, but they have still yielded wonderful artifacts and a great deal of information.

A Short History of Bahariya

The Bahariya Oasis, which lies about 225 miles southwest of Cairo, is one of five major islands of green that grace the wind-swept expanses of the Libyan Desert. Bounded by iron-rich mountains, the entire oasis covers about 1,240 square miles of desert sprinkled with spring-fed fertile areas. There are three major towns in the area: el-Bawiti, the modern capital; el-Qasr, the ancient capital; and el-Haiz, the site of a Roman fortress.

Bahariya is a uniquely romantic place. In addition to the spectacular antiquities, a visitor to the area can travel to the White, Flower, and Black Deserts, about forty miles south of el-Bawiti. In the Black Desert, the mounds of sand are actually black, and in the Flower Desert, the thousands of rocks that litter the surface are shaped like different types of flowers. But my favorite is the White Desert, where over the millennia the wind has carved the rocks into fantastic shapes—sphinxes, elephants, chickens, ducks, and all sorts of other magical creatures. During our second season at Bahariya, I arranged a surprise trip to these deserts for our team, topped off by a wonderful picnic. I was absolutely amazed by our drivers, who were able to navigate in the desert just as if they were driving on the streets of their own villages.

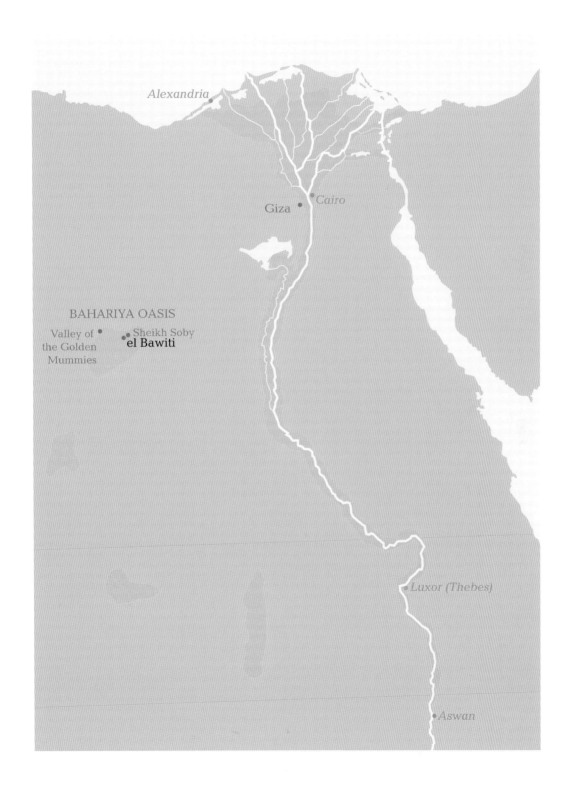

Alexandria

Giza • • *Cairo*

BAHARIYA OASIS

Valley of • •• Sheikh Soby
the Golden   el Bawiti
Mummies

Luxor (Thebes)

• *Aswan*

183

Over the millennia the wind has carved the rocks in the White Desert, which lies about forty miles from the site of our excavations, into fantastic shapes—sphinxes, elephants, chickens, ducks, and all sorts of other magical creatures.

In January 2001, as I traveled from Cairo to Bahariya to begin my third season of excavation, I relaxed in my government car, driven by Masry Bayumi. It took us only three hours from downtown Cairo to el-Bawiti on the new and beautifully paved road. I always sleep well in cars, trains, and airplanes, so I had time to close my eyes and think about how people had traveled to Bahariya before this road had been built, and how fortunate I was to be reclining in comfort in an air-conditioned car rather than jouncing along on the back of a donkey or camel. As I rode, I reviewed what I knew about the area. Bahariya was almost completely neglected by most early archaeologists. At the beginning of the nineteenth century, the region was visited and described by Belzoni, the circus performer and adventurer who explored so many Egyptian sites. He stayed for eleven days, thinking the whole time that he was at the Oasis of Jupiter (Amon), really the Siwa Oasis, about two hundred miles further west. He and his strange Italian handwriting made a great impression on the villagers of el-Bawiti, who thought he was a magician. His servant even stole pages from his diary to sell to the ladies of the village who thought that this writing would cure their diseases and help them capture the hearts of men in the town.

Apart from short visits by several other nineteenth-century archaeologists and explorers, it was not until the twentieth century that Bahariya began to be investigated in any serious fashion. The great Egyptian archaeologist Ahmed Fakhry dedicated much of his life to excavating in the Five Oases, and he had a special love for Bahariya. (He even received a marriage proposal here, although he does seem to have accepted it.) I feel a special affinity for this man, who excavated, as I do now, at both Giza and Bahariya. Fakhry first came to el-Bawiti in January 1938, at which time it took him two days to travel from Cairo to Bahariya. He had a good relationship with the people of the region and gave rewards to villagers who guided him to archaeological sites in the area. He started excavating five days after arriving at Bahariya and almost immediately discovered tombs from the 26th Dynasty (the ones we rediscovered) and cemeteries dating to the Greco-Roman Period. Before the discovery of the Valley of the Golden Mummies in 1996, I had done some excavation in the region, but we have only just begun to uncover the splendors that lie beneath the sands of this practically virgin territory.

The oasis was inhabited as early as the Paleolithic Period. It has enough water to support agriculture, although it cannot maintain a large population; the range of ruins in the area suggests that the water level was much higher in ancient times and would have supported a larger population than it does today. In pharaonic and Greco-Roman times, Bahariya was known for its wine, especially its date wine, and for being an important stop along the caravan route through the Western Desert to the Nile Valley. Although Predynastic, Early Dynastic, and Old Kingdom remains have never been found at Bahariya, there is evidence for activity during these periods at two of the other oases, and I believe that there was probably an early settlement near or at the current location of el-Bawiti.

Records from the Middle Kingdom refer to Bahariya as the intersection of two major trade routes to the Nile Valley, and two 12th Dynasty kings mention having to watch the area to secure Egypt's western border against marauding Libyans. However, the only artifact from this period is a scarab bearing the name of Senwosret I of the 12th Dynasty, which Fakhry bought from a local man. The strategic importance of the region to the Egyptians during the Second Intermediate Period is brought to life in an important inscription found at Karnak (ancient Thebes), which tells the story of Kamose, the warrior king who fought to reunite the country at the end of the Second Intermediate Period (c. 1550 B.C.). Apophis, king of the foreign Hyksos who had taken over the north of the country, sent a messenger from his palace at Avaris in the eastern Delta to the king of Kush, far to the south, proposing that they join forces and crush the Egyptians between them. The messenger took the western route through the oases, but Kamose had sent troops to Bahariya, and they caught the Hyksos messenger, thus averting disaster for the native Egyptians.

In the New Kingdom, the oasis was known to the Egyptians as both Djes-Djes (which we cannot translate) and the Northern Oasis, and it was an important site from which to maintain the southern and western borders of Egypt. During the reign of Tuthmosis III of Dynasty 18, governors were sent from Egypt to oversee the oases under the jurisdiction of the mayor of Abydos, although they probably spent most of their time at home in the Nile Valley.

We know of at least one native governor from the New Kingdom: Amenhotep Huy, whose tomb lies at the site of Garet-Helwa, about two miles south of el-Qasr. This tomb was first mentioned by Georg Steindorff in 1900 and was explored more thoroughly by Ahmed Fakhry, who dated it to the transition between Dynasties 18 and 19. This tomb is cut into a sandstone ridge and follows the same architectural style as Nile Valley tombs of this period; the carved and painted reliefs depict traditional tomb scenes featuring Amenhotep Huy and his wife Ourly. The colors had been protected by the sand and were still vibrant when seen by Steindorff and Fakhry, but they have now deteriorated badly and many of the scenes have been lost. In 1999 we began to survey the area around this tomb, and we have discovered both earlier and later tombs.

There are other mentions of Bahariya from late New Kingdom sources in the Nile Valley. In an inscription in the Temple of Amon at Luxor, Ramesses II refers to it as a place of mining; several references from the reign of his son Merenptah describe attacks by Libyan forces; and Ramesses III fought the Libyans, defeated them, and brought them back to Egypt as slaves. In an important papyrus from this last king's reign, there is mention of Bahariya's wine, which evidently compared unfavorably with wine from another oasis. Ramesses VI, on the other hand, thought it was good enough to offer to Amon.

From Dynasty 21 to Dynasty 25, the centralized government of Egypt began to collapse and the power of the priests of Amon began to grow. Libyan chieftains began to settle in the Oases during this period and become Egyptianized. In about 945 B.C., the Libyans took over the Nile Valley and founded the 22nd Dynasty. An unfinished sandstone chapel at the site of el-Eion (within the boundaries of el-Bawiti) contains funerary stelae that have been dated to the reign of Sheshonq IV of the 22nd Dynasty; other monuments from the reign of the same king mention an official named Weshet-het, whose title was "Superior Libyan Chief." Still others were constructed

In 1947 Ahmed Fakhry discovered a series of 26th Dynasty rock-cut tombs under the village of el-Bawiti. Houses were built illegally above these tombs, and they were lost to archaeologists until we were led to them at the end of our first season in Bahariya. This is the tomb of Ped-Ashtar, a high priest of Khonsu and priest of Horus during the reign of Apries (589–570 B.C.).

by a Libyan named Arcawa, who became priest and governor at Bahariya at the end of this dynasty.

No monuments, have been found at Bahariya from the half-century between the end of the 22nd Dynasty and the beginning of the 26th Dynasty. This may be owing to the difficulties that Egypt experienced during this period: when there was internal trouble in the Nile Valley, the kings paid little attention to the western borders. It may also be due to lack of excavation. Fakhry did find a stone inscribed with what he believed to be a cartouche of King Shabaka of Dynasty 25.

Bahariya prospered during the 26th Dynasty, especially during the reigns of Apries (589–570 B.C.) and his successor Amasis (also known as Ahmose II, 570–526 B.C.). The economy of the region was bolstered by a strong trade in the local grape and date wines, which were in great demand in both Upper and Lower Egypt. The main trade

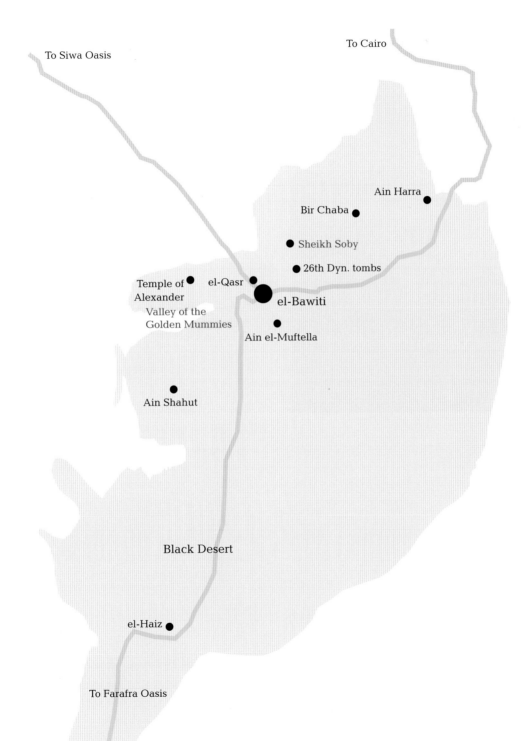

To Siwa Oasis

To Cairo

Ain Harra

Bir Chaba

Sheikh Soby

26th Dyn. tombs

Temple of
Alexander   el-Qasr

Valley of the
Golden Mummies

el-Bawiti

Ain el-Muftella

Ain Shahut

Black Desert

el-Haiz

To Farafra Oasis

There is a great 26th Dynasty temple at the site of Ain el-Muftella, built by members of the most powerful family in the Bahariya Oasis, including Wah-ib-Renefer, the second priest of Khonsu, and Djed-Khonsu-efankh and his brother Shepen-Khonsu, both of whom served as governors. We have recently discovered the tombs of several key members of this family, including Djed-Khonsu-efankh himself. Here we see the late archaeologist Mohammed Tayieb, who did excellent work at Bahariya, inside the temple.

route ran from Bahariya to Bahnasa in Middle Egypt—about 120 miles, or five days by camel.

A number of important monuments dating from the 26th Dynasty have been found at Bahariya. There is a great temple in el-Qasr, at the site of Ain el-Muftella, which was begun during the reign of Apries and completed during the reign of Amasis. The local officials responsible for this construction were Wah-ib-Re-nefer, the second priest of Khonsu, and Djed-Khonsu-efankh and his brother Shepen-Khonsu, both of whom served as governors of Bahariya. At the site of Sheikh Soby, within the borders of el-Bawiti, we have now found eight tombs belonging to this powerful family (see p. 214). Fakhry also found two tombs on the outskirts of el-Bawiti belonging to Djed-Amun-efankh and his son Bannantiu, wealthy merchants of the 26th Dynasty: I have described these tombs in my previous book *Valley of the Golden Mummies.*

During the Persian 27th Dynasty, a garrison was established at Bahariya, and more additions were made to the temples of Ain el-Muftella. In 332 B.C., Alexander the Great took over the Persian Empire, including Egypt, and had a temple built about three miles west of el-Qasr, the only one known in Egypt from his reign. This temple is built of mud brick encased with sandstone and comprises at least forty-five chambers. I first visited this site in 1977 and came back to do some excavations from 1993 to 1994. We found a number of artifacts from the Ptolemaic Period: pottery sherds, fragments of bronze statues, amulets, a small statue of the priest of Re, and a bronze statue of a royal female who we believe was the wife of Alexander the Great. We also found pottery sherds from the Greek, Roman, and Coptic Periods and later, as well as evidence that the building was reused by squatters until the Middle Ages.

The area prospered under the Ptolemies (Alexander's Greek successors), and trade routes and more military outposts were set up through the oases, increasing Bahariya's prosperity. There are some mud-brick structures from this period, recorded by both Steindorff and

Fakhry, sporting inscriptions on some of the entrances and walls; these are scheduled to be fully excavated in the near future and should provide important material for Greco-Roman scholars. I believe that the cemetery of the golden mummies, which lies near the temple of Alexander the Great, was established early in the Greek Period, perhaps even during the reign of Alexander himself.

One of the most interesting Greco-Roman structures at Bahariya is the recently discovered temple of Bes, god of pleasure, sexuality, mothers and children, and grape and date wines. This temple was found in 1988, when a villager from el-Bawiti found a basalt slab carved with the name of the New Kingdom pharaoh Akhenaten lying on a small mound among the houses of el-Bawiti. This temple was excavated by the late Mohammed el-Tayieb and yielded, among other things, the largest known statue of Bes. This was made of terracotta and stands about four feet high. It is very well preserved and still bears traces of the colors in which it was originally painted.

Bahariya hit a rough patch during the battles between the Ptolemies and the Romans but then flourished again. Most of the burials in the Valley of the Golden Mummies date from this period. There are many Roman remains from Ain el-Siwi (now known as Ain el-Geblia) and also from el-Qasr, where there is evidence of houses, churches, another cemetery, and even a victory arch. Another fascinating site, at el-Haiz, has yielded a fortress, a church, a palace, cemeteries, and a newly discovered wine factory. Nearby are also the remains of ancient aqueducts. In 1996 an antiquities inspector named Farag Allah Abdeen was walking in the desert south of el-Bawiti when he noticed some pottery sherds and stones littering the sand. A small team worked on this site for several months in 1997 and uncovered a Roman temple with three chapels, the central one of which appears to have been dedicated to Hercules. We are planning to do a great deal more excavating at all of these sites, which should provide an invaluable window into life in Egypt during the Roman Period.

For most of the last century, the villagers of the Bahariya oasis lived the lifestyle of a different era and maintained their ancient heritage and traditions. However, the relatively recent introduction of many modern amenities, including television and an improved road system, has destroyed most of the ancient culture. This mother and daughter demonstrate both: the daughter wears the traditional embroidered black dress and jewelry while her mother favors plainer, more modern attire.

The Valley of the Golden Mummies

You have already heard the amazing tale of the discovery of the cemetery of the golden mummies. We have now spent three seasons excavating here and have barely scratched the surface of this vast site. In the first season, we excavated five tombs, containing a total of 105 mummies. In the second season, we unearthed another four tombs and 103 mummies, and in the third season added eight more tombs and 46 mummies to our total. The tombs that we have found so far can be dated, through the architecture and style of mummy wrappings, to the Greco-Roman Period, most of them to sometime around the end of the first century B.C. Some may be older, and we will know more as we analyze the associated artifacts. This is the largest sample found so far of tombs and mummies from the Greco-Roman Period, although, unlike mummies from earlier periods of Egyptian history, the deceased are not identified by name or relationship to one another.

The entrances to the tombs usually lie about fifteen to twenty feet below the desert surface. The subterranean chambers are carved roughly into the sandstone bedrock, without the carefully oriented and finely cut walls common to earlier periods. The rock surfaces, with only one minor exception (two roughly painted figures of the canine god Anubis which flank the entrance to Tomb 1), are free of decoration. The tombs were family vaults, used by multiple members of the same family, often over the course of a generation or more. This cemetery was used from sometime after 332 B.C., when Alexander the Great added Egypt to his empire, through the period of Roman rule, and perhaps into the fourth or fifth century A.D.

The tombs fall into three principal types: tombs with staircases, tombs with entrance shafts, and surface burials. In the first type, a rock-cut staircase to the north leads down into a small delivery room, where the body of the deceased was passed from the family to the mortuary staff during the funeral. In several tombs, we found evidence for a wooden door that would have closed this room off from the rest of the tomb. The delivery room leads in turn into one or more burial chambers with niches in the walls. Inside these niches, the builders left stone benches, or mastabas, on which the mummies were laid, with up to six bodies on each bench. In the shaft tombs, the entrance shaft leads to a number of burial chambers that differs from one tomb to another; again, the mummies were buried inside niches.

Some surface burials consist simply of a shallow hole dug into the ground just big enough for one mummy; others are larger, cut in a square shape to a depth of about one and a half feet and leading to long pits containing one or more mummies. A few are cut in the shape of a flower or an ankh with burials in each arm. These surface tombs were usually placed near the large tombs so that the people buried there could benefit from the offerings and rituals made for the rich.

The poorest mummies, which are mostly found in superficial graves, were carelessly wrapped in linen, which in many cases has come unraveled. Some skeletons are covered with a single piece of cloth, with only the two hands

Valley
of the
Golden
Mummies

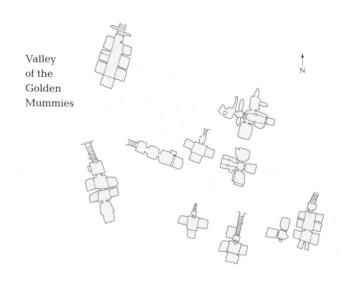

and the penis wrapped separately. Some of the mummies
have more elaborate wrappings, with the linen woven
into geometric patterns. The wealthiest individuals, probably prosperous local merchants, may also have painted
and gilded cartonnage, a type of plaster of Paris, covering
either their entire body, the upper body and head, or, as
is often the case for children, just the head. These were
always the most extraordinary mummies to find. I remember one day in particular during the first season when we
were all very tired and hot and our energy was flagging.
As the sun moved directly above us, we were getting
ready to take our short midday break, when the sun's rays
shone directly into the tomb we were excavating and
turned the gold to liquid fire.

The cartonnage on the heads of our golden mummies
is painted in the form of a portrait of the deceased. The
face is given lifelike features, including beautifully crafted
eyes made of inlaid black obsidian and white marble,
sometimes with eyelashes added in bronze or copper. The
extraordinary eyes of these mummies can make them quite
disconcerting to uncover; as you brush away at the sand,

*Above: We have now spent
three seasons excavating in
the Valley of the Golden
Mummies and have unearthed
sixteen tombs and over 250
mummies. Our work tents are
visible in the background of
this overview of the excavation
site.*

Above: Many beautiful artifacts, all dating from the
Greco-Roman Period, were
found buried with the mummies in the valley. Here we
see three bronze bracelets,
one bronze coin, and eyes
from two different mummy
masks.

Opposite: I was present when
my assistant Tarek el-Awady
found his first mummy (see
page 199). It was fascinating
to watch the battle between
his excitement over this great
discovery and his absolute
dismay at the horrible smell!
Here he is, now hardened
to the stench, examining a
mummy inside one of the
rock-cut tombs in the Valley
of the Golden Mummies.

you can never predict the exact moment the eyes will pop out from the sand and stare at you. In some cases, the eyes have shifted so that the mummy is looking in several directions at once, which can be quite unnerving. The women also have separate breasts modeled on their chest plates.

On the cartonnage that encases either the whole bodies or chest plates of these mummies are religious scenes, usually from the Book of the Dead, either modeled in gold or painted onto the plaster. The funerary gods represented include Thoth, Nut, Horus, the cobra and sun disk, and the four children of Horus with knives to protect the deceased. The mummy can also be under the protection of the winged sun disk, the cobra, Horus, and Anubis. All of the gods and goddesses are depicted according to the canon of Egyptian art, not in Greek or Roman style, and the fact that all the divinities are Egyptian is unusual for this period. All of this indicates that the deceased were Egyptian, rather than Greek or Roman. As mentioned on page 190, the only wall painting we have found so far shows two Anubis figures guarding the entrance to Tomb 1.

Some of the mummies were put inside anthropoid wooden coffins decorated with religious scenes. Most of the coffins have decayed beyond recognition, but we did find several spectacular wooden panels at the feet of mummies who had been buried in coffins of this type. A number of mummies were buried in roughly shaped and poorly fired anthropoid clay coffins. We found one example at the Valley

of the Golden Mummies that matched two more in reused tombs at Sheikh Soby (see p. 217), They were alike enough that I believe all three were made by the same craftsman. Several mummies were buried inside mud coffins covered with layers of plaster, and then painted or gilded.

We found a great many artifacts in the tombs. Many were items of food meant for use in the afterlife, such as wine, dates, onions, garlic, beans, olives, and squash. There were also pottery vessels for personal use, jewelry such as bracelets, necklaces, rings, and earrings of clay, ivory, bronze, iron, wood, glass, faience, and occasionally gold. There were statues of mothers and infants, mourning women, gods and goddesses such as Osiris and Isis, animals, and children's toys. Bronze coins were found in the hands of some of the mummies to give to the ferryman as payment for the journey to the afterlife. Analysis of these coins will tell us a great deal about the dates of the burials.

THE SEASON OF 1999

As my team for the first season, I brought Mansour Boriak, Tarek el-Awady, and Mahmoud Afifi as my archaeologists. Our epigrapher was Noha Abdel Hafiz, the only female member of our team. Noha works very quickly, and has extremely patient and dexterous hands. She is normally very quiet, although if she becomes angry (usually at the mishandling of a precious artifact), she becomes like a lioness. Every day, she would move from tomb to tomb as the mummies were uncovered, tracing each scene, and then to the antiquities tent on the site to draw whatever artifacts had been found. Keeping up with our remarkable rate of discovery was extraordinarily difficult work, and I believe she worked harder than anyone else on the team.

We had rented five apartments in a small, self-contained mining community about twenty miles from the site, and we planned to stay there for the season. Unfortunately, it took us over an hour to drive to the valley the first morning, so we decided to look for a base in el-Bawiti, only a couple of miles from the site. We ended up at the el-Beshmo Lodge, a nice cottage-style hotel, where we

Above: Poorer people were buried in shallow pits dug into the desert surface. Some, like this one, were in the shape of an ankh, with a burial in each arm.

Left: My first-season team at the Valley of the Golden Mummies was excellent, and we did amazing work together.

Opposite: Before we began excavating, we prepared the area by measuring carefully from a fixed reference point and setting up a grid, so that the location of each mummy or other artifact could be recorded exactly. Two of our grid squares are visible in this photograph.

stayed for all three seasons. When we got to the Valley of the Golden Mummies on the first morning of the excavations, we did a surface survey, walking around and collecting the archaeological debris (pottery sherds, bones, old glass, and the like), which was scattered south of the temple of Alexander the Great. The area covered by this debris stretches for almost four square miles.

Our architects, Abdel Hamid and Hamdi Rashwan, mapped out a grid of six hundred ten-meter squares over the gently undulating surface of sand and rock. I assigned each of my archaeologists a square, and we began to dig. In the initial phases, we moved many baskets of sand, the weathered workmen passing full baskets down the line to be sieved for pottery sherds and smaller artifacts and sending empty baskets back up to be filled again.

Every day for three weeks, we rose at 5 A.M. so that we could get to the site by 7 and make the most of the coolest part of the day. We would wear layers of clothing that we would gradually strip off as the sun rose and began to heat the desert sand. Our team worked intensely, taking only half an hour at midday for a light lunch. The workmen chanted as they passed their baskets from hand to hand, and the digging and brushing never stopped.

We returned to the hotel in the late afternoon, dirty and exhausted. I would wash up and go to the courtyard, where I would have a water pipe, called a "shisha," prepared for me by a relative of the hotel's owner named Sobhy. I would smoke the pipe as I planned the work for the next day, met with people, and heard Sobhy's latest update of the village news. We excavated five wonderful tombs during the first season, which I have discussed in

Above: A total of forty-three mummies had been crammed into the two burial chambers of Tomb 54. It took our workmen several days to clear the sand from these chambers so that we could excavate the mummies.

Right: Every evening, after excavating and before dinner, I sat in the courtyard at the el-Beshmo Lodge where we were staying and smoked my shisha (water pipe) while I caught up on the news and thought about the next day's work.

detail in *Valley of the Golden Mummies*. I will recap some of the high points here and describe two of the best tombs.

The greatest initial excitement in our first season came from Tomb 54, which Mohammed el-Tayieb and Mohammed Aiady, archaeologists attached to the Bahariya Inspectorate, had explored briefly in 1996. I assigned this tomb to Mansour Boriak, the best archaeologist on my team. Access to the tomb is by a flight of eight stairs leading down to a small delivery room, only about four by eight feet, with an eight-foot ceiling that had collapsed in antiquity. This leads across a threshold that bears evidence for a long-vanished wooden door to the first of two north-south chambers with burial niches in their walls.

Tomb 54 contained the most mummies, with a total of forty-three crammed into the two burial chambers, lined up wherever they would fit and sometimes even stacked one on top of the other. We are sure that this was a family tomb, used over the course of several generations. Two of the mummies found in this tomb lay next to one another in a separate narrow niche, and I believe that they were husband and wife. Both are wrapped in linen and encased in cartonnage, with gilded masks and chest plates. The man, Mummy A, has a long, narrow face, and appears to have died at the age of fifty or so. He wears a headband inlaid with colored faience and semiprecious stones with a uraeus, the royal cobra, in the center. In earlier times, the uraeus had been reserved for royalty, but by the Greco-Roman Period, common people had usurped many royal symbols. The woman, Mummy B, is gilded and decorated in exactly the same style as the man. She caught my eye from the very beginning, and her image has haunted me ever since. The most unusual thing about this mummy is that she was wrapped and modeled so that her head is tilted slightly to the right. She was laid in the niche so that she was facing her husband, gazing lovingly at him for eternity. She also has a slight smile on her face, which is a very rare feature (but is seen in several other mummies from this site).

Another notable mummy from this tomb is partly encased in cartonnage covered with painted scenes on the chest and a mask, carefully modeled in stucco and then gilded in the form of the face of a young man. He wears a crown of leaves and flowers, in the style of a Greek victor's wreath, with the royal uraeus in front, a typically Greco-Roman blend of Greek and Egyptian motifs. He has thick black curls and on the top of his crown is the image of a Horus falcon in flight, again in a complex blend of Greek and Egyptian motifs.

Two of the most interesting mummies from this tomb are of children. The first is a little boy, perhaps five years old. He was wrapped in linen and given a gilded mask, with his features painted in black and his headband colored red and yellow to look like flowers and leaves. He was found next to a small female mummy, probably his sister, wrapped in the same style. Like Mummy B, she has a small smile on her face. The children were buried with a third mummy, whom I believe to be their father.

By the end of the first season in 1999, pressure was directed at me from all sides to open the site to tourists. Unfortunately, as important as it is to the economy of Egypt, tourism is very damaging to ancient sites, and I did not want hordes of people trampling the ancient tombs. Although I do not believe in invading the privacy of the dead by putting them on public display, I finally agreed to move five of the mummies from Tomb 54 to a room in the Inspectorate building, which has since been converted to the Bahariya Museum.

Nasry Iskander, chief conservator for the royal mummies at the Egyptian Museum in Cairo, came to prepare them so that we could lift them safely from their niches. Under his supervision, conservators Moustafa Abdel Kader and Salah Ahmed Ali covered the bodies with clean linen before using sticks to lift them from their burial places. They placed the mummies into new coffins and put them onto a truck to carry them to their new home. Immediately after we had moved the children to the Inspectorate, I began to have nightmares. In my restless dreams, the babies, wrapped in the fresh linen we had used to protect them, stretched out their arms toward me and tried to grab me. I would also see the smiling face of

Many of the mummies we found wore masks and chest plates made of cartonnage, a sort of ancient plaster of Paris that was gilded and painted. This male mummy is decorated with funerary scenes showing gods that will protect the deceased in the afterlife.

Mummy B, her eyes pleading mutely with me. Only a few weeks later, still haunted by the children, I had to go to Los Angeles, where I teach each summer. I usually find my time there very peaceful and I get a lot of writing done, but the children followed me to the States, and they continued to visit my dreams.

In the meantime, public interest in the discovery had grown exponentially: photographs of the mummies appeared on front pages all over the world, I was featured in a cover story for *Archaeology Magazine;* and I was asked to do television and magazine interviews almost every day. One evening, after a particularly disturbing night, I almost told the entire world about my nightmares on CNN Live.

Things got worse. I lost so much sleep that I had trouble getting up in the morning. One night I was scheduled to speak about the golden mummies in Virginia at the Richmond Art Museum. I had one problem after another getting there, and I felt completely panicked, imagining that the little girl had her arms around my neck and was choking me. I finally gave my lecture at 9 P.M., two hours late. The next morning, I was supposed to give a lecture to some schoolchildren at 9, but I woke at 9:30 to hear people banging at my door. I knew that I couldn't ignore the children anymore, and I spent my wait at the Richmond Airport re-creating for myself every detail of the children's faces, until suddenly I realized what they had been trying to tell me: they wanted their father to come with them to the museum. When I got back to Bahariya at the end of September 1999, we moved their father to the museum, and the children never visited me again.

One of the most poignant of the mummies, whom (to my great relief) we have left in her original place in Tomb 54, wears a plaster mask carefully painted so that she looks as if she is wearing bridal makeup. I believe that she must have died shortly before her marriage, so her family prepared her for a wedding in the afterlife. I found her happy, peaceful countenance very touching and felt again the sadness that her family and fiancé must have felt at her early death.

In order to protect the majority of the mummies by leaving them in place, I agreed to move five mummies that we had moved during the first season to the Bahariya Museum, including this boy from Tomb 54 and his sister. His gilded mask is decorated with a headband painted red and yellow to look like a floral wreath. The two children haunted my dreams until I brought their father to the museum to be with them.

One thing that people who have not worked closely with freshly excavated mummies do not know is that they smell. In fact, they smell terrible; the stench is really indescribable. I have been working with mummies for so long that I barely notice it anymore, but I still remember my first experience vividly. In our first season at Bahariya, I had the somewhat sadistic pleasure of watching my assistant Tarek el-Awady struggle with the conflicting feelings that accompanied his first major discovery.

Tarek was excavating Tomb 1 when he hit a patch of the blackened sand, caused by resin and mineral from the decaying body, that tells an experienced archaeologist he or she is close to a mummy. He became more and more excited as he carefully scraped away the sand and brushed aside the pieces of outer casing that had flaked away from the mummy. I could see on his face the eagerness to work faster and uncover the mysterious piece of the past that lay beneath his trowel and, at the same time, the desire to run as far as he could from the increasing stench. The moment when he finally uncovered the golden mask that covered the mummy's face was truly priceless. This was both the most exciting and rewarding moment, and also the most unbearable!

This tomb was also entered by a staircase leading to a receiving room. An extra room lies between the receiving room and the burial chamber; this may have been a storage room or an offering room. The burial chamber contains niches cut one on top of another, which is the later Roman style. There were only four mummies buried here. In direct contrast to the later style of the architecture is the style of the mummies, one of which was buried in an anthropoid coffin, the hallmark of an earlier period. It is also the only tomb with any decoration: there are crude painted images of a canine figure, almost certainly Anubis, the god of embalming, flanking the entrance to the burial chamber.

When I left Bahariya Oasis at the end of the first season in 1999, I did not have any idea that the discovery of the Valley of the Golden Mummies would receive so much media attention. The Supreme Council of Antiquities announced the discovery to the press in May of 1999, and after that, the European press came to Bahariya almost every day for a month. The publicity for the mummies had been more extensive than for any discovery since the opening of the tomb of King Tut in 1922. What was truly amazing was that the American media did not cover it at all. There were American newspaper and magazine correspondents in Cairo, but they seemed to be too busy writing about politics to pay any attention to our discoveries.

I went to the United States in August 1999 to teach nine summer courses at UCLA. I was planning to give a lecture about the discovery of the golden mummies at the Natural History Museum in Los Angeles, in cooperation with the American Research Center (West Chapter), now called the Egyptian Exploration Organization of Southern California, headed by Noel Sweitzer. Two important reporters contacted me in Los Angeles: Tom Mough, from the *Los Angeles Times* and Mark Rose from *Archaeology Magazine*. I have known Tom well for the last seven years, and he writes frequently about my discoveries in Egypt. Mark called me from New York and told me that John Wilford, science editor for the *New York Times*, would call me. The next week there was an article in the *Los Angeles Times* and a full page with color photographs in the *New York Times*. Both stories made the front page of their papers.

For the next month, all the national television and cable networks came to Los Angeles. I gave interviews in the library of the Department of Near Eastern Languages and Culture during the day and at Marina del Rey, where I lived, in the evening. I was amazed that mummies could capture the hearts of people this way. Of course, many newspapers began to write about the curse of the mummies and ask me about accidents that had happened to me during the excavations.

Tomb 1 is the only tomb with wall paintings. Two images of the jackal-god Anubis as guardian of the cemetery appear at the entrance to the burial chamber to protect the deceased on the journey through the underworld.

THE SECOND SEASON

I received funding from the Supreme Council of Antiquities for a second season at Bahariya, which I planned for the months of April and May 2000. I would have started earlier, but my lecturing obligations in the United States and Europe and my duties to the site-management program at Giza kept me busy. I was also busy with arrangements for the Eighth International Congress of Egyptology, to be held in Cairo at the end of March. We were expecting fifteen hundred scholars from all over the world, so the preparations were extensive.

By the end of March 2000, we had the season arranged. Our plan was to continue excavating in the Valley of the Golden Mummies, investigate some newly discovered

tombs beneath the houses in Sheikh Soby, do conservation, and open certain tombs to the public, including the New Kingdom tomb of Amenhotep Huy.

At the beginning of the season, I had asked Abdel Hamid, our architect, to reestablish the grid so that we could continue in the same ten-meter squares as the year before. We built a nice camp with a tent that served as both a lab and an office. This season was terrific for me, because the press did not know that we were excavating, which allowed us to work in freedom. During the season, we discovered four tombs in different styles cut into the sandstone, containing a total of 103 mummies.

Tomb 26 is one of the richest tombs to be discovered so far, very similar to Tomb 54 from the first season. It was a

family tomb as well, and contained 42 mummies. The ceiling had fallen and lay over the hall and the niches. It took about a month to excavate this tomb because we found a number of unique artifacts with the mummies, all of which needed careful conservation. The first mummy we found was on a pedestal on the floor of the rectangular hall. It was inside a wooden coffin and was in good condition. I believe that this was the head of the family. We found a number of other interesting mummies in this tomb, including several children. There were two male mummies buried together, one a middle-aged man and one a child. The most beautiful mummy in the tomb was a woman with a gilded gypsum mask, a band of yellow and red flowers crowned by the uraeus on her head. Her eyes

Opposite: My second-season team included many of the archaeologists who had worked with me in the first season. Our second season was also very successful: we discovered four major tombs containing a total of 103 mummies.

Above: Tomb 26 is one of the richest tombs that we have discovered in the Valley of the Golden Mummies and contained many artifacts that had been buried with their owners. In this photograph, Tarek el-Awady is uncovering the mummy of the patriarch of the family buried in this tomb, who was placed on a pedestal on the floor of the main hall.

were framed in black, and on her chest was a cartonnage mask covered with painted funerary scenes. Resting on her chest was a child, who had been buried with his mother so they could be together for eternity.

On the day that Tomb 26 was found, I was at the Sheikh Soby site. I received a written message from Mansour asking me to come to the Valley of the Golden Mummies, and I could sense that something important was happening. I drove my car the short distance to the site, and Mansour showed me a mummy with something unique at his feet, a wooden panel that formed the foot of the coffin.

Every archaeologist always loses something in an excavation, especially if it is in a cemetery, where there are often fragile artifacts. Our worst enemy in an excavation is air, because when a faience or wooden artifact is exposed to air, it can turn to powder in one second. When we discover something delicate like this panel, we have to isolate the artifact as rapidly as possible by covering it with a wooden frame into which conservators carefully and gradually inject conservation material to consolidate and protect it.

I asked Salah, our conservator, to work on the panel, and he moved himself into position near the end of the coffin to begin the project. He would normally have taken it out after he finished, but I asked him to wait until I had seen it first. I moved carefully, resting on my side until I was in front of the panel. It was an absolutely beautiful example, adorned with the façade of a gate topped with cobras. The deceased was represented as a statue of gypsum, dressed in a white robe that left his right shoulder bare; he was wearing brightly colored sandals. Above his head of curly hair was the sun disk, and he held the hem of his robe in his right hand.

I came back out and told Mansour that we had another great discovery to celebrate. Mansour said in Arabic "el

Above: We found forty mummies in Tomb 26, each of which had to be carefully cleaned, as Tarek is doing here. This is very delicate work, and requires great concentration and thoroughness.

Opposite: Two of the mummies in Tomb 26, with their gilded masks and cartonnage chest plates

During the second season at Bahariya, we found three of these exquisite wooden panels, one of which disintegrated under the hands of our conservator when he tried to move it. The panel shown here is one of the best examples ever found of this type of artifact, and tells us that this woman was treasured by her surviving relatives. She is shown here emerging from one of the gates in the Netherworld in the process of being resurrected as a divine being.

Hamdulelallah," which means "thanks be to God." Salah started to move in to remove the panel, and his shoulder touched the mummy. I felt my heart drop, sensing that anything could happen, but he took the panel out, doing his job superbly. He held it in his hand and I looked at it, turned back to ask Tarek to take a photograph, then looked back at Salah and watched in absolute dismay as the piece turned to powder in less than a minute. I was so upset that I almost screamed at Salah, but then looked at his face and saw that he had turned red and that his lips had begun to tremble. Everyone can make mistakes, and it is very a delicate balance, to inject enough conservation material to consolidate a piece without destroying it. But I was devastated and retired to the lab tent for the rest of the day.

The next day, in the third niche, we found three mummies. The first was inside a wooden coffin, wrapped in linen and with a cartonnage chest shield with scenes from the Book of the Dead. The second was also in a wooden box, in good condition because it had been protected when part of the ceiling fell over it. Near the mummy we found an eye of blue glass, with the pupil in obsidian and the white of the eye in limestone. It seemed that the gods wanted to make up for the disaster of the day before, because we found another wooden panel with one of these mummies. I thought that if I did not ask Salah to do the conservation, it would end his career. So I said to him, "Come, Salah. You have to know that everyone makes mistakes. Do this work again, and do it well."

The mummy was of a woman, wrapped with linen and measuring about five feet long, a bit shorter than average. She had originally been buried inside a wooden coffin, of which only the foot panel remained. This is one of the most beautiful panels that I have ever seen, and I know of no parallels for it. To me, it is even more exciting than the golden mummies themselves. Tarek took many photographs before we tried to remove the panel.

The decoration of this artifact depicts the gate to the afterlife, guarded by a cobra. The deceased is represented in a gypsum statue, dressed in a Roman garment with short sleeves and a long skirt, painted green with black bands, over which she wears a red cloak. The right leg is extended forward as if she were about to leave her coffin and walk through the gate into eternal life. The mummy itself wore a short wig, which we removed for conservation. I thanked God for letting us find another panel and for giving courage back to Salah.

After we had finished the excavation, I stayed at the site to record and document the artifacts. I went to the lab tent to see how the wooden panel looked and found that Salah had done an excellent job and kept all of the original color. At the end of the day, we carefully covered the colored wooden panel with cotton, laid it on a wooden sledge, and took it to the Inspectorate building at Bahariya, where we were storing all the artifacts from the excavations. The storage magazines are under the care of Khaled Salah, who graduated from the Faculty of Archaeology at Cairo University and became an inspector at Bahariya. He talks very little and wears a big beard that covers everything except his eyes. Because he is a very honest man, I had put him in charge of the artifacts.

One of the two rooms in the building contains all the treasures, such as gold artifacts, that have emerged from the sands of the valley. The room is sealed with Khaled's name; no one can open it except him, and, when he does, he must be accompanied by a member of the police and two other people from the Inspectorate of Antiquities. The other room is for items under study or conservation or for objects that are being photographed. Near this is the large hall in which the five mummies we brought from the valley in 1999 are displayed. This will become a site museum, where visitors can view the mummies and some of the artifacts from the excavations.

After we had placed the wooden panel in the storage magazine and sealed the room again, I came back to the hotel to smoke my shisha. During the time I devote to smoking and relaxing after a hard day's work, I usually think about what I will do the next day and the instructions I will need to give to my colleagues at the two sites we are excavating. But that day, I could not stop thinking

Above: This child mummy from Tomb 15 shows the elaborate wrapping techniques that were used for the linen bandages. At his feet are pottery vessels in which food and drink for his afterlife were placed.

Right: Another wooden foot panel, found in Tomb 26, shows the deceased dressed as Osiris, god of the dead, and flanked by Anubis, god of embalming, and Horus, who will help him on the dangerous journey through the nether-world.

Opposite: Dr. Azza Sarry el-Din, our anthropologist, used a portable X-ray machine to examine the mummies that we found in the valley. We were amazed to discover that this young boy from Tomb 26 had a golden amulet of the protective goddess Wadjet in the form of a cobra on his forehead.

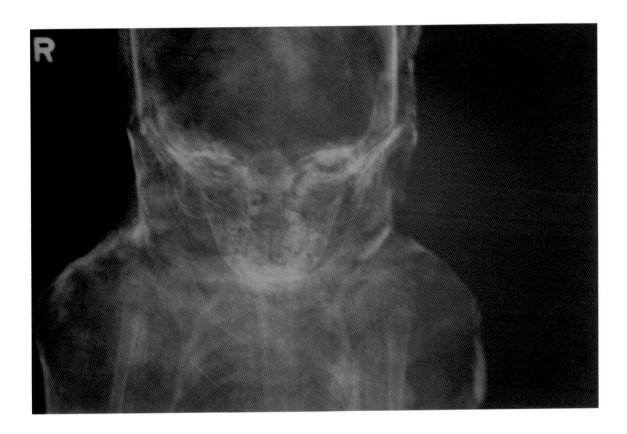

of the golden lady; I was upset at the thought that we had taken from her the special panel that was meant to insure her resurrection. I do not look at this from a religious point of view, but I feel strongly that these ancient people have the right to be left in peace. Perhaps this woman's husband told her before she died that he would not only cover her mummy with gold but would also make this special panel for her so that she could travel safely to the afterlife.

Perhaps there are archaeologists who do not care about such things, but I know many archaeologists who feel as I do. I thought that perhaps after the wooden panel had been conserved properly, I should return it to its original location. On the other hand, it might not be safe to leave such a precious artifact in the field. I argued with

myself for a long time, but finally decided that keeping this precious artifact safe and that telling the story of this lady and how much she was loved was more important. If we left these tombs unexcavated and undisturbed, the mummies would be damaged by the falling ceilings or destroyed by tomb robbers. We as archaeologists come here to preserve these artifacts and learn from them. We are not looking for glory or victory, simply for the best way to preserve and understand our ancient past. Many people think that I am crazy to leave most of the mummies in their tombs rather than moving them to the museum, but I say no, we leave them in situ because that is where they belong. The mummies that are in the museum are being sacrificed to keep their relatives safe. There are many people who agree and others who disagree; I must do what I believe is right.

The next tomb we excavated is actually the tomb that was first stumbled on by the donkey. The architecture is wonderful and the ceiling is intact. The tomb is entered from the north by a flight of seven stairs leading to a delivery room, and then one progresses to two burial chambers, each containing two niches, and a third burial chamber with one niche. About seven feet from the entrance is a niche that was used for the burial of a child.

Unfortunately, this tomb was excavated in 1996 by poorly trained archaeologists from Bahariya. They did not know how to handle and conserve the mummies properly, and they did a great deal of damage. In Niche A in the first burial chamber, we found the remains of two mummies covered with linen and a pottery lamp. The second niche contained the remains of skulls, bones, and wooden coffins. In the first niche of the second burial chamber, we found a wooden foot panel from a coffin decorated with a scene of the deceased in the shape of Osiris (wrapped like a mummy and wearing a crown) flanked by Anubis and Horus performing the proper rituals for the resurrection of the deceased. In the second niche were the remains of bones. In the only niche of the third burial chamber was the mummy of a woman with a cartonnage shield on her chest.

For this season, I decided to bring the X-ray machines that we used at Giza with us to the desert. I spoke with Dr. Azza Sarry el-Din, our radiologist at Giza, who told me that the machine costs about thirty thousand Egyptian pounds ($8,000), and that if anything happened to it, it would be a great loss. I told her not to worry and asked Abdel Hamid to prepare the guardroom for the machine and to bring it from Giza in his truck. He did a good job, and we set up the machine without any problems. I was so happy to have this machine there; it was the first time such a machine would be at an excavation, and it would enable us to get more information about the people we were finding. Dr. Azza also sent her assistant, Aiman, who is studying for his master's degree, to help us. I told him

that we would only examine seven mummies, since I did not want to move all of them. We still need a smaller X-ray machine to take inside the tombs so that we can examine all the mummies in place.

We wrapped each mummy to be X rayed carefully and took it to the lab to be examined. Tarek would take photographs, and then we would return the mummy to its resting place. Several of the mummies we examined were children, which is always heartbreaking. One of the mummies was a woman who had died between the ages of fifty and sixty from undetermined causes. She had had a great deal of dental trouble and some osteoporosis. Another mummy was a man who was between thirty-five and forty at his death; one leg was shorter than the other. Yet another had terrible sinus problems, which would have given him a constant headache. For the last two examinations, we X-rayed two separate heads, one of a woman between eighteen and twenty and the other, a man over fifty. We found a number of other health problems among both the children and adults, including cancer.

X rays of one of the children found in Tomb 26, the first tomb we excavated this season, showed that he wore a gold headband with a snake at his forehead. I decided to move this child to the museum, since leaving him in the tomb with such a precious artifact would make him vulnerable. I was afraid that this child would come to visit me, but nothing happened.

After we finished the excavations for the season, we made a big announcement in the newspapers about the discoveries. At the same time, Fox TV produced a two-hour-long film live from Bahariya with Bill Pullman and Hugh Downs. This was one of the network's highest rated shows and helped to capture the imagination of the American public. After that, television stations from all over the world sent teams to Bahariya. I am happy that the Valley of the Golden Mummies has become an important focus for media attention, because it represents a wonderful opportunity for us as archaeologists to keep the public informed and engaged in this once-in-a-lifetime discovery.

A week after we began our third season in the Valley of the Golden Mummies, I left Tarek in charge while I went back to Cairo. While I was gone, he discovered one of the best tombs at the site, which he named Tomb N. It contained thirteen mummies, distributed in family groups, like the husband and wife we see here.

THE THIRD SEASON

I felt that this season would be a great one for us. We still had many treasures waiting for us at the Valley of the Golden Mummies, and I was also looking forward to continuing our search for members of the Djed-Khonsu-efankh family at Sheikh Soby. I planned a long season, from mid-January 2001 until the beginning of May.

For this season, I decided to spend four days at Bahariya and three at Giza, running the excavations at the tombs of the pyramid builders and the site-management project at the Giza Plateau. I put Mahmoud Afifi in charge during the three days I was away from Giza.

A week after the excavations started, I left Tarek el-Awady in charge at Bahariya in my absence and went back to Cairo. When I returned, I found that he had discovered one of the best tombs at the site, which had wonderful mummies. I also found that Tarek was beginning to understand that archaeology is not just about explaining the past, it is about letting people see your passion. I am convinced that he has the same enthusiasm for archaeology as I have. He had come to the site at 8 A.M., as usual, to take photographs before the sun became too strong, and he was talking to Sheik Saber, one of the guards. Sheik Saber told Tarek that there was a place in the valley that all the donkeys avoided, because there were holes there. Since it was still early, they went to see this site, and Tarek began to examine the terrain. He found an

liminary investigation, finding that the doorway was still sealed with blocks of stone. There were four niches, all filled with mummies. The sandstone ceiling was weak, so he called in the restorers to begin working on the mummies, and then he closed the tomb until I could be informed of the find.

Tarek called me on the telephone and, with passion in his low, polite voice, described the discovery to me. I came early in the morning on the next day, and we decided to move the best-preserved mummies to another tomb cut into the rock (Tomb D), which is in good condition but has no mummies. We then called the workmen and carpenters to prepare Tomb N so that we could take the mummies out. We put a wooden ceiling over the tomb, built wooden doors for the niches, and placed a ladder to go up and down the shaft.

There were thirteen mummies in the tomb, most distributed in family groups (often a man, woman, and child). Some of the most beautiful mummies from the entire site were found here. A woman found in one niche with a man and a four-year-old child wears a magnificent mask, perhaps the most beautiful we have found so far, with wide eyes, black eyebrows, and red lips. Her child also wears a mask, which is decorated with a small necklace. He has a long nose, and his mouth and eyes look sad. The artist added dots under his eyes to show tears, and we have

opening in the rocks and cleared away sand until he had enough space to look in. He brought his flashlight and peered in. This is how he described what he saw in his excavation diary: "To my surprise, I saw faces full of life, looking at me and smiling as if they were welcoming me. It seemed as though they were happy to see the light after living in the dark for two thousand years. I could not tear my eyes away and stayed for about five minutes just looking at them. I did not feel anything around me, but finally I heard the noise of the car and the voices of the workmen. I left the niche and ran to bring the workmen to this place." Tarek labeled the new tomb N and did some pre-

Upper left: The ceiling of Tomb N was weak, so we had to move the mummies to this nearby shaft tomb for safekeeping.

Left: Some of the most beautiful mummies in the valley were in Tomb N. Here is one of the loveliest of the female mummies, adorned with a plaster mask.

nicknamed him the Crying Child. We do not know why he is shown crying; perhaps he suffered from cancer or some other disease. We hope that X rays can help us determine the cause of his death. In another niche we found a female mummy wearing a beautiful smiling mask decorated with a necklace similar to the one found on the crying child and a cartonnage chest shield bearing religious scenes. I have nicknamed this woman the Mona Lisa for the smile that she wears on her red-painted lips.

We decided to continue the excavations on the northwestern and eastern sides of the cemetery. Tarek began to have problems with his ears caused by the sand, and he is also sensitive to the sun. I asked him to go back to the office at Giza, and Ramadan Badry and el-Hussein came to work in the Valley. We found another large tomb, which we labeled Tomb 0. This tomb was unusual in that it had two axes. The ceiling had fallen in, so the mummies were not in good shape. We found nine of them in the western burial chamber, but seven of the heads had become separated from their bodies.

Above: This four-year-old boy was found in a niche with his mother and father. He has a long nose, and his mouth and eyes look sad. There are even dots under his eyes, perhaps representing tears, and we have named him the Crying Child. Perhaps X rays can help us learn why he is so sad.

Below: Tomb 0 was the last tomb we excavated in the Valley of the Golden Mummies. It is unusual in that it has two axes. The ceiling had fallen in, so the mummies were not in good shape—of the nine in the tomb, seven of them had lost their heads, which lay nearby.

About two feet northeast of Tomb 0, we found a surface burial containing two mummies wrapped in linen. In the southwest part of the valley we found two skeletons near each other in surface burials. Below the head of each skeleton were a bronze bracelet, an iron bracelet, and a pottery wine jar.

By the end of this season, we had found an additional 26 mummies, giving us a total of 234 mummies for the three seasons. We continued to work on conserving and recording the new finds, as well as on the mummies and tombs from previous seasons.

The Valley of the Golden Mummies holds many more secrets and treasures for us to find. This is truly one of the most important archaeological finds of the past hundred years. We will be able to learn so much about the population of the oasis during the Greco-Roman Period from studies that we will do with X rays, DNA testing, and CT scans, technology that has only become available to us recently. And we are finding so many treasures. Each mummy is a fascinating person, and the beautiful masks that so many of them wear and the artifacts that were buried with them help to tell us their stories.

Sheikh Soby

In September 1999, at the end of our first season at the Valley of the Golden Mummies, two young men came to me and said that they knew the location of all the antiquities in the area. They told me that they spent all their time wandering in the desert and had met a religious man who knew lots of secrets about the pharaohs. They claimed to have told Ashry Shaker the location of the Temple of Bes and the Temple of Hercules. Something told me not to trust them, but I kept talking to them. They said they could tell me something very important that would help me make a big discovery, that they could lead me personally to the location of some ancient tombs. I asked them

An overview of the site of Sheikh Soby.

Above: Ahmed Fakhry discovered these 26th Dynasty tombs in 1947, and we rediscovered them in 1999; some of them had been reused in later times. Mansour Boriak is holding a Greco-Roman offering table that we found in front of the tomb of Thaty, a 26th Dynasty priest of Khonsu.

Opposite: I noticed this space under one of the walls in the tomb of Thaty's wife, Ta-Nefret-Bastet in October of 1999. I wiggled through and found myself inside a small tomb chapel with a vaulted ceiling. A hole in the western wall of this chapel led to a burial chamber, in which I could glimpse an anthropoid limestone sarcophagus. From the moment of this discovery, I hoped that we had found the lost tomb of the Governor, Djed-Khonsu-efankh, but I had to wait until the next season before we could enter the burial chamber and confirm my suspicions.

what they wanted from me, and they said they wanted jobs in the Inspectorate, perhaps as security officers. I thought to myself that this might be like giving the keys to the cash register to thieves, but I told them to meet me that evening at the hotel to talk more about it.

I called for Ashry Shaker and repeated what the two young men had told me. I said, "Tell me frankly, are they telling the truth, or are they lying?" Ashry said that they had indeed told him many things, and that he had even caught a thief breaking into a tomb one evening because of a tip from these two. The two men came that evening and sat beside me while my shisha was being prepared. The one who did most of the talking, who has a very thin face and large eyes, said that they would talk only to me, no one else. His friend, who is shorter and darker, nodded. I agreed to listen.

My informants told me that five local men were planning to dig under some houses near the cenotaph of Sheikh Soby, who was a local religious leader, in el-Bawiti, in order to find artifacts to sell so that they could get married. According to my informants, the five potential thieves had collected for a long time what is called marriage money, but one night they had gambled it all away. They got very upset, and some other people told them that if they sold some antiquities they could get their money back. These same people promised to show them the location of some ancient tombs under some houses in return for 50 percent of the proceeds. I asked, "Are you sure of this information?" The young men swore they were telling the truth. I told them that if we found the tombs, we would give them both jobs at the Antiquities office in Bahariya, but that these would not be security jobs, which required special training.

The next day, I called Ashry to the excavation tent to talk as we were preparing to leave for Cairo at the end of the season. I asked him to keep the news completely to himself and to go hide beside the houses at night to look out for possible thieves. Ashry kept watch for one month. I came to Bahariya about once a week during this time to do interviews with various European media. I went one night with Ashry to the site at Sheikh Soby and watched for a few hours, but nothing happened. The next day, Ashry and I went into one of the houses and saw a hole in the floor. We looked inside the hole with a flashlight, and were amazed to see painted scenes from an ancient tomb chapel about fifteen to twenty feet underground!

When we did a more formal investigation, we discovered at the bottom of a shaft a maze of rounded rooms forming the chambers and corridors of three tombs from the 26th Dynasty. These tombs had been entered and described in 1947 by Ahmed Fakhry. The first belonged to Ped-Ashtar, a high priest of Khonsu and priest of Horus who lived during the reign of Apries (589–570 B.C.). The second tomb, which was connected to the first by a break in the north wall, was carved out of the rock for Thaty, also a priest of Khonsu and the grandson of Ped-Ashtar. Next to this was the tomb of Thaty's wife, Ta-Nefret-Bastet.

These tombs were decorated with religious and funerary scenes painted onto the plaster with which the sandstone walls had been covered. The women in these tombs are seen in vaguely foreign dress, with fringed shawls; Ta-Nefret-Bastet's skin is pink and she has black eyes, features that suggest she was originally either Greek or Phoenician. Fakhry found that the tombs had been reused for multiple burials during Roman times and robbed again in modern times. He only had time to describe the three tombs briefly; in the ensuing years, which included a revolution and much turnover in the Antiquities Department, the tombs disappeared beneath the shifting sands and the houses of the villagers (perhaps built

there on purpose by people hoping to find treasures that they could sell to support their families) and were lost to archaeologists. I myself had never heard of them when I became inspector of Bahariya in 1977. It was a thrill to rediscover these ancient monuments, although it tore at my heart to see how badly damaged the paintings had been by the water that had leaked down from the houses above. More than 80 percent of the scenes had been damaged, and the people who built the houses had also stolen everything that had not been already been taken before Fakhry found them.

One morning in October 1999, I crawled through a narrow passageway into the tomb of Ta-Nefret-Bastet to sur-

Naesa

Ped-Isis

Djed-Khonsu-efankh

Ta-Nefret-Bastet

Uninscribed Tombs

Thaty

Ped-Ashtar

Site Plan of Sheikh Soby

217

The area above the entrance to the burial chamber of Djed-Khonsu-efankh was decorated with a scene showing the mummy of the governor receiving the ankh from the sun disk.

vey the current status of the excavations and plan the work for the day. The air was still cool when I entered the first burial chamber and stood within its brightly painted walls. Suddenly I noticed a space under one of the walls, and my heart began to beat faster.

The family to whom Ped-Ashtar, Thaty, and Ta-Nefret-Bastet belonged was a large and important one, with at least sixteen members, several of whom had been governors of Bahariya. We know a fair amount about them from inscriptions in the temples at Ain el-Muftella; Fakhry had even reconstructed a family tree and spent time searching unsuccessfully for the lost tomb of the most powerful of these men, Djed-Khonsu-efankh, who ruled Bahariya during the reign of Amasis. I suspected that there might be more to these tombs than Fakhry had discovered, and this new space confirmed my suspicions. I knew that there must be another room behind this wall, and that if I were lucky, it might be an intact tomb, perhaps even the missing tomb of Djed-Khonsu-efankh.

On that morning in October, too excited and impatient even to wait until some of my workers could dig out a larger entrance for me, I decided to climb under the wall, bringing along Mohammed el-Tayieb, who was in charge of the dig, for safety. With great difficulty, I wriggled my way through the small opening in the red sandstone and then tried to stand, but I found that the space beyond was less than five feet high. Mohammed came through after me, and when we held up our light, we found that we were covered from head to toes in red sandstone dust, which made us both laugh. Our laughter stopped when we looked at the low vaulted ceiling above us and saw that it was painted with scenes from the Book of the Dead, which told us that we were indeed inside another tomb, one without signs of water damage or robbery. The south entrance looked like the pylon of a temple. Above it was a scene showing the deceased lying on his back, mummified, with the sun disk above him offering him an ankh (the hieroglyphic sign for life).

I saw a hole in the wall measuring only four inches square and brought my light closer so that I could peek inside. Mohammed was right next to me, about to burst with excitement. I saw an incredible sight: the face of a huge sarcophagus. The nose was broken, but in the dark, it looked like a royal figure. I put my hand further in. Mohammed asked me: "What do you see?" I could only think of the moment that Lord Carnarvon asked Howard Carter this same question, and I smiled, saying, "It seems that we are going to discover a great tomb. . . ."

It was very difficult, but I managed to get a small camera into the hole and take ten photographs of the face. The room in which the sarcophagus lay was about twenty feet long and six feet wide. This looked to us like an undisturbed burial chamber, an archaeologist's dream. The entrance seemed to lead to an area under some modern houses, putting me in a difficult situation. I brought Ashry Shaker back the next day, and he agreed that the only way to excavate the tomb properly was to remove the houses above it. Ashry is a native of el-Bawiti and is active in politics there, in addition to his position as director of Antiquities at Bahariya. He is highly regarded by the people in the town and maintains excellent relationships with the mayor and the chief of police. He is somewhat severe and very correct in his manners, and because of this he has had his share of trouble with other people in the Inspectorate. However, the Antiquities Department has never found any evidence of wrongdoing on his part, and I hold him in great esteem.

Ashry keeps the guards at Bahariya under very tight control, and he reports immediately to the Antiquities Department if anyone takes Antiquities land, builds above an ancient tomb, or is involved in any theft. It quickly became clear to me that the houses had been built illegally, and that the owners would have no legal recourse if we were to demolish them. Ashry and I went back to the Inspectorate, and I wrote a report about what I had seen and took it with me back to Cairo. The permanent committee of the Antiquities Department agreed that ten of the houses in the area should be removed so that the tombs could be excavated. We asked the police to protect the antiquities until the houses could be moved. I met

Above: A great deal of information about the most powerful family in the oasis during the 26th Dynasty was contained on the walls of the temple that they built at Ain el-Muftella. In this scene from the temple wall, King Amasis is followed by Djed-Khonsu-efankh (shown at the same scale as the king!) and his wife, presenting offerings to the gods and goddesses of the Oasis.

Right: Here I am inside the chapel that we found in 1999 and that we later confirmed belonged to the governor, Djed-Khonsu-efankh. I am examining the painted decoration on the walls, which depicts scenes from the Egyptian Book of the Dead to aid the deceased on his journey through the netherworld.

Opposite: In order to excavate the new tombs that we found safely and effectively, we had to demolish the houses that had been built illegally above them. The old woman who lived directly above the tomb was very angry with me, but I personally made sure that a beautiful new home was built for her.

with the mayor to discuss what to do about the people whose houses were to be torn down, and we agreed to offer them land, although we could not give them money. To my surprise, the house owners were very happy with this offer, evidently, according to Ashry Shaker, because most of them had other houses in the town. We left the cenotaph of Sheikh Soby standing so that his spirit would guide us in our excavations.

I came back to Bahariya in October and the owners of all the houses came to meet me. Ashry did not want to give the villagers land in exchange for their houses, but since I knew we would be excavating in the area for the next fifteen years, I thought it best to make peace with these people. The Supreme Council quickly issued a decree ordering the removal of the modern structures, and I asked Ashry to guard the area day and night until we could take down the houses. I could hardly wait until the next season so that we could begin our investigations. And I kept my promise to the two young men and gave them jobs in the Inspectorate.

The Lost Tomb of the Governor

Before I went to excavate in the Valley of the Golden Mummies, it was my dream to discover the tomb of the most powerful governor of the Bahariya Oasis during the 26th Dynasty, Djed-Khonsu-efankh. This had also been the dream of Fakhry before me. As I have mentioned, I have always felt a special affinity with Fakhry, whose books about Bahariya I had read while I was a young man in college. When I read about the "Lost Tomb," I always stopped—something about it captured my imagination. I took Ahmed Fakhry as my guide, and I was determined to discover this tomb as a dedication to him. I liked his adventures in the desert and his sense of humor. My mentor Gamal Mokhtar gave me a letter that Fakhry had sent to him right after he came back from a lecture tour in the United States. Fakhry was very pleased that his lectures had been so well received, and he felt he was doing good things for his country. This was soon before he died.

Djed-Khonsu-efankh served as governor of Bahariya and high priest of Amon under Amasis, fifth king of the 26th Dynasty. In 1900 Georg Steindorff, who was the first to discover the New Kingdom tomb of Amenhotep Huy, found an alabaster statue of Djed-Khonsu-efankh in front of some houses in el-Qasr. We also know of this man from scenes and inscriptions in the 26th Dynasty temple at Ain el-Muftella, where he is shown accompanying the king and making offerings to various gods. The scene I always remember from these chapels shows Djed-Khonsu-efankh as the second and third priest of Amon. He is depicted as equal in size to the king, demonstrating that he is a very important figure. The name of his father is listed as Ped-Isis and both his mother and wife were named Naesa. His brother was called Shepen-Khonsu; he too was a governor of Bahariya. The family had sixteen members altogether; the tombs of three of them, Ped-Ashtar, Thaty, and Ta-Nefret-Bastet, had been found so far.

On the day we got back at Bahariya to begin excavating again, I thought about the tomb and the face I had seen. I said to myself, "I am a lucky archaeologist. I always

reveal secrets from the sand," and I felt I might unveil the legend of the lost governor's tomb. The next morning, I got up at 5:30 A.M. and took the first part of the team to work at the site. I decided that this morning we would work on the consolidation and restoration of the tomb.

However, I had two important tasks to complete before I could open the burial chamber of this room. The first was to meet the old woman whose house was above the tombs. Ashry Shaker and I went to knock on her door. She opened the door a crack, covered her face with a black cloth, and said, "Mr. Shaker wants to destroy my house and throw me into the street. I have no family or relatives and no one to help me." Without giving me a chance to answer, she continued: "If you destroy my house, you will never find anything at all and I will call on God to close all the roads in front of you."

I finally got a chance to speak and said, "Please listen to me carefully. We will demolish your house because it is built above an important tomb. But we will build a house for you somewhere else. This new house will be built of stone, not of mud brick like this one, and we will even put electricity in it." The old lady did not reply, but I could hear that she was crying. Right after this, Ashry Shaker and I chose her a piece of land and asked Abdel Hamid to build a house there. I arranged everything from the stones to the workmen. I even went with Ashry to see the mayor of

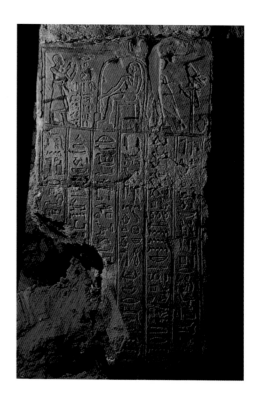

the town so we could arrange for electricity to be run to the house, which was to have two bedrooms and a hallway.

The second thing I had to do was to ask the architect to open up a space in the wall, so that I could enter the burial chamber, and to send a telegram to Saqqara summoning my sarcophagus experts, Ahmed and Talal el-Kriety, who had opened the sarcophagus of Tetiankhkem at Saqqara (see p. 143). I told Mahmoud Afifi and Abdel Hamid that I would enter the tomb the next day.

I went back that evening to the hotel and could see that the archaeologists from the Valley of the Golden Mummies had good news: they had found the opening to a new tomb full of mummies. I didn't speak with anyone at dinner and left early to go to my room, thinking of the morning, when I would finally enter the tomb and see the face that I had dreamed of every day for a year. That night I had another sort of dream. I saw myself inside a dark room. I walked and walked through the room, and found that it had no end. I was very afraid, because the room was full of smoke and I couldn't see anything. I called for help, but my cries went unheard. Suddenly, the face that I had seen inside the burial chamber was on the body of a tall man who was coming toward me. I was ready to fight, because I saw his right hand in front of my face. I screamed

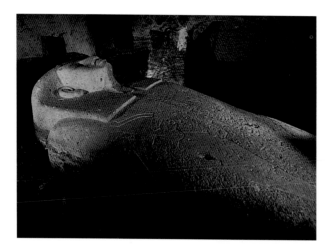

again and tried to run, but there were no doors or windows, and the face of the tall man was always in front of me. I tried again to escape but couldn't move my hands or legs. He got closer and closer to me, and I screamed again. At that moment, I woke up. It was the middle of the night and I was drenched with sweat. I put the light on and drank some water, trying to remember the dream and figure out what it might mean. I always had dreams when I went to bed early. Perhaps I was thinking about entering the room the next day and remembering my childhood fear of the dark.

The next morning I stood at the entrance to the tomb, thinking about the dream I had had the night before and also thinking that this could be the lost tomb of the governor. Abdel Hamid came to tell me that the entrance to the burial chamber was ready for me to enter. That day, a dear friend, Eloui Fareed, was visiting me to investigate the Bahariya Oasis, since his company, Mediterranean Tours, had gotten lots of requests to travel to the site. He took me aside and said, "You should let one of your assistants enter first. Aren't you afraid that the chamber could be full of snakes? Or something worse? I would never do something like this." I told him that I had to

Opposite, bottom: The burial chamber of Djed-Khonsu-efankh with his limestone sarcophagus engraved with images of the god Osiris in the center.

Opposite, top: Djed-Khonsu-efankh praying to the goddess Isis in a relief from his tomb chapel

Right: It is vital to make extensive and thorough records of every relief and painting that we find. Here we see epigrapher Nagwa Hussein copying the scenes in the tomb of the governor.

enter first; this is my habit and my ritual, and it gives me good luck always.

I went down into the first room and saw the good work that Abdel Hamid and his men had done in consolidating the room. The architectural restoration would help us examine the reliefs on the walls. Also, we would be able to open the twelve-ton lid of the sarcophagus safely. Safety is a real issue here, because the tombs are a maze of corridors, sometimes up to twenty-five feet below ground. Cracks were already apparent in the ceiling and on the sides of the walls of the first chamber. We did not want a cave-in, both for the sake of the tombs and for the sake of the archaeologists working in them!

I again examined the entrance to the burial chamber, which we were now able to see because Mahmoud Helmy had installed electricity inside. I decided to use a flashlight to enter rather than running a cable in. The entrance was shaped like the pylon of a temple, which I had never seen in a tomb from this period. The builders of the tomb had hidden the door by covering it completely with painted scenes.

As I entered the burial chamber, I shone my flashlight toward the face of the sarcophagus. I was excited and happy, and my heart was beating rapidly. When I was receiving my award of Explorer-in-Residence from the National Geographic Society in July 2001, a boy had asked me, "What do you feel when you discover something?" I told him then that these were the moments that I lived for. The moment of discovery is the moment that I think about every day of my life, and I cannot explain it in words. I felt as though arrows of fire were attacking me, and as I walked to the south toward the lid, I felt my feet sink down about a foot into dust. A cloud of yellow powder filled the room. My eyes closed, and I could not breathe because of the terrible smell. I thought that I should go back until we could do something about the strange yellow substance that was piled around the sarcophagus and now filled the chamber, but the adventurer in me would not listen, so I continued until I reached the lid. I put my left hand over my mouth and ran toward the

Above: When I first entered the burial chamber of Djed-Khonsu-efankh, I could barely breathe because of the yellow hematite powder that had been piled around the sarcoph-agus. It took six days and sixty plastic bags to remove the powder from the tomb.

Oppposite: We sieved all of the powder we collected very carefully and found a number of interesting artifacts.

sarcophagus, but the smell became so strong that I could hardly stand it. I felt as if I was dying and thought about what Eloui Fareed had just said to me. I closed my nose so that I could not smell the powder and dismissed my imag-inings and the childhood fear of the dark that rose again in me.

I continued south until I was standing beside the sar-cophagus. I could see that the face of the sarcophagus was well modeled. Although a piece of the nose was bro-ken, it still bore the stamp of royalty. On the sides were two life-size figures of Osiris with a long line of hiero-glyphs between them. I read through the lines very quick-ly, and saw right away that one of the signs in the name was "Djed," and knew that this was the lost tomb of the governor. My heart rejoiced, and I ran back outside.

I asked Moustafa Abdel Kader to put a mask on his face and go inside to take a sample of the power to send to the lab right away. I wanted to know why they would leave a powder like this around the sarcophagus. Did it have a religious meaning, or was it perhaps used for paint? I gave orders for the workmen to don masks and put the powder into airtight plastic bags to remove it from the tomb. One workman refused to wear a mask, and it was amazing to watch his face become completely yellow. I told Mahmoud that all of the powder had to be saved and gone through carefully later in case it contained amulets or other artifacts.

It took six days and more than sixty plastic bags before we had finished cleaning out the powder. Mansour had just arrived from the Valley of the Golden Mummies and was anxious to enter the chamber. So when the powder had been cleared, we went in again together and con-firmed that this was indeed the tomb of Djed-Khonsu-efankh, governor of the Bahariya Oasis and high priest of Amon.

Five days later, Moustafa Abdel Kader came back from Cairo with the results of the lab tests. The powder was hematite, which had been brought to Bahariya from a deposit in the mountains about twenty-two miles to the west. In Bahariya today, they use hematite to paint the

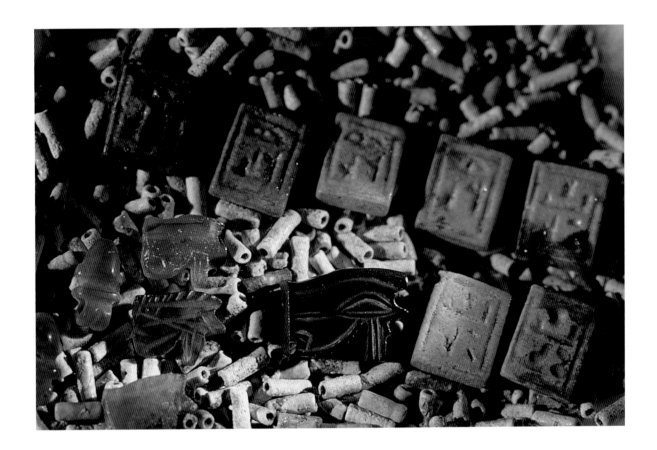

façades of their houses. But I still had no answers as to why the powder had been piled in the tomb.

By this time, the new house was ready for the old woman. I was so happy that I went straight to her house above the tomb and called her. I could only see her black dress, and I said "haga," giving her the respect due to those who have made a pilgrimage to Mecca. "I kept my promise," I told her. "You can go now to your beautiful new house, more wonderful than any other in the village. I will ask our workmen to move your belongings."

She answered me, "Son, thank you. I will tell you that God will now be on your side, and you will make great discoveries under the houses." An hour later, she had been moved and her old house demolished.

After the powder was cleared, I had time to enter and examine the architecture of the tomb of Djed-Khonsu-

efankh more carefully. The entrance leads to a domed room, which in turn leads through a passageway to the south into the burial chamber. The tomb was cut into the sandstone bedrock, and the dome was cased with sandstone blocks; the entire tomb was covered with plaster. Scenes and inscriptions were carved into this plaster and then painted. The superb decorations tell us that Djed-Khonsu-efankh was a powerful and wealthy man because he was able to bring in special sculptors and artists from Memphis or Sais (the capital of Egypt at that time) to design his tomb in the finest style of the period. A shaft at the north end of the tomb was covered with limestone blocks. Since limestone was a precious building material in that region, we knew that this shaft was very important; in fact it led to more tombs, which we investigated in our third season.

I called Ahmed and Talal el-Kreity from Saqqara to come and help us open the sarcophagus of Djed-Khonsu-efankh. We went down into the burial chamber together so they could explain to me how they would do their work.

The scenes in the vaulted chamber include an interesting vignette representing the mummy of the deceased with an alabaster vessel in front of his head. Covering the walls of this room were a number of hieroglyphic excerpts and accompanying pictures from the Book of the Dead, showing various gods and goddesses helping the deceased to travel to the afterlife. On the walls of the burial chamber are the remains of more scenes featuring different gods, all colored yellow.

A hole was dug in the center of the room for the limestone sarcophagus, which measures seven feet long by three and a half feet wide. On top is a huge lid with a human face, representing the governor with beautiful large features. The nose and the chin are broken.

Decorations on the lid and the body show Osiris, king of the netherworld, his sister-wife Isis, and his sister Nephthys, who serve as his chief mourners.

We know that Bahariya had two different names during the pharaonic period. The name Djes-Djes was used during the Middle Kingdom, when wine from the region was labeled by this name. In the New Kingdom, it was referred to as both Djes-Djes and the Northern Oasis, but in the tomb of Djed-Khonsu-efankh, Bahariya is called Wahet-Semankhet, the Deep-rooted Oasis. This is first time we have seen this name. Perhaps it was given to the oasis during this period because of the long and peaceful rule of Djed-Khonsu-efankh.

One evening, as I was smoking my shisha, Abdel Hamid told me that the el-Kriety brothers had arrived. They came to greet me and sat beside me, Ahmed with his thin face and deep eyes and Talal with his round face. Both were dressed in traditional galabia robes and *ema* headscarves. I told them that Abdel Hamid would take them to the tomb the next day so that they could examine the tomb and the sarcophagus lid, which we estimated weighed between twelve and sixteen tons. I told them I expected their usual excellent work. Ahmed said, "Sir, do not worry at all. We will move the lid without difficulty, as our father and grandfather have taught us," and Talal added that they would stay until they had finished the job.

The third night after they had arrived, Abdel Hamid came to tell me that the two brothers had gone back to Saqqara because their cousin had died and that they would be gone for a week. After they left, Sobhy came and said to me that this was the Curse of the Governor, who didn't want his tomb to be disturbed. He told me that many of the people in the town were happy because we wouldn't disturb the tomb. Ever since the excavation of the tomb of Tutankhamun, people have loved to talk about the Curse of the Pharaohs. A series of coincidences—notably the death of Lord Carnarvon, the sponsor of the dig, from an infected mosquito bite, and the supposed ingestion of a pet canary belonging to the excavator, Howard Carter, by a cobra—prompted a journalist to invent the curse. There

is no real evidence for a curse; in fact, tomb robbers have been emerging unscathed for millennia.

I must admit, however, that I have had some experiences that make me wonder, such as my dreams about the children from the Valley of the Golden Mummies and my encounter with the curse at Kom Abu Billo. I have to admit that I never shave on the day when we are to open a new tomb, but this is more practical than superstitious, a protection against the bacteria that are released when we uncover decaying organic material, which poses a risk of infection. But we were opening the sarcophagus of the governor to find out about him and his life, and about Egypt during that time; our intention was not to disturb him.

A week later, Ahmed and Talal el-Kriety came back. Mansour told them what the villagers had been saying and joked that "we archaeologists find these sarcophagi, but you open them, so the curse will never come near us." Talal answered him, "Mr. Mansour, if what you say is true, all of our family should be dead because we open sarcophagi every year! Ask Ganab el Mudier" (that was me: "Director of the Excavation"). His brother said in Arabic, "We leave it to the hand of God."

On the day before the opening, I talked to everyone on the team and was reassured that the tomb had been fully documented and restored. I told Abdel Hamid to clear the pylon-shaped southern entrance to the burial chamber so that we could move the lid. I called Ahmed, Talal, and Mahmoud Afifi to a strategy session for that evening. That afternoon, I went down alone to the burial chamber to look at the huge lid. I could see from the modeling of the face that it was the work of a sculptor from Memphis, 225 miles away from Bahariya. I believe that the governor asked his overseer of works to go north to Tura, where the fine white limestone was quarried, and to take a good piece across the river to the workshops at Memphis, where the sculptors finished it. They then would have taken the sarcophagus up the Nile to el-Bahnasa in Middle Egypt, about 115 miles to the south, and then headed west through the desert for another 110 miles, perhaps using the same route that the donkey caravans

It was an exciting moment when the lid of the alabaster inner sarcophagus was opened and the mummy of Djed-Khonsu-efankh was revealed. The alabaster would have been brought by sledge from Hatnub in Middle Egypt, a distance of about 120 miles, and was probably carved locally.

had used to transport wine. I laughed to myself and thought that we should bring the "pyramidiots" here to show them that the pyramids weren't the only amazing things the Egyptians had done. I thought about the Art Bell radio show on which he had interviewed people who had all sorts of explanations for how the Egyptians had moved stones weighing only three to five tons; this lid weighed more than twelve!

In the evening, I told Tarek to be prepared to take photographs inside the burial chamber. We were also bring-

ing Ken Garrett from the National Geographic. Ken is one of the best photographers of our time and, over the past fifteen years has become a close friend of mine. I like him to be around my discoveries because of his honest, smiling face; I always feel that he gives me luck.

The next morning, everyone was quiet at breakfast and I sat deep in thought, pondering the sarcophagus lid that we would move that day. I was so absorbed that I did not even say good morning to anyone or eat any breakfast. Everyone else ate in complete silence. I asked Ahmed and Talal to come in my car, and I also included Tarek because he is my right hand and I trust him so much. Halfway to the site, I discovered that I had forgotten my lucky hat. This hat is like my friend, and I take it with me everywhere. I told el-Masry, the driver, to turn back to the hotel. The funny thing was that no one asked me why. As I brought the hat to the car, I saw Tarek smiling.

We finally arrived at the site, and I chose Mahmoud, Tarek, Ken, and Abdel Hamid to be with me in the burial chamber, plus the five workmen that Talal and Ahmed needed. Mohammed el-Tayieb asked to come in also, and I agreed. When everyone got inside, I saw that we were too crowded, and asked two of the workmen to wait outside until we needed them.

The five hours that we spent inside the chamber cannot be described. It was beyond imagination, a true adventure in archaeology. They were among the best five hours of my life. It was very hot and everyone was sweating. Ahmed and Talal put wooden beams under the lid and began to push it to the south. I watched and wrote in my notebook about what was happening and my impressions of everyone in the chamber. Reis Talal called everyone to push. The workers began to chant, and I began to chant with them, "Hela hob, hela hob, hela hob," (an Arabic phrase to help with the rhythm). I went over to help push, and we all pushed and chanted until the lid had moved several inches to the south side. I thought at that moment about how the sarcophagus had lain undisturbed inside the chamber for twenty-five hundred years.

I asked Abdel Hamid to pass me the flashlight because I wanted to examine the lid and see whether or not it was intact. I bent down and felt the sweat trickling into my eyes and the dust drifting into my ears, but I did not care. I had to stand very still because the remains of the bad-smelling yellow powder still surrounded the sarcophagus. I continued to peer with my flashlight and Mahmoud asked me "What do you see?"

I replied with excitement, "It seems that the sarcophagus is intact and has never been opened before!" A moment later, however, I added, "But wait." I saw everyone's faces become like stone. "There is a small hole here, not made recently. It seems to me that it was opened in the Roman Period. But don't worry, the discovery is still exciting, and surely the ancient robbers won't have been able to steal everything. I can smell gold in the room, and I always say that my nose can smell what comes from the past!"

Everyone helped put the wooden beams back in place. Some pushed and some pulled the rope tied to the edges, and so we began again, with everyone invoking the names of God and the prophet Mohammed. I heard again the words "Hela hob . . . hela hob" like thunder in my ears, which were full of dust and yellow powder. Finally the sarcophagus lid was moved about two feet to the south. We saw the inner sarcophagus inside, which on closer examination appeared to be made of spotted alabaster.

Everyone screamed with joy and kissed one another. I raised my hand up, and Tarek beside me did the same. Moustafa Abdel Kader came with his people right away and began to clean the alabaster sarcophagus. We found that an attempt had been made by the ancient artist to carve a face here as well. However, the work was quite primitive, which makes me think that it had been carved locally. The alabaster would have been brought by sledge from Hatnub in Middle Egypt to Bahariya, a distance of about 120 miles.

After an hour for rest and photographs, we decided to move the inner sarcophagus to the north end of the burial chamber. It weighed about five tons and took us about an hour to move and open. Inside were the remains of a third coffin made of wood, and inside that was the mummy of the governor himself. Both the wooden coffin and the mummy had deteriorated badly because of the water that had leaked from the houses above. The irony of this is that the coffin and mummy had probably survived for twenty-four hundred years and then were destroyed in less than a century.

Mahmoud and I examined the remains and sieved every piece of dirt. We were able to collect a total of

twenty-two amulets, including eight of gold and others of faience and amethyst. They were in the form of gods and goddesses, a winged cobra, a winged *ba* (an aspect of the soul), an eye of Horus, and three hearts. We also found a large number of shawabti statuettes. We also found two canopic jars, a large quantity of charcoal left behind by the Roman thieves, and an amphora they had used to raise the heavy lid.

Above: When we explored the sarcophagus of Djed-Khonsu-efankh, we found many interesting artifacts, including a number made of gold.

Opposite: We excavated four more tombs and shafts in the area of Sheikh Soby. Here I am investigating the ruins of one of the inscribed sarcophagi found in these tombs.

OTHER TOMBS AT SHEIKH SOBY

During the same season, we excavated four more tombs and shafts in this area. The first is located in the northeast of the site, and we got to it just in time; we caught robbers from Bahariya in the act of stealing artifacts from the first chamber. Thanks to the vigilance of Ashry Shaker, whose network of informants had tipped him off, these robbers were caught and turned over to the police. After that incident, we set more guards and soldiers to protect the site day and night. I used to go out in the evening to inspect the site and make sure that everything was under control.

Tomb 1 contained three burial chambers but was uninscribed. The southern burial chamber of this tomb was intact, and I believe it belongs to one of the other members of Djed-Khonsu-efankh's family. There were two sarcophagi made of limestone from Tura in this burial chamber, which indicates that the owner was very wealthy. The first sarcophagus held a beautiful mummy in excellent condition inside. It was wrapped in the style of the 26th Dynasty. Beside the sarcophagus, we found shawabtis in typical 26th Dynasty style, and also some amulets. This is the oldest intact mummy found at Bahariya, about eight hundred years older than the mummies from the Valley of the Golden Mummies.

The second sarcophagus had been opened and the mummy "investigated" by one of the untrained archaeologists from Bahariya. Not knowing any better, he had simply dug around in the wrappings to find the amulets, destroying the mummy in the process. Before my arrival at Bahariya, no one had thought to teach the local archaeologists excavation techniques, and this was the terrible result. I gathered all of the Bahariya archaeologists and explained excavation methods to them, emphasizing that above all, they should never open a mummy. It should be

left as it is; to take what is inside is a crime and makes the archaeologist no better than a tomb robber. On the positive side, this archaeologist had not been trying to steal anything, and we were able to record the amulets and put them into storage in the Inspectorate.

The third and fourth chambers had also been used for burials, but there was much evidence of Roman intrusions. I was able to conclude that this tomb had been built in the 26th Dynasty and reused during Roman times. I also saw indications that the walls were originally cased with mortar and painted with scenes that are now gone.

Tomb 2 is not connected with the maze corridor area that contains the tombs of the family of the governor. It appears to have been built for a number of priests of Isis,

Osiris, and Thoth from the 26th Dynasty; it too was reused in the Roman Period. In the southernmost of the three burial chambers, we found five limestone sarcophagi with the names and titles of the deceased written in red ink on the lids. Three of the sarcophagi, one of which is for a child, were robbed in antiquity; we have not yet opened the other two. In the main chamber was the sarcophagus of a priest that had been robbed in the Roman Period, but we found several artifacts inside: a winged scarab made of faience, two more amulets of children of Horus, and another amulet of the god Horakhty.

Tomb 3 is a small rock-cut tomb, consisting of a shaft and two burial chambers located northeast of Tomb 1. The first burial chamber was reused in the Roman Period and also entered by the robbers who are now in prison. There were two limestone sarcophagi in this room, one of which is still unopened. The eastern room had been entered by untrained archaeologists from Bahariya, who found many amulets.

Tomb 4 consists of a shaft and four burial chambers, each one containing a limestone sarcophagus. Three of these contained mummies in good condition, all wrapped in linen; the fourth was empty.

During the third season, Mansour Boriak and Mahmoud Afifi worked at Sheikh Soby in rotation, and Mohammed el-Tayieb worked there all the time. We began the season by doing more clearing, consolidation, and restoration of the interior of the tomb of the governor. Mansour did the excavation himself very carefully. We hoped that the Roman thieves might have missed some artifacts in the dark, and that turned out to be the case. In the narrow space between the two coffins we found a large square gold amulet decorated with the image of the falcon-headed Qebehsenuef, one of the four children of Horus. We also found a 26th Dynasty shawabti, about an inch high, eight square amulets of faience bearing the name of Ped-Isis, the father of the Djed-Khonsu-efankh, and two uninscribed scarabs, one of obsidian and the other of hematite. These artifacts give us some idea of how rich the tomb had been.

THE GOLDEN TOMB

We noticed during this season that there was a broken part on the top of the shaft leading to the tomb of the governor. When we investigated, we found a room full of sand and to the north of this the entrance to another room. The entrance to the second room was closed with sandstone blocks. I began to excavate it with a lamp in my left hand and an axe in my right. After advancing about a foot, I glimpsed an alabaster head, so I pushed the lamp forward with my left hand to see better. The wire to the lamp snapped, and I got an electric shock that threw me about three feet to the east and knocked me unconscious. After a few minutes, I opened my eyes and saw all of my assistants looking down at me. Mahmoud said, "What happened? Are you all right, doctor?" I jumped up and said that I was okay. I asked them if they realized that if I had died, the main headline in all the newspapers would be "The Curse of the Pharaohs!" I could not believe that I was safe and that nothing had happened to me, although I could feel the electricity still shaking my body for the next few hours.

The excavation continued for a week, and after we removed the sand from the room, we found the sarcophagus and the treasures of the Lady Naesa II, wife of Djed-Khonsu-efankh. The tomb had been disturbed in Roman times but had been hard to access, so the thieves were not able to steal everything. Naesa's sarcophagus, like that of her husband, was surrounded with hematite powder, which blocked my ears almost completely. Even though it was February, it was very hot, and I got an ear infection, although I did not realize it at the time. I had to leave the site to go to my son Karim's graduation from the American University in Cairo (with a B.A. in economics; he is not planning to follow in my footsteps!). That evening, my friend Mark Linz gave a party so that some of the authors of the AUC Press could meet the trustees of the university. Several of us were invited to give a five-minute talk. While Mark was making his introductions, I suddenly felt that the ceiling was down and the floor was up. I was sitting next to Salima Ikram, professor of Egyptology at the

Left: My team cleaning the shaft leading to the tomb of the governor. A broken part in the top of this shaft led us to the Golden Tomb, the tomb of Djed-Khonsu-efankh's wife, Naesa II.

Below: When we investigated the break in the shaft, we found a room full of sand, and to the north, the entrance to a second room was closed with sandstone blocks. I began to excavate this entrance with a lamp in my left hand and an axe in my right. Here you can see me peering into the burial chamber, just before the wire to the lamp snapped and I was given an electric shock.

university, and said, "Salima, hold my hand, I feel dizzy." She was shocked and tried to help me, but she couldn't hold me and I fell down. Everyone gathered around, and I could hear everyone talking, upset. Mark and his assistant Nabila Akel went to call an ambulance, and I was afraid that I would die! But I recovered a bit and sat back on my chair.

The ambulance came, and Mark, Salima, Nabila, and a doctor went with me to the emergency room. That night was one of the most difficult nights of my life. They did all sorts of tests and determined that it was not a heart attack, but they couldn't figure out what was the matter. The next day I left the hospital and went home, but I continued to feel dizzy. Finally a doctor friend of mine suggested that it might be my middle ear, so I was put on antibiotics. A week later I was completely better, but it was all over the Internet that I had a heart attack; I had to write on my Web site that I was okay. Is there really a curse? I cannot answer this question!

We called the tomb of Naesa II the Golden Tomb for all of the treasures it contained. It consists of an entrance from the north; a burial chamber, which contained an anthropoid sarcophagus; and an inner chamber for the funerary equipment. The walls had been covered with plaster and painted with scenes, but the weak sandstone had let most of this fall. In the middle of the burial chamber, the ancient builders had dug a pit for the sarcophagus. The lid lay to the west and had been left unfinished except for the details of the face. The style is similar to the inner alabaster coffin in the governor's tomb and clearly came from the workshop of the untrained artisans at Bahariya. Around the sarcophagus, we found 239 shawabtis, 20 of them broken but the other 219 in good condition. They were inscribed with the name of the tomb owner, Naesa born of Itieb. The mummy inside the sarcophagus was about four and a half feet long and in bad shape, but we were able to ascertain that Naesa

Here I am with my assistant Mahmoud Afifi in the vaulted sandstone chapel of Naesa II.

Right: We found a number of beautiful golden artifacts in the burial chamber of Naesa II: golden nail stalls, a heart amulet in the shape of one of the names of King Apries, a djed-pillar amulet, bracelets, and other amulets.

Below: The anthropoid limestone sarcophagus of Naesa II in her burial chamber at Sheikh Soby

had lived into old age. The Roman robbers had taken off the linen that covered the head and the chest to search for jewelry. They did this roughly, breaking the skull of the mummy in the process.

When we cleaned the mummy and looked inside the sarcophagus, we found that the thieves had missed a great deal. We found 103 pieces of gold, 33 amulets of different sizes and shapes, one of precious stone, one copper eye with obsidian for the pupil and alabaster for the white. It seems that this eye was one of a pair that graced the wooden coffin, destroyed in the Roman Period, that had contained the mummy. Under the skull was a hematite amulet in the shape of a headrest, the base covered with layers of gold. Inside the mouth were a beautiful tongue scarab of light brown hematite and a false tongue of pure gold. In the chest area were a small scarab of onyx with beautiful detailing and a heart scarab of amethyst, about eighty-four golden beads, and an amulet representing the heart with a sun disk on top. This last is a wonderful artifact, one of the best we have found. This is first time I have seen such an amulet, and I believe that it represents

Mansour led us to the tomb of Ped-Isis, the father of Djed-Khonsu-efankh, by pointing out a door on the east side of the vault in front of the burial chamber of the governor.

a graphical image of the royal name Wah-ib-Re, one of the names of King Apries.

The inner chamber of the tomb lies to the north of the burial chamber. It has a vaulted ceiling cased with blocks of sandstone covered with mortar, and inside we found the head of an alabaster canopic jar with the face of Imsety, one of the children of Horus. I believe that the canopic jars would originally have been with the sarcophagus and that this piece was dropped here by the robbers.

THE TOMB OF THE FATHER

It was Mansour who led us to the tomb of Ped-Isis, father of Djed-Khonsu-efankh. I had ordered him to supervise the clearing of the area northeast of Djed-Khonsu-efankh's tomb. I told him to be careful, since the sandstone was in terrible shape from the water that had leaked down from the houses above, but I never thought that another tomb could be here. Mansour took my hand and pointed out two important things to me—that there was a door on the east side of the vault that fronts the burial chamber of the governor, in spite of the fact that the entrance is to the north of the vaulted room, and that in front of this entrance was a large limestone sarcophagus in typical 26th Dynasty style. I told Mansour to bring the workmen in and excavate the area, and within a few days we had found the tomb of the father. This is one of the oldest tombs here. It is built in the same style as the tomb of Naesa, with a burial chamber containing an anthropoid sarcophagus and an inner chamber. The entrance to the tomb was destroyed because it was used as a sewer by one of the illegal houses. We even found sewage inside the sarcophagus. The burial chamber is rectangular, cut into the bedrock and cased with blocks of sandstone. The scenes that once decorated the walls have been destroyed by the water from the houses above; we found only remains on the ground, but these give us a glimpse into how amazing the original scenes would have been.

Fakhry believed that Ped-Isis was governor of Bahariya after his father, Ped-Amun. The anthropoid sarcophagus found in this tomb shows the deceased with a priestly beard, which tells us that he was also a high priest of Amun-Re. This sarcophagus was made of local sandstone, and measures seven feet and three inches long. The lid of the sarcophagus had been broken into three pieces, and the mummy had deteriorated almost completely.

When we cleaned the sarcophagus, we found six wadjet eyes of different sizes, two of turquoise and three of red carnelian; an amethyst scarab; four turquoise djed-pillar amulets; and five more carnelian amulets in different shapes. The biggest surprise was that we found about thirty shawabtis to the right of the sarcophagus; each is about an inch high and is inscribed: "The Osiris, Ped-Isis, born of Amun-Itieb." This last may be a mistake; instead of Amon-Itieb, it should be Ped-Amon.

I believe that the large limestone sarcophagus located to the immediate south of Ped-Isis's tomb was for his wife Naesa. If this is the case, we have now discovered eight members of the family, and hope to find the other eight in the coming season. We have not finished excavating the south side of this chamber because the rock is very weak and needs more conservation. I expect that we will find more shawabtis there next season.

Below: We found many shawabtis in the tomb of Ped Isis inscribed with "The Osiris, Ped-Isis, born of Amun-Iteib."

Opposite: When we cleaned the sarcophagus of Ped-Isis, we found a number of beads and amulets, including an amethyst scarab, a number of wadjet eyes and djed pillars, and various others.

*As I was finishing this manuscript,
we found the edge of a limestone
lintel belonging to the "King's
Acquaintance of the Palace,
Overseer of the House,
Nesy-weret."*

Chapter V. Saving our Heritage

The past thirty-three years have been enormously exciting and rewarding for me, and I look forward to whatever the future holds. My work at Giza, Saqqara, and Bahariya has yielded much important material that will help us reconstruct the past, and my focus on site management will help us to protect the monuments for the future from the many dangers that threaten them.

The Future of Giza

Giza is one of the most important sites in the world; we have accomplished a great deal, but much remains for us to do. We recently completed the construction of a new entrance to the Giza Plateau from the Faiyum Road, about four miles southwest of the pyramids. This entrance has control gates and leads directly to a picnic area located south of the third pyramid. Many visitors come to Giza, especially during the holiday season, just to picnic in the shade of the ancient monuments, and now they will be able to enjoy a spectacular view without overrunning the site. Eventually, the Pyramid Road entrance will be used only for individuals, and all the tourist buses will be rerouted to the new Faiyum Road entrance.

Plans are also under way for a new ring road leading to the recreational area and the new entrance. I have proposed that this should be a one-way road, so that people can look at the pyramids without running head on into one another. I want to be very certain that we have enough time to excavate the entire site of this road properly before it is built. I am also concerned, because a sixty-foot swath of village houses will have to be demolished on the east side of the plateau, and I am afraid that this part of the plan will meet with such resistance that the project will have to be canceled.

Educational programs for tourists and residents will be offered at a new cultural center, which will be located in the desert south of the third pyramid, near the new Faiyum Road entrance. This Desert Center will include bookstores, souvenir shops, cafés, and various other tourist facilities. I am very excited about a new educational museum that the Ministry of Culture is planning to build in the shadow of the Giza pyramids, the Grand Egyptian Museum. This will be the largest antiquities museum in the world. Wonderful as it is, the Cairo Museum

is really a huge treasure warehouse. The world has changed since it was founded, and we must educate our children, not just show them beautiful objects. We need to build model tombs for them to visit and explore; we need classrooms, cafeterias, and places for them to sit and rest when they are tired. We are also talking to the National Geographic Society about building an IMAX theater near the new museum, which will help to introduce the world, especially Egyptians themselves, to the ancient heritage of this area.

As soon as possible, all modern structures on the plateau, including paved roads, will be demolished, and gas-powered cars will be banned. I am certain we will make some remarkable discoveries when we execute this part of the plan. Electric vehicles, all in yellow to blend with the desert sand, will be available for use by people with limited mobility and for Antiquities Department staff who have to move around the plateau quickly. A new conservation laboratory and Antiquities Department offices will be built at the northwest corner of the plateau.

An important issue for me has always been the aesthetic impact of the plateau. The site has traditionally been crammed with visitors, most of whom don't seem to

have been taught to take away their trash, and by camel and horse drivers and hawkers trying to sell souvenirs. All of this is very colorful, but it is also very distracting for people who want to experience awe in the presence of these great monuments. I have taken several steps to improve this situation. First, I hired a private company to clean the site regularly. (In 1988, we won a prize from the British Guild of Travel Writers for this.) Another part of the plan is the construction of a new wall around the plateau. This wall will provide protection for the site and will keep the camel and horse drivers from entering. The camels and horses will be transferred to new stables south of the plateau, near the new Desert Center, and they will be prohibited within the Giza site. The pyramids will only serve as a distant backdrop for visitors who wish to ride, and

Opposite: An overview of the Giza Plateau before we instituted the site-management plan.

Above: The new entrance to the Giza Plateau from the Faiyum Road.

Left: We have made a new picnic area south of the pyramids so that people can come on feast days and celebrate in the shadow of these great monuments without overrunning the actual site.

tourists will be able to enjoy the site without harassment. The camel and horse drivers will follow a rotation system, and prices will be fixed. The most powerful of the drivers are very upset about this, because they are now able to dominate the trade, but the new system will be much fairer, and I believe there will be more business for everyone. Near the stable will be a market area for souvenir vendors and a parking lot for electrical cars.

In 1990, as a result of a successful collaboration with the archaeologists in charge of the site-management plan, an Egyptian architect named Moustafa Simbol designed and built a wall to separate the village of Nazlet es-Samman from the Great Sphinx. The wall is high enough to block the view of the modern houses that are not in keeping with the dignity of the ancient site and includes tourist facilities such as toilets, a first-aid post, and offices for the tourist police and Antiquities officials. At the same time, we have prohibited cars from parking in front of the Sphinx and established a new parking lot farther away from the site. The Civil Airline Department has also agreed to ban all planes from flying over the pyramids.

The cleaning and restoration of the nobles' tombs surrounding the pyramids will continue. Most of these have already been excavated by various scholars, but many areas between the tombs have not been investigated, and careful archaeological research must still be done. We need at least ten to fifteen years of excavation and conservation in order to do this work properly, and we look forward to having our fully equipped conservation lab operated by well-trained personnel within the next few years. As the final phase nears completion, we must ensure the documentation of all tomb decoration and artifacts within a computer database. A program to restore the exteriors of the three great pyramids of Giza will require a photogrammetric map and other documentation for each side of each pyramid, and appropriate tools and equipment.

We will continue our excavations of the tombs of the pyramid builders and the royal installation south of the Wall of the Crow. We hope we will be able to catch more glimpses of the pyramid city and workmen's settlement that lies beneath the village of Nazlet es-Samman before it disappears forever. For the first time, we are in a position to see in this exceptionally rich archaeological site the entire horizon of an Old Kingdom royal city.

We cannot have stones falling from the pyramids, or tombs that are falling apart. We cannot have camel drivers and souvenir sellers at the pyramids or they become a mess. There are many people trying to take advantage of the site, and there are hundreds of difficulties to face. Giza is one of the greatest tourist attractions in the world, and we must continue to find ways to balance the needs of the tourists today with our obligation to preserve this heritage for future generations.

The Future of Saqqara

Saqqara is an important site, and I look forward to putting a new site-management plan into effect. We are continuing our excavations in the Teti pyramid cemetery. There may be more queens' pyramids here, and perhaps more tombs of royal relatives; we also hope to find Teti's causeway and valley temple. We may even find the pyramid of the usurper Userkare and thus bring the history of the early 6th Dynasty into better focus.

I also plan to re-excavate the elite tombs of Dynasty 1 that lie at the eastern edge of the plateau, for these will help clarify the early history of the Egyptian state. These were uncovered in the last century by Walter Emery, a scholar who dedicated his life to his work at Saqqara. He hoped to discover the tomb of Imhotep, architect of the Step Pyramid, but he died without discovering it and asked to be buried in Egypt in the hope that his soul would one day hear about its discovery. Our excavations in the area of the Early Dynastic tombs should reveal more information about the officials and courtiers who helped to rule Egypt during Dynasty 1, about 3000 B.C. (The kings of this period were buried at Abydos.) The conservation and the restoration of the tombs of Dynasty 1 will be one of our most important projects.

We will also continue to excavate in the area north of the Step Pyramid, where we found the tomb of the physician Qar, so that I can clarify the relationship of the newly discovered stone-rubble wall and the pyramid complex of King Sekhemkhet of Dynasty 3. It is also very important to continue to excavate in this area so that tomb robbers will be forced to stay away.

In spite of the fact that Saqqara is one of the most important sites of the Old Kingdom, it has not been well managed and is in grave danger. This is in many ways still a virgin site; anywhere you dig, you will find a tomb. You do not need to be a trained archaeologist to make a discovery here—you almost cannot avoid it. Until recently, there was no site-management plan; everything was very haphazard. Currently, more than twenty foreign and Egyptian expeditions are working at Saqqara; some do restoration, others do not. The new site-management plan includes an evaluation of the most important expeditions and a concentration on conservation and documentation rather than excavation.

We have many problems at Saqqara. Since 1988 large cracks have developed on the ceiling of the Serapeum (the vaults where the Apis bulls were buried); the north entrance of the Step Pyramid of Djoser is in terrible shape; the southern tomb of Djoser, where many tiles have fallen, is at risk; and the buried pyramid of Sekhemkhet has a crack in the ceiling of its burial chamber. None of our experts has been able to explain these problems; we need outside help to both understand and correct them.

Although in many ways Saqqara is a forgotten site, and many visitors to Egypt do not even know that it exists, the regularly visited monuments here are in grave danger. Guides come with groups of thirty tourists and stand inside the most famous tombs for half an hour to explain the layout and point out the most important scenes—and this is terrible for the reliefs. The humidity inside the pyramid of Unas, whose walls are covered with carved and painted Pyramid Texts, has increased to more than 80 percent, and the burial chamber has been closed since 1993. In order to combat this problem, we are making

large signs to put outside the principal monuments, showing the plans and outlining the key scenes. This way the guides can do their explanations outside, and the tourists can move through the actual tomb quickly. This important project should be finished by the time this book goes to press.

The Future of Bahariya

Much of our work at Bahariya during our third and fourth seasons was focused on preservation and conservation. We have treated all of the mummies in situ to protect them from deterioration and infestation by insects, and we have carefully recorded all the artifacts that we have found at both sites. We have also made ceilings and doors for the four tombs excavated in the Valley of the Golden Mummies during the 1999 season and done some architectural restoration in the temples at Ain el-Muftella and at the temple of Alexander the Great.

In 2001, during the third season, we opened several new tombs for the public. This is a big job, which requires landscaping on the outside and the installation of electricity and ventilation inside. Two of the newly opened tombs belonged to wealthy 26th Dynasty wine merchants, Djed-Amun-efankh and his son Bannantiu. In the 1930s, when Fakhry entered and described these tombs, the scenes were preserved. Many of them have now been lost to weathering and erosion, but the colors are still vivid. The third tomb we prepared for visitors was the New Kingdom tomb of Amenhotep Huy at Garet el-Helwa, south of el-Bawiti. All three of these tombs are described in more detail in the *Valley of the Golden Mummies*.

My long-term plan is to have a major site museum at Bahariya, the first of its kind built for a major discovery such as the Valley of the Golden Mummies. My fear is that tourists from all over the world will come to Bahariya wanting to visit the tombs themselves: this would be an archaeological disaster, because the mummies will be rapidly destroyed by the rise in humidity caused by their breathing, not to mention the damage resulting from their touch. I also feel that the mummies deserve peace. The ancients buried their dead for spiritual reasons, and to disturb them to this extent is to go against their values and wishes. That is why I agreed to move the six mummies to the Inspectorate, to sacrifice them for the sake of the others. Now anyone who comes to Bahariya can go to the Inspectorate and buy a ticket for thirty Egyptian pounds ($6), which will allow them to see the mummies and several artifacts, to visit the 26th Dynasty tombs of Djed-Amun-efankh and Bannantiu, the New Kingdom tomb of Amenhotep Huy, the 26th Dynasty temples at Ain el-Muftella, and the temple of Alexander the Great.

In our fourth season at the Bahariya Oasis, we decided not to do more excavations in the Valley of the Golden Mummies. My best estimate is that the valley holds about ten thousand mummies, but I feel that we should let them rest undisturbed. The 234 mummies we have uncovered have given us an enormous amount of information to sift through and produced more gold than was found in King Tut's tomb. Rather than excavating further, we need to continue our analysis of what we have found. We have greatly increased our knowledge of the daily lives and religion of these people, and additional study will tell us even more.

About ten thousand tourists travel to Bahariya each year, and the region is finally entering the twenty-first century. There are hotels, cafés, markets, and cars, and it is now possible for the first time to dial directly from Bahariya to anywhere in the world. My friend Sheikh Rashed, who had a café near the gas station on the main road of el-Bawiti—the first one you see upon entering the town—recently told me that he was opening an Internet café, so that everyone can check their e-mail from Bahariya. I never thought anything like this could happen in an oasis deep in the western desert of Egypt!

The Future of Egyptian Archaeology

Many spectacular finds still await us buried under the soft sands, green fields, and modern buildings of today's Egypt. I believe that what has been discovered to date represents only about 30 percent of what remains and that 70 percent is still hidden. But many dangers threaten the ancient monuments, both those that have been excavated and those that still remain to be uncovered. Tourism, urban development without proper precautions, the rising water table, lack of education, improper or inadequate excavation or restoration: these are some of the problems that face us. To deal with them, we must have well-developed site-management plans at all major sites, and we must work to find a balance between excavation on the one hand and publication, restoration, and conservation on the other.

TOURISM

Mass tourism is one of the greatest threats to the monuments. More than three thousand tourists each day visit the tomb of Tutankhamun, and this number increases to five thousand during the peak tourist season. If the tomb continues to be visited at this rate, it will be destroyed completely. The problem in the Valley of the Kings is made more acute by the fact that tourists are visiting the same tombs that they have been visiting for the past ninety years. We must keep in mind that there are sixty-two tombs in the Valley of the Kings, but tourists concentrate on visiting only the most famous of these. There has been such deterioration in the tomb of Seti I—dangerous cracks have appeared in its interior—that it has had to be closed. Damage is so acute in the tomb of Ramesses III that the inscriptions in the inner half are now gone.

The damage caused by tourism is well documented in the sites that are visited by large groups. For example, an average of two to three thousand visitors visit the temple of Abu Simbel every day, all at the same time. It is impossible to control such numbers of people. Some touch or rub against the walls; others take flash photographs; and all of them exhale carbon dioxide, raising the humidity in the tombs.

Vehicular traffic is one of the most obvious problems at many antiquities sites, because visitors like to park their cars directly in front of the monuments. Tourist buses, trucks, taxis, and private cars are all allowed to enter and drive near the monuments. As they meander around the sites, their exhaust increases the air pollution in the area and the vibrations they create contribute to the deterioration of the tomb paintings. In addition, the presence of vehicular traffic increases solid waste pollution around the sites, while the multicolored buses parked in front of the temples and pyramids create visual pollution unworthy of the noble monuments.

URBAN DEVELOPMENT

The problem of urbanization is evident in many places. For example, the temple of Esna is completely surrounded by the city of Esna. The temple is located on low ground, and the city is on the higher ground around it. None of the modern houses is connected to a sewage system, so the waste leaks down from the houses into the temple, and salt has started to appear on the lower part of the temple walls. The same process is occurring in Edfu, where cracks have begun to appear in the walls of the temple. In 1988 this resulted in a huge block falling down from the top of the first pylon.

This urban encroachment also threatens archaeological sites in Qurna (the Valley of the Kings), Akhmim, el-Ashmunein, Heliopolis, and Giza. Many new houses have been built recently near the tombs of nobles and around the tombs of Dynasties 4 and 5 at el-Tarif (near the Valley of the Kings), but the villagers of Qurna refused to move to the new state-of-the-art village built by renowned architect Hassan Fathy. A temple of Ramesses II has been found inside the city of Akhmim, and to date the villagers have prevented excavation of this monument. The village of el-Ashmunein is also growing rapidly; as I described in the introduction, in 1968–69, it was discovered that people were excavating in the courtyards of their houses and

selling the artifacts on the black market. The village of Nazlet es-Samman, which houses approximately two hundred thousand people, is located just at the foot of the Giza pyramids. The village expanded in 1984 following a decree from the Antiquities Department granting villagers permission to build sporting clubs on Antiquities land and to raise the height of houses to three stories. All of this has impacted negatively on the pyramids.

Thousands of illegal houses and farms have been built on Antiquities land. The present law is very weak and does not provide for the removal of squatters. The people who live in these villages smuggle artifacts and sell them on the black market; many have been caught stealing antiquities. In addition to the theft of artifacts, the villages pose more general dangers to the tombs by producing acid pollution, water pollution, and fire and smoke from cooking. Education is badly needed in schools, for the parents as well as for the children. The Egyptian people should be encouraged to develop a feeling of responsibility for their archaeological, architectural, and artistic heritage, and archaeologists, especially at the highest levels, can also help by participating in educational programs. Television can be a powerful tool for education, but we should also explore ways of using sites or monuments to stimulate local involvement in a way that benefits residents as well as tourists and Egyptologists.

Another effect of urbanization is erosion from rising water caused by the lack of proper sewage systems or by leaking systems, as in Islamic Cairo, Heliopolis, Luxor, and other cities where ground water can be seen in the temples. This water is full of salt, which, when it comes into contact with limestone monuments, produces a chemical reaction that reduces the rock to powder. Some believe that the rise of the water table is a result of the High Dam at Aswan. It has been proven that this is not the case, although the fact that the Nile no longer floods does keep the excess salts in the soils from being washed away.

The problem of salt crystallization is observed in monuments all over Upper Egypt. The wall of the Luxor Temple is a good example of this problem: the scenes on the walls behind the columns in the peristyle court depict-ing the festival of Opet show changes every year. The Sphinx is another good example of this problem and how it can be solved. For many years, the level of the water table under the Sphinx was only six feet below ground because of water leakage from the village nearby. After the completion of the new sewage system in Nazlet es-Samman in 1993, the water level fell to twenty-one feet below the Sphinx.

In addition to salt crystallization, climatic elements that cause damage to monuments and ruins include biological degradation, rock swelling, rains, flash floods, wind erosion, and temperature variation. The ancient Egyptians them-selves recognized this problem: Tuthmosis IV built large mud-brick walls around the Sphinx to protect the statue from the wind and blowing sand. Temperature variation is especially severe in Upper Egypt: in the area of Abu Simbel, the temperature can change from 59° to 106° F. (15° to 41° C.) during an eight-hour period. There is no doubt that this drastic change can affect the stone surface.

Inadequate or Improper Archaeology

Improper restoration is another great danger to the long-term preservation of the pharaonic monuments. The Great Sphinx is a good example. Large stones were added as a casing to the Sphinx between 1982 and 1987 (while I was at Penn), and cement was used to hold the casing in place. In order to add the casing, many of the ancient stones that were added to the Sphinx in the pharaonic and Roman Periods were removed. The result of this improper restoration can be seen in the damage done by the workers to the original claws of the Sphinx.

Poorly designed restoration can also be seen in the temples of Edfu, Esna, Luxor, and Karnak. This type of short-term restoration has been going on since the early twentieth century. We must evaluate the long-term effect of any restoration we do carefully and make sure that it will protect rather than harm the monument. We also need to make sure that the restoration is in keeping with the fact that the monuments are ruins and should look ancient.

There are more than 250 foreign and Egyptian expedi-tions working in Egypt today, and there are no consistent rules that they have to follow in order to be granted a con-cession. In addition, permission is sometimes given to nonarchaeologists to work in Egypt. Even though they may love Egypt and Egyptology, these people have not gone through the rigorous training that Egyptologists must complete before they can excavate. They do not know enough about the problems they may face and the techniques that they need to follow to do an adequate and professional job. They are amateurs who should not be allowed to put our ancient heritage at risk.

A truly horrifying example of this problem occurred in 1986, while I was still at Penn. The Antiquities Department had given permission to two French amateurs to work with radar inside the Great Pyramid. The Frenchmen claimed that there was a room off the horizontal passage, and without asking permission, they drilled two holes inside the pyramid! In another example, a French archi-tect who thought that Khufu was buried under the pave-ment in front of the first chamber inside the Great Pyramid was allowed to work inside the pyramid. I tried to stop this man him from making a hole, but the permis-sion had come from the Permanent Committee, based on the power of the chairman, so I could do nothing. I believe that we should not permit anyone to work in Egypt with-out being associated with a reputable institution. Amateurs like these do not care about the monuments; I even read in a French paper a headline bragging about the holes the men had made in the pyramid.

Theft

History is disappearing every day at the hands of tomb robbers, who dig in the dead of the night to steal the treasures of the ancient Egyptians. This is one of the biggest problems that Egyptologists face today. We are in a race with the tomb robbers to uncover history: if we find it first, we can add it to our store of knowledge for everyone to share, but if they find it first, it will disappear forever. Each time we discover an artifact we have another piece of the puzzle, but artifacts that are stolen cannot be used by scholars or enjoyed by everyone.

Antiquities theft has been rampant since the time of the pharaohs. The ancient Egyptians tried hard to protect their mummies and treasures inside their burial chambers in various ways, but their efforts almost always failed. We have only found a couple of intact king's tombs: the tomb of King Tutankhamun and the tombs of the 22nd Dynasty at Tanis in the Delta. Many of the royal tombs were robbed almost as soon as they were sealed; thieves even made a partially successful attempt on the tomb of Tutankhamun, but they were caught almost immediately, and the tomb was resealed right away.

For thousands of years, thieves would hide among the brooding desert hills that hid the lavish tombs full of gold and silver, using the cover of the night to plunder the royal burials. They were always afraid of being caught by the necropolis police, who did not hesitate to use torture to extract their confessions, but the treasures of gold, jewels, and precious oils were too tempting to resist. We have some fascinating records of tomb robberies from ancient times. In one, a judge in the courtroom asked the thief, "Why did you steal from the tomb of the pharaoh?" The thief replied, "Everyone says that the pharaoh is a god. Why didn't he stop me from stealing from his tomb?"

One of the most interesting documents about a tomb robbery in ancient Egypt was written on papyri known to us as the Abbott and Amherst Papyri. These records date from the 20th Dynasty, at the end of the New Kingdom (c. 1186–1069 B.C.). They tell the story of a struggle between an honest man known as Paser, the mayor of the east bank of Thebes, and a corrupt man with no conscience called Pawera, the mayor of the west bank of Thebes. Pawera was responsible for the protection of the tombs of the kings and queens, as well as the tombs of the nobles and officials, but he and his chief of police were involved in a conspiracy to steal their treasures. They bribed everyone, buying silence so that no one would say anything negative or incriminating about them.

But the honest man, Paser, heard about the corruption and reported the thefts to the authorities. He reported officially to the vizier that Pawera was involved in many tomb robberies and was disturbing the peace of the pharaohs. The vizier appointed a committee that consisted of dishonest men who were loyal to the mayor of the west bank, and the committee wrote a false report to the vizier stating that all the tombs were in good condition, that all the seals were intact and nothing had been stolen. Pawera and his men marched to the east bank in a victory celebration, shouting, laughing, and screaming with happiness because they had been found innocent in front of all the people. Paser could not believe that the committee had lied and written a false report. He first reported to the vizier that Pawera had participated in this celebration march against him and wrote again to the pharaoh explaining that the committee was dishonest and had been bribed.

The pharaoh appointed a new committee of men who were not connected to Pawera and could not be bribed by him or his people. They went to the Valley of the Kings and other sites and opened many of the tombs. They were shocked to find that most of these tombs had been robbed. The *kenbet* (the council of judges) looked at the case and ordered an investigation. They extracted confessions from the thieves and found three men guilty of stealing from the tomb of King Sobekemsaf II of the 17th Dynasty (sometime before 1550 B.C.) One thief even told the court in detail about how he found the mummy of the king: "He was equipped with a sword and there was a . . . set of amulets and ornaments of gold at his throat; his crown and diadems of gold were on his head and the . . . mummy of the king was overlaid with gold throughout. His coffins were wrought with gold and silver within and without and inlaid with every splendid costly stone. . . . We stole the furniture that we found with them, consisting of vases of gold, silver, and bronze." The guilty men were handed over to the high priest of Amun, who sent a decree to capture all the tomb robbers who had escaped and have them imprisoned at the temple of Amun until the pharaoh decided their punishment.

Imagine if the tomb of Ramesses II had been found intact. What kind of treasures must it have contained? But all these grand tombs were robbed secretly by thieves who hid at night and broke the seals and the silence of the valley. We were lucky that the tomb of the Golden King was saved by pure chance: Tutankhamun was considered part of the heretical Amarna dynasty and expunged from the Egyptian history books and thus forgotten. Two hundred years later, the Egyptians built the tomb of King Ramesses VI (c. 1143–1136 B.C.) on the slope above his tomb, and rubble from this construction covered it completely, saving it until Howard Carter discovered it on November 4, 1922.

The tales of the dancing tomb robbers are not just fascinating tales of yesterday. Tomb robbing is still happening today, as we have seen at Saqqara. Egyptian antiquities are still suffering greatly at the hands of thieves who steal reliefs and statues from tombs, break into storage rooms at antiquities sites to steal objects, and sometimes raid tombs before archaeologists even see them. The police try to foil these thefts, but despite all their best efforts, they never manage to stop them completely, and the thieves continue to dance on the already tattered remnants of the past.

I have many stories to tell about my encounters with tomb robbers, apart from the stories I have already told from Tuna el-Gebel, Saqqara, and Giza, but for now I will tell one more. When I was twenty-one years old, I was the inspector of antiquities working with an Italian expedition at Sheikh Abada under the direction of Sergio Donadoni. One day thieves entered the expedition camp and stole a box full of antiquities. It was a shock to all of us, and we felt helpless. I wanted to solve this crime and return the box without informing the police. I discovered that the mayor of the village was a very powerful man, and I suspected that he held the key to the mystery. I met him and told him, "I am sure that you know who stole the box; if you do not bring it within the hour I will inform the police that you arranged for the theft." The mayor said, "I will see." One hour later the mayor came, and the stolen box

was on the back of the donkey. He said, "I brought it back not because I was afraid of the police but because I liked your courage as a young man." Donadoni was very happy; he could not believe that the box had been returned! That night we ate melokhia with rabbit to celebrate our victory.

Today Egypt is taking more action to protect the monuments and stop tomb robbers. We are beginning to guard the monuments and artifacts more effectively, but we still need to focus on educating the public and strengthening Egypt's economy so that people have less need to enter the antiquities trade and more incentive to work with the Antiquities Department.

The international community is not only cooperating by catching robbers and putting them in jail, but museums are also returning stolen artifacts that have appeared in their collections over the years. For example, Philippe de Montebello, director of the Metropolitan Museum of Art in New York, and Dorothea Arnold, who runs the Met's Egyptian department, recently returned a relief that was stolen from Saqqara about thirty years ago. The consul of Egypt, Mahmoud Allam, took the relief from the museum to Egypt, where Dr. Gaballa and the director of the Egyptian Museum received him. The reunion of artifacts with their guardians was like a feast, and everyone was very happy.

Imagine the day when we can go to the Cairo Museum and see the beautiful head of Queen Nefertiti, wife of the heretic King Akhenaten. What a day it will be, a dream come true! However, the magnificent head of Queen Nefertiti is not in Egypt. If you want to see this incredible artifact you must travel to the museum in Berlin. When I was in Berlin, I visited the museum with Dietrich Wilding, its director. When I looked at Nefertiti's face I could see and feel the aura of mystery that surrounds her. She is breathtaking. Her parents are not known and like her mother-in-law, Queen Tiye, she was probably of nonroyal birth. Her name means, "the beautiful one is coming," and she appears beside her husband on all his major monuments. Nefertiti later changed her name to Nefer-Neferu-Aten "beautiful is the beauty of the Aten." She lived with Akhenaten at Amarna, the capital, whose ancient name was Akhetaten "the horizon of Aten." How did the head of Queen Nefertiti leave Egypt? Is it legal that Germany has possession of this Egyptian treasure? I will explain the history and leave it to you to decide.

The head is made of painted limestone and has one inlaid eye. It was discovered by a German expedition under Ludwig Borchardt during the excavations at Amarna in 1925, in the studio of the sculptor Tuthmose. According to Borchardt, he discovered the head but he did not clean it; he left it covered with mud and took it straight to the Cairo Museum. At that time, it was required for expeditions to take the antiquities they discovered to Cairo to be divided between the expedition and the Egyptian Antiquities Department. The committee took two limestone statues of Akhenaten and Nefertiti and gave the head of the queen to the German expedition. Some people say that Borchardt disguised the head by covering it with a layer of gypsum to make sure that the committee would not know that the statue was an exquisite piece crafted from painted limestone, but Wilding assured me that this story was not true, and that the committee knew it was made of limestone from the beginning. In any case, Borchardt went back to Germany and took the statue with him. The Egyptian government tried later to have Nefertiti returned, but when Hitler came into power he announced that Nefertiti was his lover and would never leave Germany. In 1978, when Mohammed Abdel Kader became the chairman of the Antiquities Department, he asked again for the head to be returned, but the Germans refused.

Museums all over the world house beautiful artifacts that should be in the Cairo Museum. Not long ago I went to London to give a lecture at the British Museum and met with my friend Vivian Davies, who runs the Egyptology Department there. I stood in front of the Rosetta Stone and wished that one day it would be returned home so our children could visit it at the Cairo Museum. An officer of Napoleon's named Buchard found the stone in the sum-

mer of 1799 near the Rosetta Branch of the Nile, and the French gave the stone to the English in 1802 as part of a treaty between the two countries. This incredible stone is of basalt and the text on it, which is a decree dating from 196 B.C. that gave honors to King Ptolemy V in return for the many privileges he gave to the temples, is in classical Greek, hieroglyphs, and a later Egyptian script called demotic.

Another important artifact that should be at home in Egypt is the bust of a prince named Ankhkhaf that was discovered in his tomb to the east of the Great Pyramid by Reisner. Some scholars believe that Ankhkhaf was the architect of the Great Pyramid. If we look at the head of this sculpture we can see that it is a masterpiece; it is unique and has no parallel in any museum in Egypt.

The last piece I will discuss is the Zodiac that was discovered at the temple of Dendara and is now exhibited at the Louvre in Paris. One of the most important astronomical pieces from ancient Egypt, the Zodiac was first conceived in 50 B.C. and describes the positions of the different planets as well as the lunar and solar eclipses.

I hope to one day see all these artifacts back in their motherland, but if this is impossible, I hope that the different museums will at least agree to exhibit the objects for a year at the Cairo Museum. Then our children and the Egyptians who cannot travel to see them will have a chance to see these magnificent pieces of art. I hope one day I will open the paper and read "Nefertiti is back in Egypt." I know this is a dream—but I often see my dreams coming true!

A Plan for the Future

Even though many treasures and vast quantities of information are left to be found, I truly believe that we should stop most excavation in Upper Egypt, from Giza in the north to Abu Simbel in the south, for the next ten years—except for salvage work, where the monuments are in danger of disappearing without a trace if we do not record them immediately. Most Egyptian and foreign-expedition work has been done in Upper Egypt, from Giza to Aswan; in contrast, many fewer excavations have been carried out in the Delta. The dry climate in Upper Egypt helps to preserve the monuments, but in Lower Egypt the situation is the opposite. It is urgent to excavate in the Delta because of the threats posed to the sites by the rising water table and the increase in agriculture: if we do not salvage the monuments in this area now they will be lost to us for good. Also, the eastern and western deserts are full of sites that no one knows anything about, and temples that are not guarded. For the monuments that have already been exposed, we need to focus on preservation and conservation, recording and publishing, and site management plans such as the one I have put in place at Giza. If we do not do this immediately, the Egyptian monuments will be lost in less than a hundred years.

As I am finishing this book, I am getting ready to embark upon a new part of my journey. I have been asked to become secretary general of the Supreme Council of Antiquities, and, although in many ways I would prefer to stay at Giza, I have accepted this new position, which places me in charge of all the ancient and Islamic monuments in Egypt and will allow me to implement many parts of this solution. I will be able to make many decisions to protect our ancient heritage. It will be hard work, and many of my decisions will not be popular, but I must think about the long-term survival of the monuments. I look forward to this new challenge.

More Secrets from the Sand

The text of this book is finished, but the sand of Egypt is revealing still more secrets. Even as I am finishing this book we are making new discoveries at Giza to add to the incredible things I have found there over the last fourteen years. Recently, I went to review the conservation work that is being done under the supervision of Nevien el-Magrabhy in the tombs that we are restoring south of the causeway of Khafre, where the priests who maintained the cult of Khafre and officials from the central adminis-

tration were buried. Nevien, one of the most intelligent people I have ever met in the field of architectural restoration, is fiercely protective of these tombs. A workman was laying new stones in a course along the top of a tomb, and the stone he was lifting had a sharp edge that dug a hole in the ground. To our amazement, out of the hole peered the eyes of a statuette. When we dug it out, we found that it was a carved figure of black granite inscribed with the name Merer-nisut and the title "Overseer of the Craftsmen."

Another surprise came at the last moment in the cemetery of the artisans. We found, at the north end of our excavations, the edge of a limestone lintel. When we cleared this, we found that it belonged to the "King's Acquaintance of the Palace, Overseer of the House, Nesy-weret." In front of the lintel was a thirty-foot causeway, the largest found so far. On the façade of the tomb, the deceased is shown with his wife in a beautifully carved relief. We have now excavated this tomb, and found an intact limestone sarcophagus in one of the five burial chambers. This is the first stone sarcophagus we have found in the tombs of the pyramid builders, and we opened it on September 16, 2002, in a live program aired by the National Geographic Society. Inside was a beautifully preserved, completely intact skeleton, which we will now study very carefullly.

At Bahariya, we are working now in Sheikh Soby on the tombs of the family of Djed-Khonsu-efankh, governor of the Bahariya Oasis in the 26th Dynasty. We have found the tombs of his wife Naesa II; his father, Ped-Isis; and two other tombs of nameless merchants. Our work lies about thirty feet under the houses of the modern town of el-Bawiti. There should be about eight major tombs left to be discovered, based on the family tree that can be extracted from the wall of the temple at Ain el-Muftella. These excavations will tell us the story of this powerful family, which lived under the 26th Dynasty kings Apries and Amasis.

In the spring of 2002, we uncovered more 26th Dynasty tombs in this area. The images are gone, destroyed by the water that has leaked down from the illegal houses that

were built above. But we found two more intact sarcophagi. The first is a limestone sarcophagus that was
completely sealed with mortar, meaning that the mummy
inside has been undisturbed since its burial. All the
amulets that were placed inside the wrappings should be
in their original positions. In the summer we brought a
portable X-ray machine to see how they are laid out,
information that will tell us more about the religious and
funerary beliefs of the time. The other sarcophagus is
anthropoid and made of pottery, similar to those we found
in the Valley of the Golden Mummies; it dates to the
Roman Period and was also sealed with mortar when we
found it. Unfortunately, the body was not carefully mummified and is not in good shape.

More illegally built houses have been moved from the
site at Sheikh Soby, and I can smell that there are more
tombs underneath. I am sure that we will find the tomb of
the brother of Djed-Khonsu-efankh, Shepen-Khonsu,
who was also a powerful governor, and the tomb of their
mother, Naesa I. Perhaps by the time this book is published, we will have found these two important tombs and
learned more about this powerful ancient family.

The sand of Egypt hides many secrets, and each new
discovery changes our understanding of the ancient
world. My thirty-three years of excavation have been
exciting and fruitful, and I am proud to have added signif-
icantly to the store of information on which we base our
interpretation of the past. But there are still more secrets
buried in the drifting sand. I look forward to entering into
newly discovered tombs and shafts, and revealing more of
the magic of Egypt to the world.

*The sands of Giza recently
revealed to us this gray gran
ite statue of Merer-Nisut,
"Overseer of the Craftsmen."
We found it when a workman
was laying new stones for a
tomb south of the causeway
of Khafre. The stone he was
lifting had dug a hole in the
ground with its sharp edge.
When we peered in, the eyes
of this statue looked back at us.*

Chronology of Ancient Egypt

PERIOD	DATES	CHARACTERISTICS; KINGS	AUTHOR'S EXCAVATIONS
PREDYNASTIC	c. 5300–3000 B.C.	End of the Neolithic Period; farming and domestication of animals; permanent settlements. Simple pottery; copper and gold working. Local rulers for most of period; Egypt unified under one ruler by 3000 B.C.	Merimde Beni Salama: Predynastic settlement
EARLY DYNASTIC	c. 3000–2686	Capital of a unified Egypt at Memphis; royal tombs at Abydos and Saqqara.	
Dynasty 1	c. 3000–2890	Aha Djer Djet Den Merneith Anedjib Semerkhet Qa'a	Abu Rawash: Dynasty 1 tombs
Dynasty 2	c. 2890–2686	Hetepsekhemwy Raneb Nynetjer Weneg Sened Peribsen Khasekhemwy	
OLD KINGDOM	c. 2686–2160	Period of strong centralized government; pyramids on west bank of Nile in Memphite region; Pyramid Texts appear at end of Dynasty 5. Decline begins during long reign of Pepi II.	
Dynasty 3	c. 2686–2613	Nebka Djoser Sekhemkhet Khaba Sanakht? Huni	

PERIOD	DATES	CHARACTERISTICS; KINGS	AUTHOR'S EXCAVATIONS
Dynasty 4	2613–2494	Sneferu Khufu Djedefre Khafre Menkaure Shepseskaf	Giza: satellite pyramid, causeway; valley temples of Khufu and Khafre, pyramid harbors, settlement; tombs of Kay and Perniankhu; tombs of the pyramid builders.
Dynasty 5	2494–2345	Userkaf Sahure Neferirkare Shepseskare Raneferef Niuserre Menkauhor Djedkare Unas	Abusir: scenes of Sahure's causeway.
Dynasty 6	2345–2181	Teti Userkare Pepi I Merenre Pepi II Nitocrit	Saqqara: pyramid complexes of Iput I and Khuit; tomb of Tetiankhkem, tomb of Qar; Abusir: the scenes of Sahure's causeway.
Dynasties 7 and 8	2181–2160	Numerous kings ruling for short periods	
FIRST INTERMEDIATE PERIOD	2160–2055	Collapse of central government; country divided among local rulers; famine and poverty	
Dynasties 9 and 10	2160–2055	Kings at Herakleopolis	
Dynasty 11	2125–2055	Kings at Thebes	
MIDDLE KINGDOM	2055–1650	Reunification of Egypt by Theban rulers. Powerful central government; expansion into Nubia. Capital at Itj-tawy, near Memphis	
Dynasty 11	2055–1985	Mentuhotep I Mentuhotep II Mentuhotep III	

PERIOD	DATES	CHARACTERISTICS; KINGS	AUTHOR'S EXCAVATIONS
Dynasty 12	1985–1773	Amenemhat I Senusert I Amenemhat II Senusert II Senusert III Amenemhat III Amenemhat IV Sobekneferu	
Dynasties 13 and 14	1773–after 1650	Rapid succession of rulers; country in decline	
SECOND INTERMEDIATE PERIOD	1650–1550	Country divided, with Asiatics ruling in the Delta	
Dynasty 15	1650–1550	Hyksos kings in Delta	
Dynasty 16	1650–1580	Kings at Thebes	
Dynasty 17	1580–1550	Seqenenre Tao I Seqenenre Tao II Kamose	
NEW KINGDOM	1550–1069	Reunification by Theban Dynasty 17; expulsion of Hyksos; annexation of Nubia; empire in Syro-Palestine. In Dynasty 19, prosperity threatened by incursions of "Sea Peoples." Economic decline and weak kings in Dynasty 20; civil disturbances and workers' strikes; royal tombs robbed	Giza: Pair statue of Ramesses II Saqqara: New Kingdom tomb chapels
Dynasty 18	1550–1295	Ahmose Amenhotep I Thutmosis I Thutmosis II Hatshepsut Thutmosis III Amenhotep II Thutmosis IV Amenhotep III Amenhotep IV (Akhenaten) Smenkhare Tutankhamun Ay Horemheb	

PERIOD	DATES	CHARACTERISTICS; KINGS	AUTHOR'S EXCAVATIONS
Dynasty 19	1295–1186	Ramesses I Seti I Ramesses II Merenptah Amenmessu Seti II Siptah Tausret	
Dynasty 20	1186–1069	Sethnakht Ramesses III–XI	
THIRD INTERMEDIATE PERIOD	1069–664	Egypt in decline, fragmented and politically divided. Siamun may be the pharaoh who gave his daughter in marriage to Solomon. Dynasty 25 kings are from Nubia	
Dynasty 21	1069–945	Smendes Amenemnisu Psusennes I Amenemope Osorkon the Elder Siamun Psusennes II	
Dynasty 22	945–715	Sheshonq I Osorkon I Sheshonq II Takelot I Osorkon II Takelot II Sheshonq III Pimay Sheshonq V Osorkon IV	
Dynasty 23	919–715	Pedubastis I Iuput I Sheshonq IV Osorkon III Takelot III Rudamon Peftjauawybast Iuput II	

PERIOD	DATES	CHARACTERISTICS; KINGS	AUTHOR'S EXCAVATIONS
Dynasty 24	727–715	Bakenrenef	
Dynasty 25	747–656	Piy Shabaqa Shabitqa Taharqa Tanutamani	
LATE PERIOD	664–332	Dynasty 26 from Sais in Delta, last of strong native Egyptian rulers. Annexed into Persian empire; native rulers reemerge in Dynasties 28–30, but country is in decline and is reconquered by Persians.	
Dynasty 26	664–525	Psamtek I (Wahibre) Nekau II Psamtek II Apries Ahmose II (Amasis) Psamtek III	Baharia: Tombs at Sheikh Soby Heliopolis: Tombs of Panehsy and Wadjhor
Dynasty 27	525–404	Persian Period	
Dynasty 28	404–399	Amyrtaios	
Dynasties 29 and 30 2nd Persian Period	399–332		
PTOLEMAIC PERIOD	332–330	Persian Empire is taken over by the Macedonians under Alexander the Great; after his death. Egypt is given to his general, Ptolemy; last ruler, Cleopatra VII, allied with Mark Antony against Rome.	Kom Abu Billo Baharia: Valley of the Golden Mummies
ROMAN PERIOD	30 B.C.–A.D. 395	Cleopatra and Antony defeated by Octavian at the Battle of Actium; Egypt becomes a Roman province. Heavy taxation drains wealth from country. Christianity spreads and eliminates ancient religion.	

Glossary

Ankh: the hieroglyphic sign for life.

Ba: the aspect of a person that is individual and unique; sometimes depicted as a bird with a human head.

Ben-ben: the sacred symbol of Ra, the sun-god, kept at Heliopolis and possibly consisting originally of a lump of meteoric iron, shown in depictions as pyramidal in shape.

Cachette: a pit in which artifacts such as statues were deliberately hidden.

Canopic jars: four vessels of stone or pottery used to hold packages of viscera removed from the body during mummification.

Cartonnage: a type of plaster of Paris made with layers of linen or papyrus coated with plaster and then often painted or gilded.

Djed pillar: the hieroglyph for stability; often used in protective amulets.

False door: a niche found in the west wall of tomb chapels, carved and decorated to look like a door through which the soul of the deceased could magically pass.

Hetep: the hieroglyph for offerings.

Ib: the hieroglyph for heart.

Ka: the life force of a human being, capable of being transmitted from one person to another (for example, from one king to his successor).

Kherep scepter: long baton used as a symbol of power and authority.

Mastaba: Arabic for bench, used to refer to a low rectangular tomb superstructure with gently sloping sides and a flat top.

Melokhia: an Egyptian plant that resembles spinach.

Nemes headdress: a striped cloth worn by the king.

Phyle: a tribe or clan, used to describe an administrative unit of workers.

Pyramid Texts: a collection of magical spells inscribed on the walls of the burial chambers of kings and queens of the late Old Kingdom.

Reserve head: an image of the deceased showing him or her only from the neck up; usually found in the fill of 4th Dynasty tomb shafts.

Sealing: a gob of clay bearing the impression of a personal seal, used to close storage pots, bags, boxes, or doors.

Serdab: a small, fully enclosed tomb chamber, usually with an eye-slit near the top of the front wall, where statues of the deceased were placed.

Serekh: a rectangle bordered at the bottom by niches representing the facade of a palace and surmounted by a royal falcon enclosing one of the names of the king.

Shawabti: statuette placed in the tomb to act as a substitute for the deceased if he or she is called upon to do work in the afterlife.

Shisha: a water pipe.

Stele: an upright slab of stone, usually bearing an inscription.

Tafla: a claylike form of limestone.

Uraeus: the rearing cobra used to adorn the forehead of royalty.

Wabet: the mortuary workshop, where the body was embalmed.

Wadi: a canyon or dry stream bed.

Wadjet eye: the eye of Horus, destroyed by his enemy Seth and restored by the god Thoth; often used as a protective amulet.

Wesekh: a broad collar worn around the neck.

Bibliography

Abubakr, A. M., "Divine Boats of Ancient Egypt." *Archaeology* 8 (1955), 96–101.

Abubakr, A. M., and A.Y. Mustafa, "The Funerary Boat of Khufu." *Ricke Festschrift BABA* 12 (1971), 1–16.

Abu-Seif, H., "Dégagement de la face et de la pyramide de Chéops." *ASE* 46 (1947), 235–38.

Aldred, C., *Egypt to the End of the Old Kingdom*. London, 1965.

Badawy, A., *A History of Egyptian Architecture*, vol. I. Giza, 1954.

Bárta, M., and J. Krejčí, *Abusir and Saqqara in the Year 2000*, Academy of Sciences of the Czech Republic Oriental Institute. Prague, 2000.

Baz, F. el, "Desert Builders Knew a Good Thing When They Saw It." *Smithsonian* (April 1981), 116–22.

Bleeker, C.J., *Egyptian Festivals: Enactments of Religious Renewal*. Leiden, 1967.

Butzer, K., *Early Hydraulic Civilization in Egypt*. Chicago, 1976.

Dunham, D., and W. K. Simpson, *The Mastaba of Queen Mersyankh III: Giza Mastabas I*. Boston, 1974.

Edwards, I. E. S., *The Pyramids of Egypt*. Harmondsworth, 1961.

Erntefest and Hordjedef, *Lexikon Der Ägyptologie*, Otto Harrassowitz, Wiesbaden (1977), 1111–13.

Faulkner, R.O., *The Ancient Egyptian Pyramid Texts*. Oxford, 1969.

Firth, C. M., and B. Gunn, *The Teti Pyramid Cemeteries*, vol. I. Cairo, 1926.

Frankfort, H., *Ancient Egyptian Religion: An Interpretation*. New York, 1961.

Frankfort, H., *Kingship and the Gods: A Study of Ancient Near Eastern Religion as the Integration of Society and Nature*. Chicago, 1978.

Griffiths, J. G., *The Origins of Osiris*. Münchner ägyptologische Studien 9. Berlin, 1966.

Grinsell, L., *Egyptian Pyramids*. Gloucester, 1947.

Hassan, S., *Excavations at Giza*, vol. I, Oxford, 1932; vols. II–X, Cairo, 1936–60.

Hassan, S., *The Sphinx: Its History in the Light of Recent Excavations*. Cairo, 1949.

Hassan, S., "The Causeway of Unas in Sakkara." *ZXS* 80 (1955), 136–44.

Hawass, Z., "The Excavations Northeast of the Sphinx." Unpublished paper read at Third International Congress of Egyptology. Toronto, 1983.

Hawass, Z., "The Khufu Statuette: Is It an Old Kingdom Sculpture?" *Mélangea Gamel Eddin Mokhtar. BdE* 971 (1985), 379–94.

Hawass, Z., "Kom Abou Bellou," *SAK* 7 (1985).

Hawass, Z., "Archaic Graves at Abou-Rawash," *MDAIK* 36 (1987).

Hawass, Z., *The Funerary Establishments of Khufu, Khafre, and Menkaure during the Old Kingdom*, Ph.D. dissertation (microfilm). Ann Arbor, 1987, 53–85.

Hawass, Z., "A Burial with an Unusual Plaster Mask Found at Giza." In *Followers of Horus: Studies Dedicated to Michael Hoffman, Egyptian Studies Associated Publication* 2, Oxbow Monograph 20 (1990).

Hawass, Z., *The Pyramids and Temples of Gizah*, by W. M. F. Petrie, with an updated chapter by Z. Hawass, *Histories, Mysteries of Man*. London (1990).

Hawass, Z., *The Pyramids of Ancient Egypt*. Pittsburgh, 1990.

Hawass, Z., "The Statue of the Dwarf Pr-Ni-Ankhu Discovered at Giza." In *Kaiser Festschrift, MDAIK* 47 (1991).

Hawass, Z., "Recent Discoveries at Giza." In *Sixth International Congress of Egyptology*, vol. I. Turin, 1993.

Hawass, Z., "A Fragmentary Monument of Djoser from Saqqara." *JEA* 80 (1994).

Hawass, Z., "The Passages under the Sphinx." *Hommages dà Jean Leclant, IFAO* 1. (1994).

Hawass, Z., "The Egyptian Monuments: Problems and Solutions," *Journal of Law* (1995), 5–117.

Hawass, Z., "A Group of Unique Statues Discovered at Giza: I. Statues of the Pyramid Builders," *Kunst des Alten Reiches* (symposium), *MDAIK* (1995), 29–30.

Hawass, Z., "Touristic Management of Giza Plateau." In *Proceedings of a Round Table on Culture, Tourism, Development, UNESCO*. Paris, 1996, 26–27.

Hawass, Z., "The Workmen's Community at Giza." In *Sonder Druck aus Haus und Palast in alten Ägypten Internationales Symposium 8 bis 11 April 1992 in Cairo*. Vienna, 1996.

Hawass, Z., "The Discovery of a Pair-Statue Near the Pyramid of Menkaure at Giza," *MDAIK* 33 (1997).

Hawass, Z., "The Discovery of the Pyramidion of the Satellite Pyramid of Khufu, GID." In *Iubilate Conlegae: Studies in Memory of Abdel Aziz Sadek*, Part I, *Varia Aegyptiaca* 10, nos. 2–3 (August–December, 1997).

Hawass, Z., "The Discovery of the Satellite Pyramid of Khufu," In *W. K. Simpson Festschrift*. Boston, 1997, 379–98.

Hawass. Z., Four sections and preface in A. Siliotti, *Guide to the Pyramids of Egypt*, Cairo, 1997.

Hawass, Z., "The Pyramid Builders. A Group of Unique Statues Discovered at Giza: III. The Statues of Jnty-Sdw from Tomb GSE 1915." *Les critères de Datation Stylistiques à l'Ancien Empire, IFAO*. Cairo, 1997.

Hawass, Z., "The Pyramids," *Ancient Egypt*, D. Silverman, ed. 168–190, London 1997.

Hawass, Z., "The Dwarf Who Danced for the King," *1000 Words Magazine* (December 1998).

Hawass, Z., "Pyramid Construction: New Evidence Discovered in Giza." In *Stationen Beiträge zur kulturgeschichte Ägyptens Gewidmet R. Stadelmann,* Heike Guksch and Daniel Polz, eds. Mainz, 1998.

Hawass, Z., "The Discoveries of the Egyptian Archaeologists at Memphis." In *Egyptian Art in the Age of the Pyramids.* Exh. cat. New York, 1999.

Hawass, Z., "Excavating the Old Kingdom: The Egyptian Archaeologist." In *Egyptian Art in the Age of the Pyramids.* Exh. cat. New York, 1999.

Hawass, Z., "A Personal Account of the Discovery of the Golden Mummies," *KMT* (November 1999).

Hawass, Z., "The Pyramid Builders. A Group of Unique Statues Discovered at Giza: IV. The Statue of an Overseer of the Craftsmen and His Wife." *L' Art de l'Ancien Empire égyptien,* Paris, 1999.

Hawass, Z., "Who Really Built the Pyramids?" *Archaeology Odyssey.* 2 (May / June 1999), 49–55.

Hawass, Z., "A Unique Old Kingdom Headrest and Offering Tablet of Seven Sacred Oils Found at Saqqara." *Memnonia* 9 (1999).

Hawass, Z., "The Discovery of the Temple of the God Bes at Bahria Oasis." In *Moustafa El-Abadi Festschrift, Alexandria Archaeologie Société.* Alexandria, 2000.

Hawass, Z., "The Discovery of the Tomb of the Golden Mummies at Bahariya Oasis." *Egypt Revealed* (October 2000).

Hawass, Z., "A Female Hand Found in Abou-Rawash." In *Edward Wente Festschrift.* Chicago, 2000.

Hawass, Z., "Mummies: Emissaries of the Golden Age." *Archaeology Odyssey* 3,

no. 5 (September / October 2000), 38–43.

Hawass, Z., "The Old Kingdom Pyramidion: Is It Cased with Gold?" In *Fayza Heikel Festschrift. BIFAO* (2000).

Hawass, Z., "Recent Discoveries Near the Pyramid of Teti at Saqqara." Prague, 2000.

Hawass, Z., "Roman Mummies Found at Bahariya Oasis," in Jim Sauer, ed. *Festschrift Semitic Museum.* Cambridge, 2000.

Hawass, Z., *Silent Images: Women in Pharaonic Egypt,* rev. ed. New York, 2000.

Hawass, Z., "Site Management at Giza Plateau: Master Plan for the Conservation of the Site." *International Journal of Cultural Property* 9, no. 1 (2000).

Hawass, Z., "A Stela of the Vizer Mehu at Saqqara," *Lingua Aegyptia Journal of Egyptian Language* 7 (2000).

Hawass, Z., *Valley of the Golden Mummies,* New York, 2000.

Hawass, Z., "Site Management and Conservation." In *The Debate of Millennium.* Cairo, 2001.

Hawass, Z., "The Valley of the Mummies." In *Book of Proceedings. Eighth International Congress of Egyptology.* Cairo, 2001.

Hawass, Z., "The Biography of the Priest Kay of Giza." In press.

Hawass, Z. (co-author), "Chronology, Settlement and Subsistence at Merimde Beni Salama," *JEA* 74 (1974).

Hawass, Z. (co-author), "Builders of the Pyramids." *Archaeology Magazine* 50, no.1 (January / February 1997).

Hawass, Z. (co-author), "The Discovery of the Old Kingdom Settlement at Giza," *MDAIK* (2000).

Hawass, Z. (co-author), "Excavation Northeast of the Sphinx," *MDAIK* (2000).

Hawass, Z. (co-author), *The Valley Temple of Khafre: Construction and Discoveries.* In press.

Hawass, Z. (co-author), *The Discovery of the Causeway and the Valley Temple of Khufu.* In press.

Hawass, Z., and E. J. Brill, *Kingship in Ancient Egypt.* Leiden, 1995.

Hawass, Z. and M. Lehner, *Excavations in the Area of the Great Sphinx at Giza.* Unpublished manuscript.

Hayes, W., *The Scepter of Egypt,* vol. I. New York, 1953.

Hölzl, C., "Heliopolis, the Predynastic Cemetery." *Encyclopedia of Archaeology of Ancient Egypt,* K. A. Bard, ed. London / New York, 1999, 366–67.

Jeffereys, D. G., *The Survey of Memphis,* vol. I. London, 1985.

Kanawati, N., *The Egyptian Administration in the Old Kingdom: Evidence on its Economic Decline.* Warminster, 1977.

Lauer, J. P., *Saqqara.* London, 1976.

Lehner, M., "A Note on the Proposed Excavations at the Eastern Base of the Giza Plateau." Unpublished paper.

Lehner, M., *The Complete Pyramid.* London / Cairo, 1997.

Lehner, M., "Some Observations on the Layout of Khufu and Khafre Pyramids." *JARCE* 20 (1983), 7–25

Lehner, M., *The Pyramid Tomb of Hetep-Heres and the Satellite Pyramid of Khufu.* Mainz / Rhein, 1985.

Lehner, M., "The Development of Giza Necropolis: The Khufu Project." *MDAIK* 41 (1986), 23.

Lehner, M., "A Contexual Approach to the Giza Pyramid," *Archiv für Orientforschung* 31. In press.

Redford, D. B., *The Oxford Encyclopedia of Ancient Egypt,* vol. II. Cairo, 2001, 88–89.

Reisner, G. A., *Catalogue des Antiquités*

Egyptiennes au Musée du Caire, vol. 68. Models of Ships and Boats. Cairo, 1913.

Reisner, G. A., "The Tomb of Hetep-heres," *BMFA* 25 (1927), 2–36.

Reisner, G. A., "The Empty Sarcophagus of the Mother of Chéops." *BMFA* 26 (1928), 76–88.

Reisner, G. A., *The Development of the Egyptian Tomb Down to the Accession of Chéops.* Cambridge, Mass., 1935.

Reisner, G. A., *Mycerinus: The Temples of the Third Pyramid at Giza.* Cambridge, Mass., 1935.

Reisner, G. A., *A History of the Giza Necropolis*, vol. I. Cambridge, Mass., 1942.

Roth, A. M., "Egyptian Phyles of the Old Kingdom." Chicago, 1985. Unpublished dissertation.

Saleh, A., "Excavation around Mycerinus Pyramid Complex." *MDAIK* 30 (1974), 131–54.

Silverman, D. P., *Ancient Egypt.* Oxford, 1997.

Simpson, W. K., *Paprus Reisner II.* Boston, 1965.

Simpson, W. K., *The Mastabas of Kawab, Khafkhufu I and II*, vol. III. Boston, 1978.

Simpson, W. K., *Mastabas of the Western Cemetery: Part I*, vol. IV. Boston, 1980.

Simpson, W. K., R. Faulkner, F. Wente, *The Literature of Ancient Egypt.* New Haven, 1977.

Smith, E. B., *Egyptian Architecture as Cultural Expression.* New York, 1938.

Smith, W. S., "Old Kingdom Sculpture." *AJA* 45 (1941), 514–28.

Smith, W. S., *A History of Egyptian Sculpture and Painting in the Old Kingdom.* Boston / London, 1946.

Smith, W. S., *Ancient Egypt as Represented in the Museum of Fine Arts.* Boston, 1952.

Smith, W.S., "Inscriptional Evidence of the History of the Fourth Dynasty." *JNES* 11 (1952), 113–28.

Smith, W. S., *The Art and Architecture of Ancient Egypt.* Harmondsworth, 1958.

Smith, W. S., "Old Kingdom in Egypt and the Beginning of the First Intermediate Period." In I. E. S. Edwards, ed. *Cambridge Ancient History*, vol. 12. Cambridge, 1971.

Smith, W. S., *The Art and Architecture of Ancient Egypt.* Revised by W.K. Simpson. Harmondsworth, 1981.

Spencer, P., *The Egyptian Temple: A Lexicographical Study.* London, 1984.

Stadelmann, R., *Die ägyptischen Pyramiden.* Vom Ziegelbau Zum Weltwunder. Mainz 1985 (1991)

Trigger, B.G., et al. *Ancient Egypt: A Social History.* Cambridge / New York, 1993.

Verner, M., *The Pyramids.* New York, 2001.

Index

Acknowledgments

I was assisted in the preparation of this book by a number of people, whose cooperation and advice are greatly appreciated. First, I wish to acknowledge my classmate and friend Janice Kamrin, who edited this book and also encouraged me to finish it on time. I am also grateful for the advice and assistance of Barbara Burn, the editor of Harry N. Abrams who also did excellent work on my previous book *The Valley of the Golden Mummies*. I would like to give sincere thanks to Robert McKee, who designed this book and made it so attractive. And, of course, I owe a great deal to Eric Himmel, the editor in chief at Abrams, for his constant support and outstanding efforts on behalf of this book. I am also deeply grateful to my good friend Ken Garrett, whose photographs, especially of Bahariya Oasis, add so much to this book.

In Egypt a number of friends and colleagues participated in this book in various ways. I am especially grateful to Tarek el-Awady, who is always my right hand, for reading my work and putting the photographs in the right places. Thanks go to Mansour Boriak for his excellence assistance in all my excavations since 1988; to Noha Abdel Hafiz, whose golden hand in copying the scenes and inscriptions make this book valuable; and to Brook Myers in my office at Giza and in the office of the Supreme Council of Antiquities for her support, devotion, and help in typing my work. I am very fortunate indeed to have assistants who help me during my busy days at the office: Mohamed Ismail, Mohamed Megahed, and Sahar Mabrouk. I would also like to thank Mahmoud Afifi, who helped me in my excavations in Giza and Bahariya.

There is no way that I can repay the gracious contributions of my dear friends in Egypt, especially Dr. Ali Radwan and Dr. Tohfa Handousa. Every time I finish a project, I cannot forget my debt to my mentor, the late Gamal Mokhtar. I wish also to acknowledge another friend, Mostafa El Nager, the tourist editor of the *el-Ahram* newspaper in Cairo. Last, but not least, I would like to thank my good friend Mark Linz, who always gives me advice and help, as well as the members of the staff at the American University in Cairo Press for all their aid.

Zahi Hawass
SECRETARY GENERAL OF THE
SUPREME COUNCIL OF ANTIQUITIES,
DIRECTOR OF THE PYRAMIDS
AND EXCAVATION

Photograph Credits

Editor: Barbara Burn
Designer: Robert McKee
Production Manager: Justine Keefe

Library of Congress Cataloging-in-
Publication Data

Hawass, Zahi A.
 Secrets from the sand : my search for
Egypt's ancient past / Zahi
Hawass.
      p. cm.
Includes bibliographical references and
index.
ISBN 0-8109-4575-4 (hardcover)
1. Egypt—Antiquities. 2. Excavations
(Archaeology)—Egypt. 3.
Hawass, Zahi A. I. Title.

DT60 .H386 2003
932—dc21

2002151675

Printed and bound in China

10 9 8 7 6 5 4 3 2 1

Harry N. Abrams, Inc.
100 Fifth Avenue
New York, N.Y. 10011
www.abramsbooks.com

Abrams is a subsidiary of